DATE			
AUG 2 4 1989			
FEB 2 0 1995			
APR 1 1 1995			
NOV 2 8 2000			

CLAUDE DEBUSSY

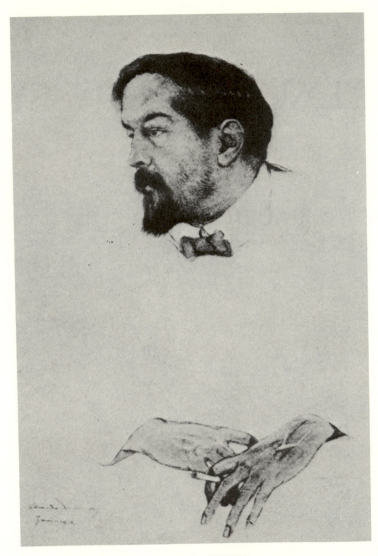

CLAUDE DEBUSSY

From a crayon by Yvan Thièle

>>>>>>>>>>>>>>>>>>>>><<<<<<<<<<<<<<<<<<<<

CLAUDE DEBUSSY

Master of Dreams

MAURICE DUMESNIL
Author of *An Amazing Journey*

GREENWOOD PRESS, PUBLISHERS
WESTPORT, CONNECTICUT

Library of Congress Cataloging in Publication Data

Dumesnil, Maurice, 1886-
   Claude Debussy, master of dreams.

   Reprint of the ed. published by I. Washburn,
New York.
   1. Debussy, Claude, 1862-1918.   2.   Composers--
France--Biography.
ML410.D28D8 1979   780'.92'4 [B]   78-23438
ISBN 0-313-20775-5

First published in 1940 by Ives Washburn, New York

Reprinted in 1979 by Greenwood Press, Inc.
51 Riverside Avenue, Westport, CT 06880

Printed in the United States of America

10 9 8 7 6 5 4 3 2 1

Dedicated to my friend
JAMES FRANCIS COOKE

Foreword

It is generally conceded that an artistic career seldom brings earthly rewards and that most composers, painters, and writers reach fame only after death.

Claude Debussy, apparently, was an exception to this rule. The latter part of his life brought to him great honors and recognition, though only a fraction of the glory that was to come. Gounod once said: "Since I hear my music hummed on the street by people who do not even know my name, I begin to believe that I have a reputation." Now, Debussy's *Rêverie* has attained that supreme consecration, and the *Clair de lune* has taken its place on all piano stands. This has created much curiosity concerning his private life. He was often called "le grand solitaire" and spent his days absorbed in his work, far from intrigues and politics. Was he happy? Yes, at times he knew hours of great joy; but his extreme sensitiveness made him vulnerable to many blows. On the whole, his life was one long struggle: misunderstood by some of his teachers, insulted by the critics, he suffered in his artistic convictions, but pursued his way serenely in spite of all attacks.

The great tragedy came when, after marrying a good woman who was poor, knew nothing of music, and bore him no child, he met another woman who was wealthy, highly artistic, and gave him a beloved little daughter. Public opinion in each case considered only the first adjective; abandoned by many of his friends, fiercely criticized, he found among his family the solace and peace necessary to his creative spirit. Soon, however, crucified by a dreadful disease, he saw his powers decline and finally departed prematurely at the age of fifty-six.

In the last years of her life Emma Claude Debussy thought of writing her memoirs; by doing so she would have dispelled many misunderstandings and put certain phases of her husband's life into the proper light. When her strength began to give way she suggested that I collaborate with her, thus alleviating the material task. But soon her health broke down completely and she passed away. From many conversations held over a period of several years, I preserved some notebooks filled with information gathered directly from her lips. Had she written her memoirs herself, it is likely that her great modesty would have drawn a veil over the part, so vital, which she played in Debussy's life. Therefore, in substituting for her, I am able to restore to her memory the credit which her profound devotion to him deserves.

Claude Debussy's music is now beyond discussion. In the Hall of Fame his name stands in the company of the greatest. Anyone can understand this music without going through a long process of technical education; but to love it best one must also be a lover of nature, of deep forests, of medieval legends which tell of old castles, of ancient walls worn by time and covered with ivy; one must have felt the spell of the declining sun on seashores and river bends, and perceived in an autumn park the exalted fragrance of dying flowers.

M. D.

Contents

CLAUDE DEBUSSY

1

Conservatoire Days

"Hurry up, Achille . . . dinner is on the table. What on earth are you doing?"

Mme. Manuel Debussy, née Victorine Manoury, was getting impatient. It was well after seven o'clock and for some time the din of the scales running up and down the keyboard had no longer been audible. Leaving the dining room, she crossed the hall and proceeded along the narrow corridor leading to the bedrooms of the old-fashioned apartment located on the Rue Clapeyron, just off the Boulevard des Batignolles, a typical dwelling for a middle-class French family: on the street side there was a parlor adjoining a dining room furnished in Henry II style, very popular at that time. A gas cluster hung from the ceiling, spreading a cozy, yellowish light on the huge soup tureen of decorated china; an appetizing smell of boiled vegetables steamed out of that container.

"What do you mean by keeping us waiting so long?" Manuel Debussy grumbled as the boy appeared. "Don't you know I am in a hurry? I'm going to the Opéra-Comique with your mother, and we don't want to miss one note. They give *Il Trovatore*."

13

Achille sat down with a guilty look on his face. He was not going with them and frankly didn't care at all, preferring to return to his room after supper and resume his interrupted task of classifying a collection of butterflies horded since the hunts of the last summer.

"Very nice of Uncle Arosa to send us those two tickets," Manuel pursued, "and for *Il Trovatore*. . . . This is great music, Achille. One of these days I shall go to the quays and see if I can find a used score. Then you can play it for me."

Achille acquiesced; he knew little about *Il Trovatore*, and once only had heard a fantasy on that opera played by a military band at an open-air concert in the Square des Batignolles.

"My brother has conducted *Il Trovatore* many times," Manuel continued. " 'Verdi is the greatest genius of our time,' he used to say. Melody, my son, is what counts in music. Verdi has that gift and that's what makes him great; besides, he never gets into divagations like so many others of the modern school: that Wagner, for instance . . . Richard Wagner."

Manuel Debussy pronounced the latter name "ouagnair," in the French way. Now he was on one of his favorite subjects and would have continued indefinitely had not the cuckoo clock burst into song three times.

"Seven-forty-five!" Victorine exclaimed. "We must rush or we shall miss the overture. Never mind the dishes; I'll clear the table when we come home."

The couple hurried down the four flights of the winding stairway, sparingly illuminated on each landing.

"Cold and foggy tonight," the concierge, Mme. Mousset, remarked as they passed her loge.

At the corner they waited for a few minutes, but the Batignolles-Clichy-Odéon omnibus failed to appear.

"Oh . . . those buses," Victorine exclaimed impatiently, "they run so seldom at this hour. Let's take a cab, Manuel, or we shall be terribly late."

They hailed one that was passing. Never mind the thirty cents, they thought. Payday was near at hand and they could afford this small luxury.

After years of uncertainty, during which Manuel Debussy had ventured into various branches of business, something had come at last which satisfied his inborn French yearning for permanence and security: he had just been appointed as an employee of the Fives-Lille company, a large concern for the building of railroad engines. The offices were located on the Rue de Londres, only a few minutes' walk from home. The salary, modest at first, would gradually increase; so life seemed to smile on him and the future looked rosy.

Up in the apartment Achille had gone back to his room. A small upright piano stood by the window; at its side was a plain mahogany table covered with manuscript paper, sheet music, books, and a number of pages taken from illustrated magazines. From these the boy selected and cut out pictures, then pinned them on the walls. He preferred the more delicate ones in pastel shades, surrounded by large margins. Above the table hung a sort of box with a glass front, in which the butterflies were carefully arranged; from time to time he altered the arrangement, not out of regard for the laws of natural history but because of some new shimmering color scheme.

The piano was an old instrument bought secondhand in a furniture outlet, but despite its age and the tarnished keys on which cigarette burns were noticeable it had a pretty good tone.

Achille was preparing for his entry examination at the Conservatoire National. His father wished him to become a virtuoso and for that purpose he drove his boy hard, insisting upon six or seven hours of daily practice; thereafter Victorine stepped in and tried to compensate for a college education by inculcating into him a few principles of grammar, arithmetic, history, and geography. But her own education was only primary; her ability with figures limited itself to household additions and subtractions, while her favorite authors were d'Ennery and Xavier de Montépin. Her greatest accomplishments were in the kitchen: like most Frenchwomen she was an expert cook and excelled particularly in the preparation of delicious entremets which appealed strongly to the refined taste of her elder son.

The clock had struck midnight when she and Manuel came home. Enthusiasm ran high and the name of Verdi echoed all over the hall.

"Quiet, Manuel," Victorine said; "be careful or you will wake the children."

Achille in his little bed had promptly dropped his book and blown out the candle, ready to "play possum" if necessary. Candles were expensive, Victorine thought, and why not read by daylight, which comes to us from God and costs nothing.

The spring was already well advanced and the chestnut trees on the Boulevard des Batignolles were in full bloom.

"How did you get along with your lesson this morning,

Achille?" Manuel asked as they sat down for lunch. "Was Mme. Mauté pleased?"

"I think she was," answered Achille, "she hopes to be able to introduce me to Marmontel before long, so that I may play for him."

"That's wonderful! Victorine, did you hear that? Achille is going to play for Marmontel."

That famous pedagogue occupied at that time an unique place in the musical world of Paris. To come under his guidance was considered paramount by young aspirants, since his class usually reaped a majority of the awards. Musically speaking, however, this elderly man was a queer mixture of good and bad taste, with his frequent inclination to recommend too many suave, or "drawing room," effects. He also was self-centered and somewhat dictatorial, though at other times quite human. His large apartment in the Rue de Calais, in the house once occupied by Berlioz, was rigidly conservative; he did not teach there, and for this purpose he had another flat in the Rue Blanche. Hanging outside the padded door a strip of tapestry set into action the most incredible little jingle bell; but since the studio itself gave on the noisy street where carriages and buses rolled continually on the cobblestones, it could not be expected that the master's ears could be reached by its tinkling. So the students used to sit on the steps and wait until the current lesson was over.

Mme. Mauté and Achille had thus been informally seated for some fifteen minutes when the door opened.

"Come in, come in. I am delighted to see you," Marmontel said affably; "so, here's our young musician."

Achille, shy and embarrassed, twisted his blue tam-o'-shanter adorned with a red tassel. His black blouse, held at the waist by a leather belt, was carefully pressed and pleated. But Marmontel paid little attention to such details; he examined the rather massive boy who stood before him, interested by the high forehead, the dark curly hair, and the deep and mysterious eyes which looked at him with mingled awe, admiration, and respect.

"Has he always been your student?" Marmontel queried.

"Oh, no, he only came to me a few months ago. His first teacher was an old Italian, when Achille stayed at Nice a few years ago. Since then and until I met him he had no teacher but his instinct. He listened to military bands, then came home and reproduced what he had heard, sometimes improvising harmonies of his own."

At the evocation of the Riviera Achille's face brightened. A vision of that magic land came to his mind: the sunny landscape perfumed by orange blossoms with the sea as a background; the road to Antibes, lined with rosebushes under a pastel-blue sky; and he could still hear, in the distance, the song of a Norwegian carpenter joyously singing, some Grieg perhaps?

"Interesting youngster," Marmontel remarked, "let's hear him."

The audition was a success and the master promised to recommend his admission.

It was with a light heart that Achille came back to the apartment and announced the happy outcome of his interview.

"Let's celebrate," Manuel said. "*Hamlet* is on at the Opéra tonight. We will go and hear it; in the meantime

I must go downtown and on the way back I'll stop at Bourbonneux's and get a pound of petits fours. How's that, Achille?"

A broad smile illuminated the boy's face; nothing could have pleased him more than a bag of those expensive delicacies! He retired to his room while Victorine, utterly happy with such a fine day, picked up *Le Petit Journal* and plunged into her daily installment of *The Two Orphans*; these unfortunate little girls had been left desperately unhappy the day before and she wanted to find out what had happened to them.

The summer passed quietly: office hours for Manuel, housework and care of the younger children for Victorine, practice for Achille. When he finished his exercises he reached eagerly for a certain package of music containing the score of Bach's *Mass in B minor*, several Mozart quartets reduced for piano, and the overture of *Tannhäuser*. But to play such music he chose the hours when he was alone, since his father detested Wagner.

"My son," he used to say, "Wagner wouldn't be anything if he had been born in France. There's nothing in his music but a lot of noise. I know, because I was at the première of *Tannhäuser*. Yes, way up in the top gallery, the 'paradise.' I couldn't hear one single passage that came from the heart. Music without melody is like a hare stew without the hare. Then, imagine having such a magnificent corps de ballet and not using it! The members of the Jockey Club got up and left. Ah, you should have heard that row! I am proud to have been one of those who shouted most."

No melody? Achille wondered; how strange! He found,

on the contrary, that melody poured through each measure. Thereafter he avoided discussing aesthetics at home
and kept his opinions to himself.

With the autumn his work grew more and more inten-
sive. Then one day in October the concierge brought up a
yellow envelope with the heading of the National Conservatory; the aspirant Achille Debussy was summoned to
appear before the jury the following Thursday at nine
o'clock.

The Conservatoire was then located in the Faubourg
Poissonnière, one block from the boulevards. Only one
wing remains now, containing the historic concert hall,
the museum, and the collection of old instruments. An
ugly post office has replaced the other parts. Former students still remember the old courtyard into which con-
verged all kinds of musical sounds: pounding of the grand
pianos; blare of trumpets, horns, and trombones; shrill
high notes of the coloraturas mingled with softer tones
from string instruments and the distant echo of the peaceful pipe organ.

The admission competitions took place in the organ
hall where the jury sat at a horseshoe table, surrounding
Director Ambroise Thomas. From the waiting room the
contestants came through a corridor nicknamed "le boulevard du trac" (the avenue of nervousness). It was aptly
named, for many careers must have been nipped right
there through inability to dominate physical reactions, and
many excellent fingers and memories found themselves
suddenly paralyzed.

It was there that Achille awaited his turn. He kept calm
and poised while his mother concealed her anxiety by
reading an installment of *The Two Orphans* over and

over. His composure did not leave him when his name was called and he walked up the steps leading to Nervousness Boulevard.

Toward the end of the afternoon the crowd rushed to the bulletin board where the announcer stood with a sheet of paper in his hand. A great silence fell. The names of the winners were called.

"Achille Debussy."

Victorine lifted him off his feet and kissed him on both cheeks while Manuel patted him affectionately on the shoulder, and they proceeded to Prévost's where three cups of the famous hot chocolate helped bring everyone back to normality.

Along the Faubourg Poissonnière, sobs and angry words could be heard. Injustice . . . favoritism . . . the first touch of tragedy among those youngsters who knew no better and imagined that their whole future had been at stake and was irremediably lost.

Having been admitted as a piano student in the class of Marmontel, Achille was assigned to the solfeggio class of Albert Lavignac. This young teacher was intelligent and understanding. At once he discovered the musicianship of his new pupil.

Sometimes the boy let his fingers roam on the keys, extracting from them some rare links of subtle harmonies. Lavignac listened and wondered. So much insight, so much intuition seemed strange in one so young.

Among the other students there was at least one who shared the bewilderment of the teacher; a slender boy with light hair and blue eyes whose name was Gabriel Pierné. Mme. Pierné often came to the classes with her son and almost invariably took the two boys to Prévost's afterward. Later Achille was invited to their home on the occasion of Gabriel's birthday.

Attired in a brand-new black jacket with a white collar and a floating polka dot tie, short pants of velvet and patent leather shoes, he boarded the omnibus ready for a fine day.

A delicious dinner was served and there was music afterward.

But on top of the grand piano Achille discovered a folder containing various prints, etchings, and engravings.

"Gabriel, let's take these to your room, I'd love to look at them"; and the two boys disappeared, unnoticed.

Seated at Gabriel's desk, Achille examined the pictures with tremendous eagerness. He held them up to the light, using his folded hand for an ocular as he had seen done by "Uncle" Arosa when the latter scrutinized some outstanding piece of his collection. There were also several issues of *L'Illustration* and a few exquisite woodcuts. Achille was quite fascinated by the latter and he contemplated them for a long time, then placed them under the pile.

"Gabriel," he said, "why don't you cut some pictures from *L'Illustration*. They would look nice on the walls of this room."

Gabriel went in search of a pair of scissors. When he came back the intensity of Achille's eyes seemed to have become appeased.

"Achille," Marmontel called as he looked at his schedule book, "play your Bach F minor prelude."

Achille opened his music as if reluctantly. He started

but soon began to stumble; his eyes were glued on the notes. Obviously he did not know his text.

"Stop!" said Marmontel. "You haven't been practicing on this. You don't even know your fingerings. Let us hear the Alkan étude. I hope it will fare better."

This time Achille blushed and nervously rubbed his hands. He simply couldn't bear Alkan's music, that "unison" étude in particular. When he admitted that he hadn't even started studying it, Marmontel's face became sober.

"How many hours did you practice each day, this week?"

"Eight hours, maître."

"And this is the result. What did you do during those eight hours?"

"Well, maître, I must explain to you. Last week at the music store I borrowed the score of Haydn's quartets. Since I had to return it today I spent all my time reducing them on my piano."

The entrance of M. Terrasse stopped the dialogue. A retired army officer, he was now the surveillant général, the supervisor, the chief policeman of the Conservatoire. One of his duties consisted of checking up on the students' presence. Regulations were strict and being absent three consecutive times meant dismissal from the class; unless, of course, some valid excuse was presented.

When the roll call was over, Marmontel's irritation had visibly calmed down.

"That will be enough for today," he told Achille, who had remained under fearful expectation, "but for the next time I want those pieces known thoroughly . . . otherwise . . ."

He always stopped at that "otherwise" and, though the students never knew what was threatened, it was enough to put them into a fever of work that would last for several weeks.

Down in the hall Marmontel met his colleague Ernest Guiraud, the teacher of composition.

"Do you see that queer-looking boy with the black blouse, there in the courtyard? Imagine . . . he came today with his lesson completely unprepared!"

"And you pushed him out of the class?"

"No. Because he had spent his time reducing the Haydn quartets. Ah, the little rascal. He doesn't seem to care much for his piano, but he certainly loves music."

Mme. Pierné had missed the folder. She looked for it all over the drawing room, on the piano, in the chests, everywhere. Finally she went to Gabriel's room and saw it on the table. The scissors were there too, and paper shavings on the floor testified to the mutilation which had taken place. Gabriel explained what had happened.

"You didn't even ask for permission," his mother scolded, "and you cut all those pages. What for? To stick them around these walls, as a concierge would do. I wonder what your father will think of the idea. Just wait till he comes in."

But as she spoke Mme. Pierné had been checking up on the rest of the contents. Suddenly she burst into indignation:

"The woodcuts! Where are the woodcuts?"

Up in the little room of the Rue Clapeyron the two exquisite gems rested peacefully on the wall. Achille had been unable to resist the temptation. Entirely unconscious that he was doing something unethical, he had slipped them under his coat, intending to return them when his artistic thirst had been satisfied.

And so he did . . .

The incident had no effect on his friendship with Gabriel, but Mme. Pierné resented it. Her husband took a different view:

"He didn't mean anything. A child, just a child. But also an artist!" he said.

In the Debussy household life went on as usual and nothing apparently troubled the course of the conventional bourgeois routine. Still, Victorine seemed to have lost some of her cheerful disposition. One day Achille spoke to her:

"Mother, it would be so useful for me if I could go to the Opéra more often. Couldn't Uncle Arosa arrange to let me have some tickets?"

Victorine looked embarrassed.

"No," she said bluntly. "Uncle Arosa cannot do anything any more. We haven't seen him for a long time. He has a wife now, and we don't know her."

So came to an end the vision of wealth, generosity and all other imaginable virtues embodied in Achille's mind by that somewhat mysterious man of the world whose interest had meant so much to him.

The months passed and one examination followed another. Once Achille presented a Bach toccata and his interpretation drew sharp criticism from Ambroise Thomas.

"Marmontel," the aged director shouted from his presidential chair, "I cannot approve of such shadings

and such expression in Bach. It isn't classical. What's
the matter with this boy Debussy? Will you see that in
the future he adheres more closely to tradition?"

Marmontel, of course, did not agree, since he liked expression to the point of being often criticized for impart-
ing to his pupils an interpretation bordering on the
"sentimental." But he said nothing.

There was also in the class a gentle, affable boy from
the South, Paul Vidal, with whom Achille had formed a
friendship. It was not long until, with Gabriel Pierné,
they constituted a sort of "trio." Often on leaving the
Conservatoire they proceeded to the home of one of
them in order to hear their attempts at composition.
They also took walks to the Parc Monceau and sat on
the edge of the pond, below the colonnade, watching the
frolics of the ducks on water and land. Sometimes, to the
bewilderment of the old ladies doing their knitting, they
sang in three voices and rather out of pitch, some in-
ventions of Bach or some of their own contrapuntal
exercises.

"Manuel, I am somewhat concerned about Achille,"
Victorine said one day to her husband. "I think he is
neglecting his piano. I have discovered in his room some
music sheets with scribbling on it. Would he want to
become a composer? That would be awful. Composers
starve during their lifetime, you know. More and more I
regret that we didn't make a sailor out of him. He liked
it and . . . that is a *stable* position!"

This time Manuel stood by his son, perhaps wanting
to show off his erudition.

"I do not agree with you, Victorine. All composers do

not starve. Rossini, for instance, and Massenet, and Verdi—"

"Why, the idea!" she exclaimed. These were the names of demigods to her. How could Achille ever aspire to such glory?

Achille had found a real friend in the person of his solfeggio teacher, Albert Lavignac, whose keen mind had soon discovered the value of his young pupil's harmonic "finds." Often he kept Achille after class and the two of them went through some four-handed score together.

One afternoon, deeply absorbed in the reading of *Tristan und Isolde*, they forgot the hour. Finally they could hardly see—there was no light in the class for fear of fire—and they were about to stop when the door opened brusquely.

"It is forbidden to stay after your teacher has left," M. Terrasse shouted. "You will be punished. Your names, please."

The supervisor's confusion was great when he recognized Lavignac; he excused himself and beat a quick retreat while Achille and his teacher groped their way along the dark corridor.

All the same, M. Terrasse could not understand why a teacher disregarded discipline and the rules of the establishment. He would have been more surprised still had he heard a conversation that took place between Lavignac and Ernest Guiraud a few moments later:

"I have a young lad in my class, Guiraud, whom I consider quite out of the ordinary. In a few years I believe he will be a wonderful recruit for you. When he sits at the piano and improvises he has me puzzled and charmed. What he does is against all reason, absurd. But believe it or not, I learn many things myself, and the illogical takes on the appearance of reason."

Guiraud was a perfect gentleman, a delicate artist, and a discriminating critic. Born in New Orleans, he had come to Paris at the age of fifteen to complete his musical education and had won the Prix de Rome, this being the only case when a father and son captured the coveted distinction. But the influence of his Creole origin manifested itself throughout his life and somewhat sterilized the development of his creative powers, which to some extent remained unused. He could spend hours in aesthetic discussions; at night he would join friends around the billiard table of some little café, smoke packages of cigarettes, and finally walk home with them in order to finish the analysis of some astonishing stroke; but upon reaching there the conversation would have reverted to musical problems; so in order to solve them the group would walk back and see Guiraud to his own home where the same process would repeat itself and continue at both ends until the breeze freshened, the tops of the trees rustled gently, the street sweepers brought out their brooms and hose, and dawn sent the incorrigible "noctambules" to a well-deserved rest.

Guiraud grew even more interested when he heard that Achille was an addict of the billiard balls, and a good player already.

"You send him to me when the time comes," he said to Lavignac. "I believe he may be just the kind of pupil I am looking for."

Meanwhile Achille became interested in the organ,

and he wished to enter the classes of harmony and accompaniment. He made his application and was admitted to all of them.

César Franck was in charge of the organ class. Quiet, unassuming, debonair, he was one of the least glamorous personalities of the Conservatoire. For years he had been making a scant living through giving piano lessons. Day after day he left his home in the morning and went from house to house, from school to convent, filling his schedule with resignation. Few musicians suspected that he was a composer, since he hardly ever spoke of his works to anyone. His class at the Conservatoire, where he dealt with advanced students, and above all the organ loft of Sainte-Clotilde, where his improvisations were much appreciated by connoisseurs, were his only relief from teaching drudgery.

But Franck's harmonic theories were not readily acceptable to Achille. Asked to improvise, it was not long until his master interrupted him.

"Modulate," said Franck.

Two measures went by.

"Modulate," Franck repeated.

Achille inwardly resented this unjustified criticism; he knew he was modulating probably more than his teacher requested, but the latter did not realize it. Finally he stopped attending the classes. No clash occurred between them. That would have been impossible with a man like César Franck, endowed with an angelic disposition.

"I had nothing to do in that class," Achille commented to Paul Vidal later. "Le père Franck is a lovely man, but musically I consider him a 'modulating machine'!"

Worse conditions prevailed in the harmony class of Émile Durand, a narrow-minded professor who loved neither music, nor his profession, nor his pupils. Nearly every week a conflict developed.

"Debussy, bring your copy."

From the first look Durand's anger was aroused. He seized his pencil and a hail of strokes fell on the paper, sometimes so excitedly that they went right through it.

"Look at this fifth . . . and that one . . . and that octave. Horror!"

"But, maître . . . " Achille tried to explain.

"Silence! It is unclean, filthy. There's no right to do that. And this here . . . that's the climax!"

It was the last measure and Achille, instead of using an orthodox cadence, had devised a system of his own to fall back on the tonic.

"I like this better," he candidly admitted; "it sounds better to my ear and I find it considerably more distinguished."

"Impudent!" Durand yelled as he completely lost his temper; and the pencil began landing on Achille's head.

Compared with such a temperamental instructor, Marmontel seemed mild and lenient. Achille was still with him and apparently enjoyed favored treatment. Despite his efforts, he could never arrive on time. When it was a matter of a few minutes Marmontel did not seem to notice it. One day, however, the delay was well over half an hour.

Slowly Achille climbed the steps, preparing his story; it was going to be something about two buses passing full up at the Place de l'Opéra transfer. But this excuse did not prove necessary.

"Ah , . . at last, here you are, mon petit," Marmontel said while the entire class gasped, wondering by what kind of wizardry Achille could get away so easily.

"Sit down and play your Pathétique sonata."

Achille, even at that early age, did not feel akin to Beethoven. He played the last movement of the famous composition and his rendition was rather indifferent, with a sort of bored attitude toward the music.

"Stop!" Marmontel ordered. "I want more expression, more feeling. Think of the title."

"But, maître, I thought the title 'Pathétique' was never put by Beethoven himself, but instead by a publisher who thought it would have more human appeal."

"Quite true, my young friend. But this is an instance when the publisher was right. 'Pathétique' fits like a glove; doesn't that mean grief, suffering, despair? You must express it. Listen."

Marmontel, improvising words of his own, started singing the theme in an incredible falsetto voice:

"*Oh, pauvre mère, douleur amère . . .* "
(*Oh, poor mother, bitter sorrow . . .*)

It was really so funny that Achille could hardly refrain from chuckling; but he controlled himself and did his best to satisfy Marmontel.

"That dear old man," he said to a classmate as they went out.

Through examinations and competitions Achille went as a good, honest student but without creating any sensation. His playing suffered from contradictory defects: at times he attacked the keys with a sort of frenzy, forcing all his effects, snorting and lifting himself from the bench; then suddenly he would return to the softest imaginable shadings, obtaining a liquid tone of rare mellowness. This disproportion was probably responsible for his stalling on the ladder of awards.

Now he was in his fifth year with Marmontel and he had to win the first prize or be definitely excluded from the class.

"Bonjour, M. Achille. I wish you the best of luck!"

Mme. Mousset, her broom under her arm and a duster in her hand, stood at the door of her loge as Achille and his mother came downstairs. The great day of the piano competition had come at last!

It was still early but the July sun already struck hard, announcing a hot day; on the streets, laborers and office workers had taken off their hats and coats and the bars of the corner cafés were well attended.

Achille was spick and span for this all-important occasion. To the students in general, this end-of-the-year contest is the long-awaited hour when everything disappears before the desire to make good, to play one's best. To Achille, in particular, it meant more, since it was his last chance. Usually so calm, today he felt impatient and wished it was over, whatever the result might be.

When they arrived at the Conservatoire there was already much animation. A few music critics paced the floor of the gallery leading to the concert hall; if any of them gathered near one of the heavy pillars, some youngster would casually linger there and finally hide himself on the other side of it, trying to steal one of the secrets which those important personages probably knew, either the composition of the jury or the author of the piece to be read at sight.

There were also the inevitable busybodies who fluttered around like flies, knew nothing but made predictions about this and that, quoting names and evaluating the chances much in the manner of bookmakers at the horse races.

Gabriel Pierné came in, sleek as a weasel and looking very sure of himself.

When Marmontel appeared the youngsters flocked around him; for each one he had a word of ultimate advice:

"Gabriel, remember . . . not too fast your chromatic passage. Achille, be sure not to exaggerate any pianissimo . . ."

But it was nine o'clock and the contestants had to be locked up in the artists' room, a barbarous custom but necessary in order to ensure the secrecy of the reading piece. There they had to wait, in a room resembling a prison parlor with its iron bars at the windows.

In the hall every seat was occupied: musicians, critics, former laureates, private teachers, society women attending because it is considered fashionable or because they had a senator friend who could give them tickets, of which two were issued to the immediate family of each contestant.

The jury came in and at once the session began. The usher stepped to the front of the stage near the grand piano, opened like some instrument of torture, and announced the name of the first boy. Then every fifteen minutes, and for hours, another would enter, sometimes so scared that he looked like a convict going to his doom. The only recess was for lunch when the adjudicators usually went to Brébant's, on the boulevard. But the boys who played in the afternoon could not go out and a waiter from some small café near by brought in a large tray: enough food to sustain them for a few hours longer! When at last the whole list had played and read, the jury retired for deliberation.

At this stage the excitement of the audience always reaches its peak. Amid loud discussion in the courtyard, an unofficial list of awards emerges, representing the "voice of the people." If the verdict of the jury coincides with it, well and good; otherwise something of a riot is likely to develop, including hissing, catcalls, and insults hurled at the jurors. All in all, a contest day is an unusual affair, hard on the nerves, the brains, and the hearts of all connected with it!

Such was the atmosphere in which Achille risked his last chance. It was aggravated by the torrid temperature.

It was late afternoon when the bell rang, calling the crowd in to hear the verdict. A few more moments of anxious expectation, then the door of the jurors' loge opened and Ambroise Thomas came in, serious and dignified, followed by the other jurors. His voice called to the usher who had advanced on the platform:

"Will you call . . . Gabriel Pierné."

A thunder of applause surged up. Pierné was a favorite and the choice met with unanimous approval.

Then other names followed for the minor awards, but for Achille it was all over and he was out of Marmontel's class.

Apparently unconcerned he stood by his mother and Manuel who had come from his office to watch what he thought was going to be the triumph of his son. The three of them walked back all the way to the Rue Clapey-ron, among the crowd of shop girls and other employees pouring out of the stores and chatting gaily as their day's work was over.

When they arrived, Mme. Mousset was seated in her armchair, reading her evening paper. But Achille passed without even looking in. Behind him Manuel's face was grave and a heavy wrinkle barred his forehead.

Mme. Mousset sank back into her chair; she saw, she understood and she, too, felt very sad.

Several days passed in a gloomy atmosphere; Manuel and Victorine were depressed and their last hopes had collapsed. More than ever they regretted not having pushed their son into a naval career.

But Achille took his failure philosophically; when the classes were resumed he continued his work with Émile Durand whose attitude, changed somewhat after an inci-dent which happened as one of the former Prix de Rome visited the class.

At Durand's invitation, he had brought a harmony les-son to be interpreted by the students. It was but a few minutes until Achille completed the task while his class-mates still struggled hard; he rose, came to the side of the piano, and presented his manuscript to the author.

"Will you play it?" the latter said.

Durand inwardly grinned in expectation of his guest's reaction. But this was as eloquent as it was unexpected. Profoundly charmed by the rare and novel harmonic flow, he took his own interpretation and tore it up, while the whole class gaped in amazement at such homage paid to the youthful genius of one of their comrades.

"Victorine! Please come here, I want to speak to you."

Manuel was seated in the old armchair near the window. His previous long silence and the tone of his voice indicated his deep concern. He crushed the butt of his cigarette on the ash tray, the last of a series he had been smoking nervously since lunchtime.

"We must talk seriously about Achille," he began. "However hard I try not to worry, there comes a time when things must be discussed. For a long time, you know, I had confidence in his musical future. But the years go by, and nothing seems to happen."

"But, Manuel, music is a long process; everybody says so. We ought not to be impatient."

"Quite right. But what about the competition last July? Pierné got the first prize and Achille got kicked out, did he not?"

"Oh, Manuel."

But he continued, more animatedly:

"That's exactly what happened and I like to call a spade a spade. Now what is he doing? Studying harmony, counterpoint, accompaniment. Where will that put him and how long will it be until he makes money? He is growing up and it's about time material results began to show up. Ah, if I still had my china shop at Saint-Germain, I would stop all this nonsense and take him in as a clerk!"

"Listen to me, Manuel; Mme. Pierné says—"

"Ah, a good joke! Mme. Pierné can talk, indeed. The Piernés have money and no financial problems to meet. They can give their son any kind of education he likes. We're not in the same position, and we have five children to feed, clothe, and send to school."

He threw a queer look at his wife, as if he resented her having brought forth such a large family.

Then the bell rang, and Mme. Mousset was at the door:

"Here's a letter for M. Achille. I brought it up especially because they said it was urgent."

Achille read it as soon as he came home.

"Hurrah!" he exclaimed. "It's a note from Marmontel; he has recommended me for a position and I'm going to see him at once."

He grabbed his hat and coat and hurried out, jumping two or three steps at a time down the stairway. It is a short distance from the Rue Clapeyron to the Rue Blanche and he ran all the way. When he arrived Marmontel had just finished a lesson.

"Come in, my child; I believe I have something nice to offer you, if you will take it."

He explained the prospective engagement and Achille, overjoyed, ran back again to the Rue Clapeyron. The atmosphere was still tense but his parents were eager to hear the result of his interview.

"I am going away," Achille announced. "There's a rich Russian family in need of a pianist to play chamber music and give lessons to the children. Not much glory in that, surely; but a nice fee!"

At the last words Manuel became attentive. When he heard the figure his gloom left him suddenly and he opened his arms:

"Bravo, my son! Now you are coming to your senses. When do you leave?"

"Tomorrow afternoon. They're expecting me and I must get there as soon as possible."

In the attic there was an old suitcase which Achille had used twelve years before when Uncle Arosa had taken him to the Riviera. He brought it to his room, dusted it, then packed in his linen, some manuscript paper, and two scores: *Marie-Magdeleine* by Massenet, and *Carmen.*

The afternoon of the next day Achille alighted from the omnibus in front of the Paris-Lyon-Méditerranée depot. He had insisted on coming alone, fearful as always of over-sentimental demonstrations. It was still early and the train had just been made up. To mark his place he put his valise in a corner of the compartment, and began pacing up and down the platform. His thoughts went back to his former trip; how young he was then! And how young he was still, despite the years that had passed so quickly. Passengers were streaming in but, absorbed in his reverie, he took no heed of them. The voice of the guard was heard:

"All aboard!"

He returned to the compartment and sat in his corner, glancing sideways at the "intruders" who had taken the other three seats. Good-byes were shouted back and forth, handkerchiefs were waved as the train began to move. How glad Achille felt that he had no active part in such a scene.

The train gained momentum as it passed the fortifications; amid a trail of white smoke it sped through Charenton. There were rowboats on the river and the cafés alongside were filled with joyous crowds. Then came the banlieue, the suburbs of Paris, the cottages with flaming tile roofs, each surrounded by a green patch, the vegetable garden where working people often spend an hour of relaxation when they come home. Farther away, rows of poplar trees lined the white ribbon of the national highway. Achille, his face glued to the window, looked at the changing picture which unrolled itself before his eyes; such a lovely one too, so purely French, so typical of the Ile-de-France.

Night came and he opened a package prepared by Victorine and containing some ham, a wing of chicken, fruit, buttered bread, and a bottle of wine. He wouldn't go hungry. Later the lights were dimmed, and everyone went to sleep.

"Vallorbe . . . All out for customs inspection!"

It was shortly after sunrise. Achille stretched himself, rubbed his eyes, yawned, then looked out. Was this Switzerland, the fatherland of William Tell, so highly boosted by the travel agencies? There was a chill in the air as he stepped out. The inspection took place in a large hall and not on the train itself, as it does now. An officer opened Achille's suitcase, fumbled through it, looked carefully through all the manuscript paper, then stuck a stamp on the outside. Soon the journey was resumed.

Now the sun was higher and he could freely admire the landscape. On both sides of the track were green pastures, hills and valleys, brooks and cascades, while in the distance one could sense through the morning mist the presence of mighty mountains and snowy peaks.

The train arrived at Interlaken in the afternoon. Achille, puzzled by the change of language and completely incompetent in German, beckoned to a cab driver and showed him the address of the Palace Hotel.

One entire wing of this imposing hostelry had been

rented by Mme. Nadejda Filaretovna von Meck, the wife of a wealthy Russian engineer who owned the Moscow-Riga railroad, a line some five hundred miles in length. In it she had installed her family, a few musicians, and a small army of chambermaids, cooks, valets, and coachmen.

As Achille was led to his room he heard the sound of several pianos and the high tones of a violin. It came from the "conservatory," as part of that wing had been pleasantly nicknamed among the personnel of the hotel. He was unpacking his valise when word came from Mme. von Meck that she would like to see him at once.

Through heavily carpeted corridors where outside noises came in as if muffled, he made his way to the grand salon. The usher announced him with a sonorous voice.

Mme. von Meck was seated in a big armchair; despite the heat in the apartment, she was wrapped in several woolen shawls adorned with beautiful embroideries; her face was serious and in the expression of her eyes there was something autocratic, almost domineering. She rose and shook Achille's hand.

"Bonjour. Won't you sit down?" she said.

She looked him over while he tried to adopt a dignified attitude; but inwardly he was terrified. Finally she broke the silence:

"How old are you?"

Achille looked no more than sixteen; he was eighteen in reality, but didn't want to admit it.

"I am twenty years old, madame," he answered with all the assurance of which he was capable.

"Oh, how lucky you are. The most beautiful age! All your life is ahead of you."

Afraid that Mme. von Meck might doubt his statement, Achille started a monologue about himself, trying to impress her with the idea that he was now a grownup. He told her of his first visit to Marmontel, years ago when he was a boy. But his hostess hardly listened; her thoughts seemed to wander far away; soon she interrupted him:

"Do you like Tchaikovsky?"

Achille remained silent; he had never heard the name.

"Tchaikovsky," she repeated, vaguely disturbed.

Once more she rose and pointed to two large photographs, one on the piano and the other on the table in the center of the room. He looked earnestly at those pictures of a middle-aged man with a kindly, pensive face.

"You will find some of his music on these shelves," Mme. von Meck said.

Achille began perusing the music. Tchaikovsky . . . Tchaikovsky . . . several contemporary German works . . . more Tchaikovsky. Then Achille stopped.

"Ah, Massenet!"

Mme. von Meck smiled disdainfully and haughtily. Poor young man, she thought, who knows Massenet and not Tchaikovsky. For the time being she preferred not to insist, and changed the subject.

"Of course, M. Marmontel told you what is expected of you. In the morning you will give lessons to my sons, Nicolas and Alexander. In the afternoon we will play four-handed music together. Then you may have several hours to yourself. In the evening we all gather in the

drawing room for a little musicale and everyone contrib-
utes. We have an excellent violinist, Pachulsky, and perhaps you can play sonatas with him."

Pachulsky was a native of Poland; he had received a
college education and this enabled him to act also as
tutor. His personality was ingratiating, though not free
from a touch of snobbery; but he had a breezy manner
and was a good talker, sure of himself and knowing how
to bluff if necessary. Of course, it all turned to meek
suavity as soon as he found himself in the presence of "la
patronne," the feminine boss, as he called Mme. von
Meck.

For some unknown reason these qualities appealed to
Achille, as did also the "grand manner" Pachulsky loved
to display; with the extra help of the sonatas they soon
became good friends.

Achille was delighted with his new surroundings: everybody was pleasant, the hotel was perfect, the service discreet and efficient, the food a marvel of culinary art.
What a change from his mediocre Paris life!

He felt deep gratitude toward Marmontel whose provi-
dential influence had made all this possible.

In the evening Achille came down to the drawing
room where Mme. von Meck was already engaged in
lively conversation with Pachulsky. Soon her elder
daughter, Julia Carlovna, joined the group; she was not
beautiful, but looked intelligent and active; already in
her thirties, she acted as manager of the household and
obviously enjoyed this responsibility. Endowed with a
small but pleasant voice, she opened the musicale, accompanied by Achille.

A few moments later Sophie, the younger daughter,

came in; she was fourteen years old; her curly hair fell over her shoulders; she wore a white dress, with patent leather shoes which squeaked as she walked nimbly on the mirrorlike floor.

When Achille saw her his breath stopped, his hands started to quiver, he blushed and lowered his eyes. Never, never before had he seen such a beautiful girl.

Mme. von Meck the next day wrote to Tchaikovsky. She had been impressed by Achille's reserved attitude and thorough musicianship. As always, she used her own writing paper, each sheet adorned with a different hand-painted water color:

"Peter Ilyitch, there is a new visitor in the house. Yesterday a young pianist arrived from Paris, recommended to me by Marmontel. I brought him here to take care of the children during the summer and to play with me. This young man possesses a real virtuosity, but it seems to me that his expression leaves much to be desired, although he is a splendid accompanist. He is young, however, only twenty. He hasn't lived enough yet, and probably has not suffered at all . . ."

Alexander (Sacha) and Nicolas had fine aptitude for music and under Achille's guidance they progressed rapidly. Sacha's attention was sometimes diverted by his taste for Alpinism, encouraged in this by Pachulsky who was a true enthusiast at climbing. Between them they had assembled enough ropes, skis, pickaxes, and other paraphernalia to arouse the jealousy of a company of professional guides.

Often they started by sunrise. If they were late in coming back, Nadejda Filaretovna became frightfully nervous, ringing the bell every five minutes, asking for her lavender salts and disturbing the calm of the household until the two excursionists finally made their entrance, wrapped in sweaters, their cheeks reddened by the exertion of a long ascent in the sunshine and by the invigorating, crisp mountain air.

After the dinner, which took place at noon according to the Russian fashion, Nadejda Filaretovna and Achille retired to the drawing room for their ensemble session. She always played the bass. At first Achille was more scared than ever when he had to sit so close to that aristocratic lady, so close that at times their arms and hands came in contact; but he soon became accustomed to it.

Tchaikovsky, of course, was kept informed of the musical developments:

"I continue making much music with my young 'musikus,' Peter Ilyitch. He has brought two scores with him, *Marie-Magdeleine* by Massenet and *Carmen* about which, he says, Paris has become crazy. I listen to it attentively, Peter Ilyitch, because I know *Carmen* must be good music, since you like it too."

As to Massenet, she could not understand the favor he enjoyed; to her it was cheap, second-rate music. Her judgment once more was biased by her partiality toward one composer, and one only. Achille showed her several of his songs but these, too, were treated with indifference; even her friendly feelings were not sufficient to prompt a few words of praise. Graceful compositions, she thought, but unimportant and almost childish.

It was when they discussed modern music that they disagreed most. It seemed to her that Achille spoke much to say nothing. With the exception of Wagner, he disliked the German school and found it heavy, conventional, and pedantic. Worse than anything in her eyes was his lack of enthusiasm about Tchaikovsky.

"My 'musikus,'" she wrote once to the latter, "is indeed a young man with strange musical ideas. I think I can define him in a few words: his whole being is an emanation of the Paris boulevards!"

When the season drew to its close Nadejda Filaretovna announced that she and her family would go to Arcachon, the resort in Southern France near Bordeaux, in order to change climate and take sea baths. An invitation was extended to Achille and he gladly accepted this opportunity to continue an existence exempt from all worries, with good financial returns which he was able to save almost entirely. And Arcachon meant the beloved sea, the mighty ocean.

The family installed itself in one of the largest villas available. The schedule was resumed, but Achille stayed less at the house during his hours of recess. He walked through the "summer town" where the business district, the fishermen's harbor, and the Casino are located, and also through the "winter city," that haven of consumptives up among the dunes. He and Pachulsky discovered the picturesque pier with its rowboats, the store of Dignac where dozens of tasty small oysters can be absorbed fresh from the beds, accompanied by a few glasses of palatable native white wine. There was also the Source des Abatilles, the spring of clear water to which the inhabitants attributed all kinds of virtues. Then the pine forest extending for miles along the lagoon and the sea.

The arrival of such distinguished visitors elicited, as might be expected, much curiosity among the native population. News of local importance was scare at Arcachon, and soon fantastic stories of unknown wealth were circulated from the fish market to the gambling rooms of the Casino where Pachulsky had made a sensational entrance. Achille never accompanied him there, however, because of his inborn dislike for quick familiarity. Instead he went for long walks along the water front, occasionally engaging in conversation with some fisherman whose simple manners attracted him more than the humbug of so many fourflushers acting to the gallery.

Half a dozen pianos had been rented from the Pleyel agency, to the amazement of the director who had never seen so much business descend all at once upon his store.

"Bussik, I have a surprise for you," said Nadejda Filaretovna to Achille one afternoon. By now she had taken the habit of calling him in this diminutive, affectionate fashion and to everyone he had become Bussik, Malenky Bussik. How soft, melodious, and caressing these words sounded when uttered by Sophie's lovely lips! He blushed, then, and hid his face in some music sheets.

"Our musical circle is going to be enlarged," Nadejda Filaretovna continued; "a cellist is coming from Moscow. His name is Danilchenko. A splendid virtuoso, but above all a real musician. You will like him, Bussik, I am sure."

This was good news for Achille; the arrival of this new element would permit him to explore that larger and richer form of musical expression: the trio.

From that day a real feast of music took place at the villa every night, to the delight of both audience and performers.

One evening Nadejda Filaretovna brought in a package which she unwrapped with infinite care. It was a new manuscript trio by Tchaikovsky! The notes were small and hardly legible, but Achille's skill conquered the difficulty superbly. He liked this work better than anything he had seen by Tchaikovsky. Perhaps this name so often repeated, the photographs he saw constantly on piano and table, the symphonies performed so much in their four-handed version, all had conspired to encircle him in a sort of suggestion. But he was too genuine a musician not to admire the power of the Russian composer; certainly he found him too much under Germanic influence and also too matter-of-fact, too facile in the choice of his melodic ideas. With youthful broadmindedness, however, he discarded such reservations.

The three partners were called downstairs one afternoon, when a photographer came and installed an enormous camera on the terrace. Nadejda Filaretovna was with him and they tried to figure out an adequate background.

"I want to have your picture taken together," she said. "A Pole, a Frenchman, a Petit-Russian. How interesting! It will be so nice to have a souvenir of this trio, the 'Von Meck Trio'!"

Naturally, her chief purpose was to send the photograph to Tchaikovsky, so that he could form a better idea of what her musicians looked like. In this way, she felt, he would be nearer to them all.

Tchaikovsky's answer came promptly:

"I was much interested by Debussy especially; it seems to me that he looks somewhat like Anton Rubinstein."

There was some similarity in the hands and face, Nadejda Filaretovna thought, as she looked at his juvenile features.

In his letter Tchaikovsky also announced the forth-coming publication of a new work, *The Maid of Orleans.* The score was about to come off the press and, of course, the first copy would be for her. Already she debated what she should do when it arrived: keep it to herself like a hidden treasure or show it to Bussik? Anxious as she was to overcome the sort of dormant reservation which, de-spite his praise of the Trio, she still sensed in Achille toward the genius of her revered friend, she was afraid to show him *The Maid of Orleans.* She consulted her elder daughter:

"Should I show Bussik the new work of Peter Ilyitch?"

"Why not?"

"For this reason: he has an extraordinary memory. I fear he might remember some passages, the most beauti-ful passages. Then, suppose they come back to his mind and he uses them in his own works? Or perhaps he might play them for some of those Parisian composers who are so unscrupulous, who would not hesitate to plunder the work of Peter Ilyitch once more and try to take from him laurels which are so legitimately his own!"

She accused Massenet who, in her mind, was jealous of Peter Ilyitch. What would he say? Who could tell what depreciating gossip he would attempt to spread about?

Finally she decided to keep the score in her own room and to read it by herself. Meanwhile she requested Achille to make a transcription of *Le Lac des Cygnes.*

The season at Arcachon was nearing its end and every day some of the summer residents left the city. Soon the von Meck party would also break up. This thought began to fill Achille with melancholy; from the present atmosphere of supreme refinement he would have to return to middle-class surroundings; he would have to listen to the trite and pretentious divagations of his father; and Sophie would be hundreds of miles away. His heart was filled with inexpressible anguish; no longer could he behold the apparition of grace and beauty.

In his room during his hours of liberty he worked feverishly, near the fireplace where a few pine logs burned cheerfully. Outside the chill of September was noticeable as twilight crept upon the landscape. Unaware of the hour, Achille worked on. Within him was a resolution to write something sensational, something that would cause the walls of Paris to shake and tremble. Then, perhaps, it would be possible to come closer to the ethereal, the divinely youthful image whose remembrance would dwell in his heart, never to be forgotten.

When Achille came down to the dining room he noticed that Nadejda Filaretovna looked preoccupied. *The Maid of Orleans* had not yet arrived. Perhaps the score had gone astray? How awful it would be if it fell into unworthy hands, with the precious dedication certainly inscribed on it . . . if someone else's eyes should desecrate the beloved handwriting.

Pachulsky had already left the villa, and temporarily at least he was in disgrace. His rambling talk, from which bits of gossip were not excluded, had been reported to Nadejda Filaretovna. But since the last week had arrived and everyone was busy with souvenir hunting, shopping, and packing, his absence passed almost unnoticed.

The Maid of Orleans arrived the very day before they

left. Once again, however, Mme. von Meck was torn between her desire and her apprehension; but in the afternoon she made a sudden decision:

"Read this work through, Bussik." She placed the score on the piano stand.

From the first, Nadejda Filaretovna was plunged into a sickly sort of ecstasy which knew no bounds when Achille concluded the "grande scène" of Dunois with the King.

"All charlatans! All fakers!" she exclaimed. "Delibes, and Massenet, and Godard too, will steal from it, fill their pockets with it. You know, Bussik, how they have already plundered the first symphony!"

Bussik preserved an Olympian calm. He said nothing, but within himself he considered that this grande scène was nothing to rave about.

The six pianos were being taken away and only the grand in the drawing room remained. Nadejda Filaretovna turned to Achille:

"May I ask you one last favor, Bussik? Please, play that scène for me once more."

He complied with her wishes and when he left she was still deep in her raptures.

It would be a few hours until suppertime. What could he do? No more writing, for sure, on this eve of his departure. His scant packing would require but little time and he could attend to that in the evening. The weather was magnificent. A walk through the pine forest would be the best thing to do.

Past the spring of Les Abatilles he went to Le Moulleau and began to wander through the woods. The

thought that this was his last day at Arcachon made him
feel depressed; he had been happy here, but now it must
end. When would he see this land again, if ever?

Soon he reached the higher dunes. As he came to the
top of one of them the sea appeared before him. There
were two tall pines and their tops waved gently in the
soft breeze. Between them Achille stood, his eyes fixed
on the seascape as if he looked into the future, and this
future was bright.

Yes, the road to success was free before him. His wallet bulged with bank notes. Now his father could criticize him no longer!

The sun still shone brightly on the wavelets, playing
among them and throwing up myriad scintillating gems.
The saline atoms of the sea blended themselves with the
strong perfume of the forest, creating an exhilarating
fragrance along the shore.

For a long time Achille remained between the two
pine trees, unaware of earthly surroundings. His depressed feeling had disappeared.

When the breeze freshened and the sun began to sink
on the horizon, he left, his heart expanding with enthusiasm, courage, sheer joy.

The courtyard of the Conservatoire presented its accustomed aspect of reopening days when Achille, freshly
landed from the South, pushed open the heavy door.
Next to the newcomers he felt like an old-timer. Upstairs, in the corridor, he waited for Guiraud, with a
note of introduction from Marmontel in his pocket.

"Oh, I remember your name very well, my boy,"

Guiraud said when he came out. "So you wish to enter my class. Let's see, have you any of your compositions? I'd like to look them over."

Admission to these higher classes depended almost entirely on the discretion of the teachers and these naturally were on the lookout for sensational finds. They went back into the class and Achille unfolded his roll of music. As Guiraud read the songs his smile reflected great satisfaction. His decision was soon taken:

"All right, my boy, I will go and speak to M. Réty, the general secretary. But you may take it for granted that you will be admitted."

Achille thanked him and took his leave; but Guiraud caught up with him in the courtyard:

"I've been told that you play billiards. If you'll wait for a few minutes, perhaps we could have a game together?"

A few moments later Guiraud came out of Réty's office with the good news that the proposed candidacy was accepted.

"Well, my new student, let's go to the Pont de Fer and have our game."

The Pont de Fer was an old-fashioned café around the corner, patronized mostly by store owners of the neighborhood who played cards, chess, billiards, and dominoes in clouds of smoke.

They had their game and Achille lost, since Guiraud was an experienced player. When they parted they had become good friends. Many years earlier Guiraud himself had been a student of Marmontel, and he earned his living by playing cymbals in the orchestra of the Opéra-Comique, at the time when Massenet acted as a drummer at the Théâtre Lyrique. From his difficult debut Guiraud had derived a kindly disposition and a great understanding of conditions as they confront young musicians. Achille could have found no better instructor; their natures agreed perfectly. A new era had begun for him.

Eager to make money in order to satisfy his parents, he accepted the position of accompanist at the vocal studio of Mme. Moreau-Sainti. This was regular employment and it could probably last as long as he found it agreeable; though modest, the salary was permanent through ten months of each year. The Cours Moreau-Sainti was flourishing and catered to a distinguished clientele; one of its features was the cultivation of choral singing for women's voices. Among those who attended, Achille noticed a young and handsome lady. She was Mme. Vasnier, the wife of an architect. Her voice was of genuine coloratura type with an unusual range and crystalline high notes which justified Mme. Moreau-Sainti's contention that it was the finest "nightingale" organ she had ever heard. Of medium height, with brown hair and large expressive eyes, her face revealed a highly artistic and cultured intellect. She sang with feeling and musicianship and, contrary to many other students more socially inclined, she took her work seriously though with no intention of becoming a professional. Once she conversed with Mme. Moreau-Sainti, when the latter called Achille:

"M. Debussy, I want you to meet Mme. Vasnier. She was asking me if perhaps you would consent to help her with her songs. I shall let you talk it over together."

Left in the presence of this gorgeous creature Achille stood silent, overpowered by her radiant beauty. Already he had made up his mind to accept her offer whatever it might be. He would do without any fee, if necessary, for the privilege of looking at her, of making music with her. But this was not the case.

"I hope you will agree to what Mme. Moreau-Sainti said. I hate to interfere with your personal work and to ask you to give me this coaching at my house. I live on the Rue de Constantinople and hope it will not be too disturbing for you, nor too far."

"Oh, no, madame, I live quite near, on the Rue Clapeyron."

"Is that so? Well, then, everything is perfect. And it is understood that your fee will be the same as here."

Achille went home and entered the dining room exultantly:

"Some news! I have a private pupil, Mme. Vasnier."

"How much are you going to charge her?" asked Manuel.

Absorbed by the lovely vision still lingering in his mind, this came as a brutal shock. But Manuel did not notice this reaction and was highly pleased with the arrangements that had been made.

The day of the first lesson Achille entered the stately apartment house and knocked at the concierge's door.

"Mme. Vasnier?"

"Fifth floor, monsieur."

There were no elevators and he had to climb five long flights of stairs. He went up the first two at a breath, then he slowed down and climbed step by step, as if wanting to make his expectation last longer. On the landing he paused for a moment, afraid, apprehensive, and his hand shook slightly as it reached the bell.

Mme. Vasnier extended her long, delicate hand toward him:

"I am very happy to see you again. It is really so nice of you to come here."

The lesson started and she stood beside him, coming closer and leaning forward at times, when she wanted to look at the notes. He could then feel her body touching his and he inhaled the intoxicating perfume that came from her hair. It was an hour of enchantment that passed too soon. When the music was over they sat in the petit salon and talked. The door opened.

"My husband," she said. Then she introduced Achille: "This is my accompanist, M. Debussy."

Achille shook M. Vasnier's hand and looked at him as they exchanged the customary conventionalities. Truly he was amazed! How could this elderly, official-looking gentleman be the husband of that superb young creature?

M. Vasnier was a typical high-class architect embodying all the characteristics of this profession where art and business meet. Of the artist he preserved a few features: his almost white hair kept rather long and brushed back, a beard worn in "member of the Institute" style, a necktie somewhat too wide; the businessman showed in the black cutaway and in the tone of the voice, courteous but at times incisive, a voice which reminded one of technical discussions and board meetings. But he was a man of great culture, equally at ease in discussing architecture, the theater, letters, music, or the politics of the day. Achille impressed him favorably. M. Vasnier hated the conceit and pretense so often noticeable in artistic personalities. He was from old French stock and had been reared in surroundings where home and family virtues still occupied a place of honor. In his wife's accompanist he found that unobtrusive attitude, that restraint which almost bordered on bashfulness. His artistic eye had also remarked the dark curly hair brought forward and down on the brows, the delicate outline of the fingers as they stretched over the keys.

"I like that young man," he commented to his wife when they were left alone. "He seems so much above the type of the average salaried musician."

Achille's thoughts rambled as he walked home; in his mind the glorious image appeared more and more adorned with divine grace. But why, oh, why had she married such an old man? It seemed strange, incomprehensible, almost against nature.

Too young to explore far into psychological considerations, he did not trouble to analyze his feelings. But soon another reaction came: as he thought of the abnormal couple it was no longer with an obscure undercurrent of unconscious jealousy; a mysterious notion of satisfaction had taken its place.

The apartment in the Rue Clapeyron was not far from the Saint-Lazare station and one great advantage of this location was the knowledge that there were trains close at hand, which within an hour or less could take the family to Saint-Cloud, Ville d'Avray, Saint-Germain, and all the green-clad resorts on the banks of the Seine. When Sunday came, Manuel often proposed an excursion, which was gladly accepted by all. He was tired after six days of office duties and the prospect of a picnic in some picturesque spot by the river appealed to him as much as it did to Victorine, equally weary of household work. Achille, too, was delighted at every opportunity to wander leisurely through the Ile-de-France, this chosen land which stretches around Paris and toward the north-west some thirty miles between the Seine, the Marne, and the Oise. The harmony of its horizons, its valleys, rivers, and rolling hills from which he would later derive such inspiration, already enchanted him. A historian once called the Ile-de-France "a garden of flowers and stones." This is adequate, and tourists will always love it for the forests, the parks, the old fortresses and historic churches which give it charm.

Wherever Achille and his family went, the devotion of artists and writers surged up with each new mile of the road. Many of them had selected some untouched corner and built a summer home there. One could see Victor Hugo's old house at Bièvres; Gounod's estate at Saint-Cloud, Corot's atelier at the lake of Ville d'Avray. Sometimes they went as far as Mantes la Jolie, "the pretty one," a name well deserved by this charming little city built in a nest along the Seine and in olden times a border town of France which William the Conqueror, Duke of Normandy, plundered and burned, finding his death in a fall from his horse as he galloped through the flames and the crumbling houses.

On each occasion Manuel acted as cicerone and explained all the landmarks with a luxury of detail borrowed from a secret reading of guidebooks the night before. From time to time he took the family to Saint-Germain where for a few years he owned his little business on the Rue au Pain. They left early enough to have time to take a walk on the terrace which extends along the forest from the historic birthplace of Henri IV to Maisons-Laffitte. Achille loved this excursion best of all. From the terrace his eyes gazed on one of the loveliest landscapes in France; below the Seine stretched as a silvery ribbon on which some barges glided softly, towed by a tug letting out a long trail of smoke; farther out were the white villas of Le Pecq and Le Vésinet; back of him, the park of the château with its venerable trees, the kiosk where the military band played on Sunday afternoon. How freely Achille breathed as he contemplated the lovely valley and far away, the outline of the Mont Valérien and Montmartre. His reverie was interrupted by Manuel:

"Let's go and eat; if we wait too long we won't find any place at the restaurant."

They hurried to the Restaurant du Château, on the square facing the magnificent historic building, and sat outside so as to enjoy the view. From the adjoining station crowds of excursionists began to pour out, many of them carrying picnic baskets which they took to some clearing in the woods. Achille would have preferred that to a restaurant overfilled with noisy Sunday diners who seemingly could not enjoy themselves without disturbing the tranquillity of others. There were the peddlers too, the Arabs with their fake rugs, the inventors of all sorts of gadgets, the newsboys with the latest edition of *Le Petit Journal*.

Sometimes when the meal was over—a meal "in series" and at a fixed price—Manuel hailed one of the cabs which stood in line on the other side of the square. The family took its place in the antiquated victoria and Achille climbed in front, near the coachman, an old

Frenchman with disorderly white hair surrounding a bloated face flushed with red wine and apoplexy. The old man was fully conscious of the dignity of his profession and showed it in his majestic, tipsy air and the respect with which he held his whip. Manuel entered into political discussions with him and it always ended by the same phrase: "Ah, were not those the grand old days!" By this they meant the Empire of ill-fated Napoléon III whose name often recurred in the conversation. The old cabman never failed to recall one particular visit of the emperor to Saint-Germain when he had the honor of driving one of the official carriages.

If he felt more sentimentally inclined, Manuel proposed a visit to the parish church.

"It is right here that your christening took place, Achille," he said as they reached the baptismal font. No mention was ever made of Uncle Arosa, however, nor of Octavie de la Ferronnière, the godmother whose name was inscribed in the church records next to that of the wealthy financier.

Then they walked to the Rue au Pain and Manuel evoked old memories as he stood on the cobblestones of the narrow street: the creamery, the grocery store, the meat market, all so familiar; they were closed on Sunday afternoon but the same proprietors were still there, as he could see by the names painted above the doors.

To wind up the excursion the family took a walk through the old district where the narrow sidewalks, the pointed roofs, the bulging attics, the massive doorways revealed the presence of a glorious past; and when night closed in they went back to the station and climbed into a car already jammed by a multitude singing joyously and carrying bouquets of wildflowers. Bodies were exhausted, but hearts were satisfied as the train crossed the Seine on the high railroad bridge at that lovely hour when the broad black hillsides disappear in darkness and the suburban landscape begins to twinkle with innumerable lights.

"Chère Madame,
"Summer will soon be here and I am remembering the lovely months I spent at Interlaken and Arcachon last year. It was a joy to find myself in such an atmosphere of refinement and discrimination. Would it be indiscreet to ask you if perhaps your projects for this season might include a renewal of activities for your 'pianiste ordinaire'? Nothing could make me happier . . . It is with anxious expectation that I will await your answer, and I eagerly hope it will be favorable."

Overcoming his shyness, Achille had decided to write to Nadejda Filaretovna. Memories of his stay lingered persistently in his mind, over which neither his studies nor his newly acquired friends were able to cast a shadow. The heavenly vision of Sophie often came to his mind, and not even the beauty of Mme. Vasnier could chase it away.

Nevertheless, he saw the Vasniers more and more. M. Vasnier had taken a great interest in Achille and he tried to mend the deficiencies of his education through long, instructive fireside talks. The old architect's turn of mind was decidedly pedagogic; during these hours he did not attempt to initiate the young musician into the dry intricacies of orthography and syntax; instead, he led the conversation toward literary subjects and Achille, whose aptitudes were extraordinary, surprised him by instinctively knowing what to others would have meant long and careful pondering. They used to sit in the petit salon which Achille preferred to the cold drawing room furnished in typical bourgeois style, a drawing room in which no work was done and where everything was too orderly: no books, no papers on the central table; instead, a large bronze occupied it in solitary majesty, polished as if it were going to a show window; in a corner, a bust of white marble, a present of some fraternity. A few conservative canvases by Meissonier and Harpignies hung on the walls, together with framed medals recalling competitions from which M. Vasnier had emerged victorious. One livelier spot was the grand piano. After a few weeks Achille was using it copiously. Having told his hosts of the disturbances at home, they invited him to come any time he wished to work in quiet. The only sounds he heard were a few distant whistles from Saint-Lazare station and the muted noise of the carriages on the street below.

The Vasniers also invited him to come to Ville d'Avray where they were going to take summer quarters; then a letter came from Russia. Achille opened it eagerly.

"Oh, I am so happy! I am welcome and they will expect me soon," he said, much to the surprise of Victorine and Manuel who hardly understood how anyone could wish him to come and find any interest in his visit.

The von Mecks were installed for the summer in their large estate at Brailovo. Apart from this change of scenery, the existence of the family was exactly as the year before. But when Achille arrived another pianist was already there: Pachulsky was back in favor and he had brought his brother. This did not interfere with the hearty welcome extended to "Malenky Bussik." Never mind! The work would be divided between the two, Pachulsky taking care of the lessons and Achille turning his attention to chamber music and the afternoon sessions with Nadejda Filaretovna.

The audience was augmented by several listeners, since Countess Bennigsen, her eldest daughter, was visiting at Brailovo with her family. As to Sophie, she was now fifteen years old. Upon seeing her again Achille's heart beat at an accelerated tempo, but now he was able to control his blushing. From time to time he met her in the garden. They chatted in French, which she spoke like a born Parisian with no accent and a beautiful deep voice. Since her English governess also spoke French, Achille had a chance to learn a little about Sophie. Surely a governess ought to know the character of her pupil. Why he sought such information he did not even question.

Thus he learned that Sophie was a good student; that her disposition was usually cheerful, with at times a moment of reverie. She took pride in her elegant wardrobe imported from the Rue de la Paix. Once the governess found her in front of a "psyché" mirror, posing as a mannequin would do and so satisfied with her looks that she started humming the "Waltz of the Jewels" from *Faust*.

"With all that, M. Bussik, Sophie is the most adorable girl I have ever known," concluded the governess. "And isn't she beautiful! Oh, so beautiful; but, M. Bussik, she knows it. Yes, and sometimes I am afraid that when she grows to be a young lady she may become—how do you say it in French?—a coquette, M. Bussik, a little co-quette!"

At the end of the season Nadejda Filaretovna presented Achille with a beautiful gold watch and chain as a parting gift; and she wrote to Tchaikovsky:

"Can you imagine, Peter Ilyitch . . . This young man felt so sad at leaving us that his cheeks were wet with bitter tears. He had become so used to our company! From this house of plenty he must return to Paris, to a life of semibeggary, where he is expected by an almost estranged family, much work and perhaps hardships. This summer he had become more of a grown-up man, more self-controlled, more independent. He even has learned not to blush! To him this house was the best spot in the world because he was treated as a friend, almost as a relative, and his ego was never hurt."

Achille landed at the Gare de l'Est in a drizzling October rain; it fell in soft patter on the glass of the station veranda and dripped from the awnings of near-by cafés. The multicolored lights were washed into watery shades and the humidity penetrated everyone and everything. He turned up his collar as he headed for the Trocadéro-Gare de l'Est omnibus and his hand felt his vest pocket to make sure that the precious timepiece was still there. The melancholy grayness gripped him in its chill and he thought of Brailovo where perhaps the sun shone and Sophie, in the garden, picked flowers; but where Nadejda Filaretovna certainly did not suspect the real cause of the tears she had noticed streaming down Malenky Bussik's face.

At the Conservatoire Achille continued to work in perfect understanding with his teacher. Guiraud was broad-

minded, interested in whatever was new, original, and
progressive. What difference did it make to him if
Achille's most recent effort in harmony had been a complete fiasco; if in his interpretation of twenty-eight measures of bass there had been at least half a dozen consecutive fifths and octaves? This was an unforgivable crime
for such adjudicators as Ambroise Thomas, kindly but
rigidly theoretical, and Ernest Reyer, who ferociously op-
posed any modernistic tendencies, dozed off during most
of the competition, and awakened only to mutter a few
profane words and vote a zero to all the contestants. But
Guiraud's vision had immediately recognized an astonishing natural ability in his new student; besides, had they
not in common that love for billiards, aesthetic discussions, paintings, cigarettes? Achille still hated to hurry and
he continued to arrive late at class, but this did not matter
since Guiraud himself always arrived considerably later.

Sometimes teacher and pupil had interesting discussions:

"Your theory rests on a basis that is absolutely inad-
missible," said Guiraud. Achille wanted to know why.

"Because you discard the most elementary principles
of traditional harmony; your system is a rebellion against
accepted methods."

"But," Achille persisted, "who set those rules? Consecutive fifths and octaves are forbidden. Why, and by
whom? Parallel motion is condemned and the sacrosanct
contrary motion is beatified. Please, by what right?"

Then he would sit at the piano and improvise cascade
upon cascade of unorthodox chords. Guiraud smiled
gently, because he secretly admired the "discoveries."
Without discouraging their inventor he strove to keep

him from excesses, for the time being at least, and as long as he would be subject to examinations and competitions.

Meanwhile the "new ideas" were making their way into other classes where they caused the despair of several less discriminating professors. These innovations even began to haunt the older generation. One night Reyer, Réty, Guiraud, and Théodore Dubois, organist at La Madeleine and future director of the Conservatoire, had gathered at the studio of Marmontel. The conversation turned to young Debussy. Marmontel went to the piano:

"Listen. Here are a few of his pranks."

He begin improvising a bizarre succession of chords vaguely reminiscent of Achille's cascades. Réty was horrified and Reyer, exasperated, swore. As to Théodore Dubois, he smiled enigmatically.

"I think I can beat that youngster at his own game," he stated. "I can do what he does, but with one finger only."

"I'll treat you to a nice dinner if you do," said Reyer.

The following Sunday the same friends met at La Madeleine, and watched as Dubois played a melody with his index finger. The "mutation" stops which he used produced a superposition of harmonics imitating indeed the famous cascades. A dinner at Weber's followed, during which Achille's system came once more under fire and Reyer, as always, told a few jokes of questionable taste. But it dawned clearly on Guiraud that the one-fingered improvisation sprang from the great medieval art of the "organum" cantors and that what had taken place was the most eloquent, though unconscious glorification of the daring methods invented by the budding genius of a young student.

Paul Vidal lived at the Hotel des Messageries, in the street of the same name. His room opened on a courtyard which served as a protection from the noise of the trucks loading and unloading in front of the commercial houses near by. It was a modest hotel patronized by clerks and some students of the Conservatoire who selected it because of its proximity to the school. Pierné came from time to time; clever and quick in everything he did, he already showed the qualities which were to make him one of the most talented musicians of France. But on many occasions Achille visited alone with Paul Vidal whose cordial nature was most congenial to his own disposition. Each delighted in playing his new compositions for the other. They were mostly songs and Vidal, who was prolific, wrote a number of them each week. Achille, however, composed slowly. This led to mystification, quite harmless at the time but followed many years later by unexpected consequences.

One day Achille had nothing to show and he feared that Vidal would be disappointed; so he copied several songs from a book by Émile Pessard, the *Joyeusetés de bonne compagnie*. One of them was called "La Chanson d'un fou." Then, with a twinkle in his eye, he played them for his friend as being his own. Back at home he placed them on his shelf and they began what would be a long, but not everlasting sleep.

When Vidal came to the Rue Clapeyron he usually stayed to dinner. Liking sweet dishes, Victorine prepared some of her entremets, chocolate custard, "eggs in the snow," and other delicacies. Manuel made him pay for his meal by playing some opera for them: *La Dame blanche, I Puritani, Lucia,* or something similar. He was in great favor with both Manuel and Victorine and they considered him a member of the family. Vidal and Achille were going to take the test for admission to the Prix de Rome competition and this made the connection still closer.

Both passed it successfully in the spring, and they entered the "loge"—the studio-room in the Conservatoire where they had to live for one long month. In order to ensure fairness they were kept under guard during those weeks when they composed their cantata. It was really a prison life, since meals were brought to them and they could go no farther than the courtyard. This regime was unbearable to Achille. How could he write under such conditions? He complained to Paul Vidal:

"I hate this way of doing things. They ask us to be inspired at a certain given period of the year. What if we are not in the mood? It is arbitrary, and frankly I don't see how it can have any significance for the future. And this stupid text concocted by the brain of some official semipoet. It's idiotic! Whoever the author may be, he'd better keep anonymous if he's alive. If he's dead, peace to his ashes!"

Vidal took first prize, and Achille second. There was a celebration at the Rue Clapeyron and Guiraud presided. As the French saying goes, Victorine "put the small platters into the big ones," which means that she outdid herself. When the champagne arrived Guiraud got up and turned to Vidal:

"This is to your great success, my young friend. May the future bring you all that you desire."

Then he raised his glass to Achille's health:

"And to you, many returns of the day for what is more

than a fine achievement: an assurance that next year will see the complete fulfillment of your ambitions."

Vidal was too deeply moved to answer, and so was Achille. The effect of the champagne created an effusive atmosphere. When Mme. Mousset came up to put out the lights on the stairway, she was invited to take part in the general rejoicing.

It was getting late, however, and when the tenants above pounded on the floor by way of protest the party broke up amid renewed congratulations and cheers.

By the early eighties, Charles Gounod had reached the climax of his glory. *Faust* had conquered the world and it brought a rich financial reward. He left his house on the Rue de la Tour-des-Dames and migrated to the new and fashionable district of La Plaine Monceau where he built a palatial mansion on the Place Malesherbes, at the corner of the Rue de Montchanin. His glory did not lessen his kindness and affability. Every Saturday he went to the meeting of the Institut de France, then proceeded to the rehearsal of the Concordia of which he was president. The conductor had just appointed Achille permanent accompanist and it was a great day for the young man when he was introduced to Gounod. The master was much impressed by his skill at transposition, and he remembered having heard his cantata at the Prix de Rome competition the preceding spring. He treated Achille in a fatherly way and expressed a desire to see some of his more recent compositions. Consequently Achille found himself one morning in front of Gounod's new home. He looked at the building in amazement, calculating the fabulous amount of royalties which it represented. But who could tell? Perhaps one day he too would be able to own a house like that.

He rang the bell and a liveried footman showed him upstairs into the immense drawing room, used by the master as a studio. As he waited he admired the inspiring collection of relics adorning the walls: a lock of Beethoven's hair and his small cross of the Legion of Honor; flowers picked by Gounod himself on his grave; there were also sketches and water colors painted by Gounod who in his early years had developed a real talent and even thought of becoming a professional painter. In a corner stood a pianoforte of black mahogany, transformed into a writing desk and on the lid these Latin words were engraved with a needle point: "Hic laboravi, non tanquam volui, sed tanquam potui."

"Good morning, my young friend," Gounod said. "You are welcome to my home and I am anxious to hear what you are doing."

They sat at the piano and the audition began. Gounod seemed delighted with the melodic grace of these new songs.

"Very nice . . . charming . . . bravo!" he exclaimed here and there. And spontaneously he offered his help for the publication of these numbers.

This first meeting marked the birth of a friendship which was to mean much to Achille. Gounod exerted great influence in musical circles; at the Institut his opinion was law. Achille was aware of that, but apart from these utilitarian motives he was fond of Gounod himself. Often on Saturday they walked home together after rehearsal and Achille learned much from so renowned and experienced a man.

As to his relations with the Vasniers, they were becoming more intimate all the time; so much so that a sort of jealousy had developed between them and Achille's parents. Nearly every day he went to the Vasniers and most of his work was done in the petit salon where a table had been installed on which he left his sheets of manuscript paper. Perhaps he had overemphasized the lack of atmosphere at home and conveyed the impression that he was unhappy between the limitations of his father and the commonplace ideas of his mother. In his younger years he loved sympathy and in order to get it he would not hesitate over the means to be employed.

Achille had a peculiar way of composing: he walked around the room, hummed, played, smoked cigarettes. Then, when Mme. Vasnier saw that the spell was over, she entered discreetly and they had tea together. He also coached her on the interpretation of his songs and she liked them so much that she decided to put them on her programs when she appeared at charity concerts. His feelings toward her were a mixture of admiration for her stunning beauty, appreciation for her artistry, and a respect created by his consciousness of the distance that still separated them socially. But his timidity was much less than in the presence of Sophie, probably because Mme. Vasnier was a pure Parisian who belonged to his own race and held no enigma for him.

One day he came in all excited and told her about a scandal he had caused at the Opéra the night before; he was proud of it, however, because it had arisen from his admiration for a work by Edouard Lalo, *Namouna*, which had been given in first performance. He sat in the box reserved for the students of composition.

Hardly had the ballet begun when many socialites began a demonstration against music which they absolutely failed to understand. They talked aloud, scoffed, and a number of them ostentatiously rose from their seats and walked out. Achille leaned out of his box and shouted:

"Imbeciles!"

There was a moment of stupor. The members of the Jockey Club, the same persons who had acted so disgracefully at the première of *Tannhäuser*, looked up in amazement through their monocles.

"Imbeciles . . . idiots . . . crétins!" he roared, reaching a climax. There was an uproar and one could no longer hear the orchestra which was trying to weather the storm. But a policeman rushed upstairs, called by M. Vaucorbeil, the director, who had nearly fainted at the thought of the terrible stain which these insults stamped on his directorate, though he was in no way responsible for them!

The representative of the law grabbed Achille's arm, pulled him from his advanced position and unceremoniously dragged him down to the office of M. Vaucorbeil, an extremely urbane and affable gentleman.

"Young man, how dare you abuse the privilege which is yours to come here without paying for your seat? You are an invited guest and your behavior is most objectionable. I could ask for your exclusion from the Conservatoire!"

"Excuse me, sir. I just couldn't bear the insulting attitude of those people. Why don't they get out if they don't like *Namouna*? They have no right to dictate their opinion to others."

"I want an apology for your disgraceful words."

"I will gladly give it and I sincerely regret what happened; but please be sure that I did it entirely out of artistic conviction."

Achille promised he would not do it again and they released him. As to M. Vaucorbeil, he felt very much as Achille did, but a little later he had to meet the protests of his subscribers with suavity and a diplomatic smile. Such are the necessities of life, above all the life of a theatrical director.

The Vasniers were amused by Achille's picturesque account of this incident. All the same, they advised him to be careful and to refrain from such public outbursts until they held no further danger for him.

In the spring Mme. Vasnier took part in a concert given by a violinist friend and Achille figured as a composer, publicizing his name as "Achille de Bussy." The songs were received with gratifying success; indeed, a few days later, after a visit to the office of a publisher, he came home proudly and exhibited to his parents an order for fifty francs, the product of the sale of one of his songs.

At once Manuel started calculating, and declared it was too bad Achille couldn't compose as fast as Paul Vidal did. Otherwise, at fifty francs a song . . .

Achille left him "counting his chickens."

In May the Vasniers moved to Ville d'Avray. Everywhere around Paris the gardens shimmered with early verdure and lilacs were in bloom. At that time the people of Paris renewed their outings to the near-by woods, but for M. Vasnier Sunday was a day of rest which he spent mostly in the garden, stretched on a long chair under the trees. Every weekday he rose early in order to catch the first train, and he disliked having to go to a restaurant at noon. So when Sunday came he enjoyed the relaxation it brought him.

Achille went to Ville d'Avray two or three times a week. The fifty francs from the sale of his song represented a considerable number of round-trip tickets. Unfortunately Bourbonneux was just across from the Gare Saint-Lazare where he took his train and the petits fours often exercised their irresistible lure. Never mind, he thought, he would soon sell another song! There was also the prospect of another trip to Russia, which would replenish his purse.

How Achille loved Ville d'Avray! He woke early, walked to the station in the delightfully cool morning air; should the weather be very fine, he climbed to the impériale, the upper story of the antiquated railroad carriage. The train stopped at the little station, so cheery with the small square in front, the tobacconist on the corner, and the cafés with tables on the sidewalk and under the green arbors. Then he walked to the Vasniers', along rows of modest cottages and gardens adorned by a fountain or the traditional large, colored globe, around which some pacific-looking retired "functionaries" pruned their fruit trees.

Mme. Vasnier, who knew Achille's tastes, always served a delicious meal. Ville d'Avray was rather limited as to shopping and it was impossible to secure anything unusual or exotic, such as could be found at Hédiard's on the Place de la Madeleine. But what Achille appreciated most in any cooking was quality. He enjoyed thoroughly a conservative French luncheon: fried eggs, lamb chops with French fried potatoes, Brie cheese, fruit, on condition that every part of it was exactly right. The Vasniers' cook was pretty good; besides, Mme. Vasnier herself superintended the preparation of the meal while Achille took a stroll in the garden or did some work at the piano. The company of Mme. Vasnier and her daughter had a favorable influence on him; he usually was gay and carefree, sometimes even exuberant.

In the afternoon they often went for a long walk along forest roads and rustling lanes, grass-grown in spots and lined by rows of whitethorn with its pungent odor; birds chirped everywhere and now and then one could hear the distant rumble of a train in the valley.

When they returned the rays of the setting sun empurpled the sky and the call of the cuckoos began their duet with the trills of the nightingales. Sometimes they called at the station and met M. Vasnier.

One evening Achille was in a particularly cheerful mood and he turned comedian, sat at the piano and improvised some chansons in the style of the Chat Noir. Then he went to get his cane and announced:

"Ladies and gentlemen, you will now hear the most famous Italian tenor of the day, who has just arrived from Florence with his guitar."

Taking the pose of an opera singer from beyond the Alps and using his cane as a guitar, he improvised a "canzone Napolitana," with high notes, gruppetti, and all the trimmings. Seeing how amused his listeners were, he chuckled:

"Perhaps one of these days I can make a fortune with songs à la Tosti!"

On another occasion they were having coffee in the parlor when three street singers started a serenade in front of the villa.

"Here comes reinforcement for our musicale; shall we let them in?"

M. Vasnier was in good humor and he consented. Then Achille presented them:

"To this distinguished audience I have the honor to introduce a trio of celebrated vocalists. They will sing soli, duets, and trios. There will also be a quartet with the assistance of the pianist of the company, your humble servant, who has no voice but plenty of good will. Now: one, two, three, four, let us go!"

He improvised a snappy overture, caricaturing Rossini for whom he had little esteem.

The singers were having a wonderful time, especially since some wine had been brought up. They sang popular Italian songs with real feeling, accompanied by Achille who finally told them they were greater artists than many stars from La Scala of Milan, and the music they sang was better than most of the operas from the peninsula.

He had given them all his cigarettes too, but M. Vasnier had a stock of caporals; he gave a package to Achille and stuck another one in his pocket. As Achille stood in the hall, ready to take leave, Mlle. Vasnier noticed a strange odor. "My hat . . . my new hat!" Achille exclaimed. In his excitement he had held hat and cigarette with the same hand, and a clean round hole was burned through the felt. Everyone laughed and Mme. Vasnier mended it with a patch of black velvet so neatly that it hardly showed.

Alone in his compartment, Achille still hummed some of those sentimental ballads which called to his mind the sunny Neapolitan landscapes that he knew only through pictures, but which the simple and expressive cantilènes evoked so vividly.

The competition in fugue and counterpoint was about to be held. He and Paul Vidal were hard at work on this technical phase, somewhat repulsive to a musician like Achille who reveled in the "pleasure of the ear." Pierné, on the contrary, felt "like a fish in water." There were many discussions among the three friends.

"Bach's own fugues are admirable," Achille stated, "because they express perfectly the musical atmosphere of his time. It is because of this that he reached in them such a degree of expression and even emotion. This is no longer possible, now that the musical language has changed, and that's why modern fugues are so dry and so uninteresting. I accept them as a sort of gymnastics for penmanship, and nothing more."

Pierné, the eternal scholar, defended the "form." Vidal, never wanting to assert himself, agreed with both. In conclusion, they all went back to their desks and continued to drill with the inevitable mathematics.

It was something of a surprise when Achille won a "second mention." He derived no special pride from it, and the matter had slipped out of his mind when once more he found himself at the Gare de l'Est, ready to board the night train to Moscow where the von Mecks were expecting him for the third time.

Looking back on the last year he realized the value of his association with the Vasniers; after those many hours of conversation with such a learned man he felt more confidence in himself. He had read the great classics, Molière, Racine, Corneille, and also some moderns. Then there were those two enormous volumes: the *National*

Dictionary by Bescherelle, considered as a Bible of the French language and affording so much information, so much documentation.

"I like the dictionary very much," Achille used to say. "One may laugh at my statement, but I insist: I learn a lot of interesting things from the dictionary."

As the train entered Germany he was again impressed by the law and order which reigned everywhere, from the cleanliness of the customhouse to the way in which the officers' uniforms were kept immaculate and shining. What a contrast with the carefree way on the French side of the border! Nevertheless, Achille much preferred the latter, even if the gendarmes did not shave every day, if they stood nonchalantly along the platform, a cigarette hanging informally from their lower lip. He knew that in an hour of need this apparent carelessness would transform itself instantaneously into sheer courage and determination and that the gift for improvisation, so typical of the Gallic race, could advantageously substitute for preparedness in which all details are meticulously but too rigidly set in advance.

There was also the word "verboten," used so profusely in Germany. Everything was verboten. Forbidden to lean out of the window . . . forbidden to step out before the train came to a complete stop . . . forbidden to disregard the cuspidors, ash trays and other gadgets . . . everything forbidden, everywhere. It was regimentation, a stifling of the personality, and instinctively he felt like doing just the opposite, in a spirit of contradiction; but he prudently refrained, scared by what might happen in a land inhabited by people whose characteristics were so strange to him.

After a long and slow journey through the barren steppes of Russia he found the superintendent of the von Meck estate waiting for him at the Moscow station with a carriage. They drove through avenues dominated by the towers and walls of the Kremlin.

"We are so glad to have you with us again, Bussik," Nadejda Filaretovna said as she greeted him in the hall of the palatial house. "I have been informed of the stir you are creating in Paris with your new ideas. It is very interesting and I am anxious to hear some of your new works. Let me look at you. How you have changed since last year!"

Indeed, Achille had undergone a transformation; no longer had he that boyish appearance, nor that mixture of timidity and spontaneity which made him so awkward at times. He had grown mentally and physically. His hair was cut shorter and he kept it more orderly; a light growth of beard was noticeable around his cheeks and under the chin, making his complexion still more pallid. One thought of some young Venetian prince, painted by Titian among the sumptuous settings of a palace on the Grand Canal.

Again the schedule was resumed; but they were in a great city, not in the country, and that made it somewhat different. Toward the end of the afternoon they often went sightseeing and also visited some of the smart cabarets where society folk gathered and listened to the music of the tziganes, then in great favor. To Achille it came as a sort of revelation: he leaned forward and gazed at the violinist who began to play, apparently improvising. Music seemed to come to him on the wings of inspiration; it might be a reverie, or a love song, depending upon whether he thought of a starry sky or of a lovely maiden. As he played on and on, changing his moods while his partners also improvised their accompaniment, Achille had a vision: the splendor of those nights in Hungary when the country people, dressed in their finest garments, gather around the musicians on the village square; the flashing colors of native costumes; the exaltation which permeates the whole celebration. Then the music increased in vitality and intensity; it became a lively dance in which the crowd joined, seized by a frenzy that would keep them dancing until dawn. Achille's imagination pictured all that as he listened to the languorous or fiery bowing; he was charmed by these popular tunes so distinctly representative of a nation and of a race. He came back several times, anxious to hear again those musicians who still retained their ancestors' secret, that singular power to evoke from their fiddles the echoes of heroic deeds, the sighs of the lovelorn, the glory of reddening sunsets over the horizons of their fatherland.

The musicales still took place every evening. Once Julia Carlovna asked Achille to accompany her in some modern songs; they were by Alexander Borodin, a professor of chemistry who devoted part of his time to composition. A member of a group of five musicians considered leaning toward dangerous revolutionary tendencies, he was almost entirely unknown in Paris. Even in Russia no one suspected the fame that he would acquire.

The songs which Julia Carlovna interpreted made a deep impression upon Achille; he sensed what an advancement their harmonic coloring represented, particularly in *La Princesse Endormie*. He borrowed this song and studied it during the next days, fascinated by a certain formula of dissonant seconds. To him it testified that here in Russia, hundreds of miles from the "City of Light," was a man who also looked for novel ways and found them. This discovery both delighted and encouraged him, and when Nadejda Filaretovna invited the chemist-composer to tea it was an unforgettable experience for Achille.

As they sat around the steaming samovar, Borodin spoke:

"Glinka is the father of our national music. Before him no Russian music existed except folklore. This may seem strange to you if you consider that other European countries were so flourishing. The first real piece of Russian music was A *Life for the Czar*, after which Glinka wrote *Russlan and Ludmilla*. How do you like the overture?"

"I have never heard it . . . I am so sorry . . ."

"Glinka founded our group," Borodin continued. His intuition told him that Achille "spoke his own language." So he gave him more information about the Russian school then in the making: Rimsky-Korsakov, Balakirev, Moussorgsky, César Cui. How attractive these names sounded! Achille wished he could investigate their works right away; but this was so difficult in view of Nadejda Filaretovna's exclusive admiration for Tchaikovsky. She felt no particular taste for the songs sung by her daughter and she, too, considered Borodin an amateur whom she received more for social reasons than anything else.

"There is an episode that will also interest you, M. Debussy," Borodin pursued. "When I mention Glinka I should not omit to associate his name with John Field's."

A look of surprise flashed from Achille's eyes:

"Field? The same Field of the concertos and the nocturnes used in the conservatories?"

"Exactly. As a pianist he took our country by storm. He
was lionized, led the 'great life,' spent lavishly and became something of a popular idol. But in 1814 a young
Russian, only twelve years old, asked him if he would consent to be his teacher. Field accepted. The young man's
name was Glinka. On that day our national music was
born."

Achille was captivated by all he heard and promised
himself to look up the works of the new Russian school as
soon as he returned to Paris.

He had not long to wait for this opportunity, though he
had been in Moscow only a few weeks.

During the musicales his eyes drifted more and more
toward the heavenly silhouette of Sophie. She was sixteen now and she fascinated him more than ever. When
she sat near the piano he played with greater feeling, as if
wanting to say something in music which he did not know
how to express in words, or more likely did not dare.

One afternoon as he had tea with Nadejda Filaretovna,
he felt within him a big wave of resolution. Why should
he lack courage, after all? Wasn't he treated as one of the
family? Why could he not become one of the family?

Suddenly it dawned upon him that Sophie herself demonstrated more than a sisterly inclination toward him.
Yes, there was more than mere friendliness in her affectionate attitude. He felt it . . . he was sure of it. Now
was the moment to act; now . . . or never! Mustering all
his courage, with a determination that banished all fear,
he spoke.

Nadejda Filaretovna rose; her face and lips were pale and there was in her eyes a strange glitter, which told of her grief, her regret, her repentance for the unavoidable words she had to pronounce, and which would hurt.

"Bussik . . . dear Bussik. What is it that has come into your mind? You are so young . . . too young. And Sophie is a child. No, it is impossible! Besides, it would be a case for long reflection . . . long pondering . . . and there is no time for it, since your departure is so near at hand . . . since you are leaving . . . tomorrow!"

Achille understood and felt the ground collapsing under his feet. Heartbroken, his spirit crushed, he bowed slowly and retired to his room, forgetting on the music shelves several manuscripts of songs and the sketch of a symphony which he meant to dedicate to Nadejda Filaretovna.

The Vasniers were at Ville d'Avray and Achille's absence was felt keenly; so it was a cheerful surprise when the morning following his return he rang the bell at the front gate.

"Mother . . . mother . . . it's M. Achille!" the little girl shouted when she saw him standing there.

Hurriedly Mme. Vasnier came down. This was so unexpected; in his last letter, received only two days before, he had announced that he would remain in Moscow another month. Had anything happened to make him leave so soon? Was there anything wrong with his family?

Achille reassured her; everything was all right and his family had been as surprised as she was. The reason for his change of plans? Nothing but his nostalgic feelings. Russia decidedly was too great, too immense. He could no longer stand that depressing vastness, that colorless sky, that life, so different, to which he could never adapt himself. And the Russians . . . How could a Parisian ever understand the intricacies, the complications of the Slavonic soul? The Île-de-France was the only place where he could be happy and if he went abroad it only fortified his belief. Then—and he looked at her with eyes that were no longer those of an adolescent—was there not the "melodious fairy," the source of inspiration without whose presence his creative faculties became thwarted? No, he could bear Russia no longer and unexpectedly he had left.

Mme. Vasnier looked at him; this absence had lent perspective to the change in his appearance; he was almost a man now and looked like one already with this budding beard that gave his features a virile appearance. Twenty years old . . . the spring of life . . . the age of hopes and enthusiasms.

The luncheon was improvised and it took place in the garden. There was no more gloom in Achille's mind. It was one of those marvelous summer days when everyone is optimistic. The sun shone in a cloudless sky and its rays made the outline of the distant hills tremble in a vibration of light. Between puffs at his cigarette he breathed deeply, inhaling the perfume which came from the flower beds and the orchards beyond the road. In the afternoon they went to the piano and tried to have some music; but the heat had increased and the atmosphere was stifling. Achille proposed a promenade into the forest, and on the way back they would meet her husband at the station. They smiled, thinking of his surprise at the sudden appearance of the long-distance traveler.

They started out and after walking for some distance on the main road, entered on a path leading directly into the woods. From time to time they passed a signpost, half-effaced by the winter rains: "Road to Chaville' . . . "Road to the hunting lodge." They did not know their way but were not afraid of losing it because of the clearings where more explicit directions could be found on the tablets.

How they enjoyed this walk! It was nice and balmy beneath the shade of those lofty trees crowded so closely that the sky was no longer visible. They passed a spot where the woodcutters had recently accomplished their work of mutilation; an old, venerable oak lay there amid chips, twigs, and fragments of bark. Looking up, they saw that dark clouds had invaded that patch of sky. When they came to the crossways some swallows soared by, flying low.

They sat on a trunk lately felled, but soon heavy drops of rain began to fall while the treetops rustled under a sudden gust of wind. Achille rose and took her hand:

"Come, let's hurry. I fear there is going to be a bad storm!"

They followed a bridle path, walking on the moss which carpeted the side. The rain was increasing all the time and now it had soaked the foliage and dripped heavily around them. Suddenly Achille stopped:

"The lodge!"

An abandoned hunting cabin stood in front of them, only a few steps from the path. Hurriedly they made their way through the shrubbery, pushed the crumbling door and stepped inside; not much of a shelter assuredly, but it would do for the time being, if this shower did not last too long.

As they stood by the window, gazing through the shattered panes Achille still held Mme. Vasnier's hand and they remained silent, listening to the pelting of the rain on the roof. He began to feel intoxicated by the subtle perfume which emanated from that superb creature whose shapely breast and shoulder appeared in their sculptural beauty and molded by the drenched summer dress which fitted her closely like a tunic. The pressure of his hand became more firm and he quivered under the fascination of that lovely body so near his own, under the onrush of temptation that came to his brain.

Suddenly a peal of thunder crashed, while a flash of lightning illuminated the room. As she uttered a shriek Achille seized her and frantically kissed her neck, her shoulders, all the gleaming flesh which for so long had inflamed his desire.

Overpowered by the magnitude of that instant, she had neither the time nor the will to resist, perhaps not even a clear perception of what had taken place.

When the storm subsided it was too late to meet the train. They went directly to the villa where M. Vasnier nervously paced the floor.

"Ah, here you are, you children . . . naughty children!" the old architect remonstrated, as he caught sight of their dripping clothes and muddy shoes.

Ernest Guiraud was a composer somewhat lacking in inventive genius though always picturesque and colorful; but it was as a teacher that he distinguished himself. His sense of psychology made him handle each student in an individual way, which was particularly important in the case of Achille. Guiraud "canalized" him, kept watch over him and never failed to impress him with the necessity of acquiring a solid technical foundation. He knew, for instance, that Achille's failure to take the first grand Prix de Rome had been due mostly to his inexperience in orchestration; so during the winter he trained the young man in that special direction. He was helped in this task by the revival of *Carmen* at the Opéra-Comique after an ostracism of seven years. This opera was, and remains, an astonishing masterpiece of instrumentation. Guiraud had been a close friend of Bizet and he loved to recount the details of the première, always insisting that the version of the fiasco was unfair and unjust.

"That story is nothing but a lie," he said emphatically; "on the contrary, it was a great and immediate success with the public. I know, because with a number of my friends I attended all the performances."

"But wasn't *Carmen* taken off?"

"Of course it was, because of the summer season; but it reappeared in September and the success grew steadily until the following January when the fiftieth performance was given."

Achille was greatly interested by these things of the theater and he questioned further:

"Why was it ostracized for seven years if it was a success?"

"There were several reasons: the director ran into financial trouble and the Opéra-Comique closed its doors for eight months. It happened, unfortunately for Bizet, that the wife of a new director was Mme. Miolan-Carvalho, a renowned opera singer; the keeping of a work on the active list depended much upon the likes and dislikes of that important person."

"Didn't she like *Carmen?*"

"That was not the question; it simply did not include a part suitable for her voice. Ah, Achille, if you knew the intrigues, the politics of a great theater!"

Guiraud was on his pet subject and, since Achille showed such interest, he laid down his billiard cue and continued:

"Of course, Achille, no one can kill a work of genius. *Carmen* was bound to be revived and I am positive it will never leave the repertoire any more."

And he proceeded to tell Achille the story of that first night. It had been far from auspicious. At one moment, as Mme. Galli-Marié sang pianissimo, the bass drum player who had counted his bars wrong, broke out with two formidable thunderbolts! The orchestra played without conviction. The chorus was worse.

"Imagine, Achille, those poor women accustomed to the ensembles of *La Dame blanche*, suddenly obliged to fight, to dance, to smoke cigarettes! Then, as always happens in Paris, the public was split in two: society, the nobility, the financiers, downstairs; the intellectuals and the musicians, upstairs. . . . That's where I sat," Guiraud interrupted with a smile. "Downstairs the libretto was judged immoral, but upstairs the enthusiasm was enormous. As to Bizet, it is a sad story. Perhaps he had based exaggerated hopes on that first night. Anyhow, he retired to the director's office. When we rushed backstage after the performance we found him a prey to grief, almost despair. He took my arm and until dawn the two of us wandered aimlessly through the streets of Paris. I tried to transmit to him some of my own confidence; but it was useless and the whole evening appeared to him in the light of a disaster!"

"In any case it broke his heart and killed him," Achille concluded.

"No, not at all," Guiraud protested. "That is another legend. Bizet died naturally. He was in the habit of attending to some duties of the household. Early one morning at Bougival, he left his bed and went down to the kitchen to settle the bill of the washerwoman. You know how chilly it is by the river, even in June. Scantily dressed, he caught cold and pneumonia took his life within two days."

Once more spring had come and soon it would be time to re-enter the dreaded loge, that semijail. Achille had worked hard all winter, and now he felt better grounded. M. Vasnier had continued his artistic coaching and he was surprised at the young man's gift for appreciation of paintings and etchings. "Had he not been a musician he would have made a fine art dealer," the architect sometimes declared jokingly.

Gounod continued to visit the Concordia and Achille met him every week. Sometimes he went to the Rue de Montchanin with a package of new manuscripts under his arm. The old master appreciated Achille's songs and certainly was one whom the "innovations" did not scandalize; in fact, he was charmed by them but he, too, advised Achille to be careful until he should be free from competitions.

Gounod's friendship meant much to Achille in many

ways. A matter of much importance at the Prix de Rome
was the selection of the interpreters. Each contestant tried
to secure famous names in order to make an impression
on the jury. Naturally Gounod was powerful among the
singers of the Opéra who catered to him in the hope that
he might consider them for some new role.

Achille wanted to secure the services of Mme. Krauss
and he approached Gounod on the subject, but the master answered rather evasively. A few days passed and finally he decided to call on him and find out what could
be done, if anything. The tall, uniformed concierge looked
down majestically:

"Monsieur is not at home."

"But I saw him standing at the window. Surely I am
not mistaken."

"I am sorry, sir. Monsieur is not at home."

Without further discussion he shut the heavy door.

"Now what . . ." Achille thought. "Hasn't Gounod
wanted to receive me? Has anything happened, some intrigue, perhaps, stirred by some other contestant jealous
of my friendship with the great man?" And he began to
fret, as one always does in such a case.

The next morning Mme. Mousset brought up a letter; it was from Gounod:

"My dear child: I didn't know it was you. Had I been
informed of your visit I would have given instructions to
receive you. What you wish to obtain of Mme. Krauss is
very difficult indeed, not because of her good will but on
account of the direction of the Opéra which is inflexible
and, I must say, absolutely obliged to be so. I will make
the request, however; but I don't guarantee anything, or
rather I guarantee . . . failure. Why don't you go and

see Carvalho? Mention my name and I am sure he will give you someone. Affectionately, Gounod."

Achille uttered a sigh of relief; at least there was nothing wrong in that direction. At once he saw Carvalho and through the magic name succeeded in getting a trio of admirable artists: Rose Caron, Van Dyck, whose Parisian debut had been sensational, and Taskin. With such names he could await the great event with confidence.

The cantata had to be composed, however. The libretto was by E. Guinand and the title *L'Enfant prodigue* (The Prodigal Child). Once more the drudgery of writing against time . . . the prison life . . . the bad ventilation. He found the whole process still more objectionable than formerly, possibly on account of the unusual heat. During the recess hour he talked to his friends who came to see him, and always grumbled vehemently.

"Look at that window up there. That's where I have to live. Can you see the iron bars? Probably they think we are a bunch of wild animals!"

And worse still, smoking was prohibited, as in all other parts of the ancient building. This regulation was strictly enforced by M. Terrasse who came unexpectedly and sniffed along the corridor.

Following an old army custom, Achille had hung part of a tape meter along the wall. It was thirty-one centimeters in length when he entered the loge. Every day he cut one of them and as the tape dwindled he could visualize the coming of his liberation. It served also as a reminder that time was measured, that the cantata at all costs must be finished.

2

The Prix de Rome

O~N~ the old Pont des Arts, the narrow bridge for pedes-
trians which crosses the Seine opposite the Institut de
France, Achille stood, watching the evolutions of the
bateaux-mouches, those picturesque river boats which by
now have fallen into oblivion but in 1884 enjoyed great
popularity among Parisians of all classes. Leaning on the
rail as if fascinated by the pretty spring light shimmering
through the drifting waters, he appeared as just one more
of those delightful Paris badauds, eternal loafers who,
with nothing of particular importance on their minds,
occupy themselves day after day by contemplating street
landscapes and derive occasional excitement from the futile little happenings which occur at every turn in the
busy life of a great city.

No special emotion was noticeable on his features. Still,
under the cupola of the Institut, only a hundred yards
distant, the members of the illustrious company were
gathered. His immediate fate was being decided; the Prix
de Rome competition was in progress.

Suddenly a man rushed out of the venerable structure,
ran across the embankment and along the bridge; pant-

ing for breath, he excitedly clapped Achille's shoulder. It was Paul Vidal:

"Hurrah! You got the prize!"

The new laureate's reaction was most unexpected. At receiving the big news, all his joy collapsed. He began to realize the worries, the troubles, the complications which never fail to come with an official title. All he felt was that his cherished freedom would soon be lost.

Both friends went back to the Institut. A crowd poured out into the courtyard. He heard his name everywhere . . . Debussy . . . Debussy . . .

A hard battle had taken place among the jury. Conservative members with old-fashioned ideas objected strongly to his tendencies, mild as he had tried to keep them. The debate had been passionate, almost violent at times. But a master was there, whose authority and prestige swung the balance: Gounod. Valiantly he had fought the Philistines and carried the decision. Kissing the young man on both cheeks and with tears in his eyes he exclaimed:

"Bravo, my dear boy, bravo! You are a genius."

And Guiraud was there too; at the last moment he had been called to substitute for one of the jurors who was taken ill; he smiled radiantly and was happy beyond words.

So Achille was officially consecrated, by the Academy at least. Now what would happen? He was at the foot of the musical ladder; could he climb it without losing faith in himself, without sacrificing to the public's taste, without descending from his high standard of ideals? What did the future hold in store for him: an easy way or a hard struggle?

In the midst of congratulations and embraces he could not repel these thoughts, and they cast a shade of melancholy on his triumph.

Achille was now entitled to a three years' stay at the Villa Medici in Rome. There he would live at the expense of the French government, together with other laureates in painting, sculpture, and architecture. Nothing in particular would be required of him except to send in a few compositions now and then, to testify to his continued artistic activities, and to be examined by the Institut. It was without joy that he looked forward to this stay. He cared nothing about that kind of life, in an official establishment where everything goes on schedule from the hour of breakfast to the hour of bedtime. Then there were those meals in the refectory, with the other inmates, which shocked his desire for privacy.

But Manuel and Victorine were delighted over the whole prospect. What pride, what exultation gleamed in Manuel's eyes when the morning after the competition he stepped into the office and announced to the other clerks that his son had won the Prix de Rome; and that soon he would leave for the "Eternal City" and stay at the famous villa. This brought to him great prestige all over the Fives-Lille administration building and even the director in chief, the "big boss," offered his warmest congratulations.

More than anything else, however, the prospect of the inevitable separation from the Vasnier family prevented Achille from sharing the general rejoicing. He felt depressed and gloomy. The "melodious fairy" had become a precious element in his life and although the issue was not imminent since he would not leave until January, the mere thought of leaving her frightened him.

Once he put a "feeler" to M. Vasnier during one of their fireside talks which still took place regularly:

"I am just wondering if this privilege of staying in Rome is going to do me any good. I am afraid not. For the past few days I have been thinking seriously of sending in my resignation. . . ."

The old architect remonstrated; kindly but firmly, with the authority of his age and his position, he warned Achille of the disastrous consequences such a move might involve, explaining that a young musician at the dawn of his career should never do anything likely to be considered slighting by the Immortals, as the members of the Institut are pleasantly called in France. He succeeded in convincing him, at least for the time being. Did not six months remain until January, Achille thought; plenty of time to reconsider the whole affair. Meanwhile he was going to live intensely, ardently; he would extract from each hour all the joy, the beauty, and the inspiration it contained; he would write songs for "her" and try to make them worthy of being expressed by her incomparable voice.

The period which follows a competition is always one of relaxation contrasting with the high degree of nervous tension inseparable from such events. At the suggestion of M. Vasnier himself Achille decided to go oftener to Ville d'Avray:

"Take it easy for a while now. Come as often as you please. We want you to feel completely at home. Rest in the garden or walk in the forest . . . suit yourself."

Achille was perfectly agreeable to the idea, as it always

included the "melodious fairy." He had already written several new songs for her and they were trying them at the piano when a detail attracted her attention:

"What is this? 'Music by Claude-Achille Debussy.' "

"Yes, I think Claude-Achille will be very much better."

He did not care for the name "Achille" any more; in fact, he had disliked it for a year or two. It sounded so ordinary, so plebeian; then there was that facile joke heard in the courtyard of the Institut: "le talon d'Achille," Achille's heel, the famous heel. And they made a pun, saying "le talent d'Achille" with a sneer in the corner of their mouths. How much more distinguished, elegant, and, he thought, adequate to the character of his music was his other name: Claude, so French, and tasty like a juicy fruit. For the time being, however, and in order to avoid confusion, he decided to use both.

One evening, as the night was peaceful and clear, he and Mme. Vasnier walked to the lake of Ville d'Avray; a light mist enveloped the hillside and the glistening moonlight descending calmly upon the placid water made it shine like a pool of silver. Slowly they went along the lane, hand in hand. There was profound repose everywhere, a sense of remoteness, the untroubled stillness of dreamless slumber. They remained silent, not wanting to break the spell, and as they stood among the high grass and wildflowers, gazing at the poetic landscape, her head reclined tenderly on his shoulder.

Back at the villa, they went to the salon illuminated only by the moonrays and Achille improvised softly, dreamily; he had found the idea of the *Clair de lune*.

Summer weather, however, was not always propitious; sometimes a shower came from a stray cloud and sometimes a drizzling, penetrating rain set in during the early hours and lasted the whole day. On such occasions there was other entertainment besides music: M. Vasnier was very fond of card playing and he had taught Achille (they continued to call him so) how to play écarté and bézigue. They played for small stakes, of course, just enough to make the game interesting, and a difference of a single franc meant considerable gain or loss. But Achille was an impossible card player, excitable, temperamental, especially when he reached his last pennies and lost. Should this happen, a package of tobacco was discreetly placed under his napkin and when he sat at the table and found it his good disposition was restored.

One day a pleasant surprise awaited him; as he came into the salon he noticed a new score on the piano. It was *Manon*, the work of Massenet which had scored such a great success at its recent presentation. Achille had not had an opportunity to hear it yet, as all tickets for the few remaining performances of the season were sold out; but Guiraud had given him a glowing report; he had been one of the guests at Philippe Gille's house the preceding year, when Massenet brought his manuscript, sat at the piano with his inevitable liqueur glass on the side, and gave the first audition to his librettist. According to Guiraud, hearing Massenet under such conditions was an unforgettable experience: Manon, Des Grieux, the chorus, he was everything, sang everything, acted everything, at times caressing the keys, then breaking into great passionate outbursts, for instance in the "scene of Saint-Sulpice." A great artist indeed, a musician to his finger tips!

Achille was enchanted with *Manon*. Before suppertime Mme. Vasnier had already learned several arias and when her husband came back she surprised him by singing them for him. He was particularly fond of the gavotte and asked her to repeat it several times:

"*Profitons bien de la jeunesse,*
Des jours qu'amène le printemps;
Aimons, chantons, rions sans cesse,
Nous n'aurons pas toujours vingt ans!"

(Let's profit by our youth, by the days which spring brings to us. Let us love, sing, laugh without ceasing; we will not always be twenty years old!)

From his piano bench Achille cast a look at the old and grizzled architect, with an imperceptible twinkle in his eye.

"Today I want to wear my gold watch," Achille declared as the Debussy family sat down for breakfast.

It was Assumption Day, a great festival in France, and he was going to the Vasniers' in his new black suit purchased the day before.

"I put it in a small wooden box way back of the bed sheets, in the cupboard of your room," said Victorine.

Achille had never asked for the watch since his return from Russia when his mother, afraid of his carelessness, had taken it from him to hide it in authentic French fashion.

He went to his room and came back all excited:

"The watch is not there!"

Victorine's face turned pale. Having had it appraised, she was aware of its high value.

"Impossible!" she exclaimed. "Your father and I are the only ones who knew where it was; you didn't even know it yourself!"

Strangely enough, Manuel's face had turned as red as his wife's had turned white. She noticed it and asked Achille to retire for a moment, which he did gladly, feeling that a scene was coming.

"What have *you* done with the watch?"

Poor Manuel presented a pitiful sight, his chubby cheeks and his lips hanging down like those of a disgruntled little boy. Full of confusion, he had to confess: the household budget had been quite heavy lately, with those expensive celebrations; then there was Achille's new suit, and he had bought one for himself too; all that had made him short of cash. Victorine flared up:

"And then you sold the watch! Shame on you, you wretch!"

Manuel begged her to keep calm; when he could make himself heard he assured her that the watch would soon be back, in fact, in exactly two weeks, on his payday.

"You see, Victorine, I didn't sell it . . . just went past the Place Clichy, up one block, you know . . . that little street on the left."

"You pawned it!"

"Right!" Manuel exclaimed with a big sigh of relief.

All dressed up, though watchless, Achille walked down to the Gare Saint-Lazare. With that incident the day had started badly. It continued when he had to wait in line to buy his ticket, then found the platform crowded with Sunday excursionists. Baskets of provisions, fishing paraphernalia, butterfly nets, folding chairs, one could see every type of accessories without which a true Parisian of the working class would not consider his outing worth while. More than ever Achille hated promiscuous crowds, their heavy laughter and their cheap jokes, and he felt most uncomfortable during the trip, half crushed between a fat woman, whose voice sounded like a bugle, and one of her boys, who never kept quiet and whose dangling feet threatened constantly the polish of his shoes.

There were also three elderly men, apparently retired functionaries, who whiled away the time by telling funny stories. One of them had a high-pitched voice and his diction resembled that of a circus clown.

"There once was a man went to a café," he began, chuckling already at the good joke; "he sat at a table and ordered a big glass of beer. But before he even began to drink he was seized by an irresistible urge to pay a visit to the end of the corridor. Of course, he was afraid that during his absence someone might drink his beer. So he wrote 'I have spat in this glass' on a piece of paper and placed it on top. When he came back the beer was still there, sure enough, but there was more writing on the paper; an unknown hand had traced these words: 'So have I!' "

Followed by his companions, he burst into a fit of giggling that could have been heard at the other end of the train.

When Achille reached the villa he learned to his dismay that some friends of the Vasniers were expected in the afternoon. Decidedly the day—perhaps the planets too—was against him. Instead of the quiet Sunday he had anticipated, he would have to submit to introductions, listen to futile chatter, hear idle gossip concerning people or facts that did not interest him in the least. Really, he regretted he had come and wished he could have gone to Paul Vidal's instead. His disappointment showed so clearly that Mme. Vasnier noticed it.

"Please, Achille, don't be sullen. Wait till our friends come. You will like them, I am sure."

It happened exactly as she predicted. She was a tactful woman and, knowing Achille's tastes so well, would never have invited anyone who would not fit in harmoniously. The family who came in the afternoon were delightful people, highly educated but unpretentious; they were musical too and could talk intelligently on the subject.

Achille's attitude changed instantly. He became gay, affable, demonstrative; and he, usually so reluctant to play for strangers, went to the piano spontaneously, sang fragments from Wagnerian operas and from his own Prix de Rome cantata. Carried away by his joyous mood, he wound up by caricaturing several composers including the pompous Ambroise Thomas, the commonplace Reyer, and last but not least the suave Massenet. To these sketches he brought a delicate sense of humor which made them fine bits of observation.

After supper and until the hour of the last train, they played cards and probably the planets had changed, for Achille won every game; so it was a lucky day after all and when he left his new friends at the Gare Saint-Lazare he expressed the hope that it would not be long until he met them again.

After an uneventful autumn during which Achille spent most of his time with the Vasniers, the day came when he had to leave for Rome and the Villa Medici. All morning there was great animation at the apartment. Victorine went busily from one room to another as with motherly solicitude she helped him pack his trunks. He was going away for a long time and she had to see that he was

provided with everything necessary to his comfort and
health.

"Don't forget your woolen underwear," she insisted;
"they say that when the snow falls in Rome it is much
worse than in Paris."

The gold watch had been redeemed; wrapped in cotton, it was placed in a soft spot among the linens. There
was also the brief case which Achille wanted to over-
crowd to at least double its capacity, and the additional
encumbrance of several walking sticks bought mostly for
the attractiveness of their handles, but which he declared
indispensable to the enjoyment of his walks. Finally everything was in order and they were about to lock the trunk.

"My books!" Achille suddenly remembered.

But there was a dozen of them or more, which he said
he absolutely needed; so they were packed separately in
heavy brown paper and tied with string. Victorine looked
distressed at the steadily mounting bulk; trunks, valises,
packages, all that meant a nice little sum to be paid for
excess baggage! They might be soaked in the rain too,
with those transfers from the cab to the train. She listened to the gentle patter on the zinc of the balcony
above. The fine, drenching rain had started during the
night and probably would not stop for a long time; the
sky was completely overcast and the light so dim that
the gas lamps were burning in many windows.

In the afternoon Achille bade a fond farewell to his
"Muse." He had just completed the copy of her song
cycle, and it was a work of beautiful musical calligraphy.
On the front page and at the top was the dedication "To
Mme. Vasnier."

When he presented his offering, however, he realized

that these words did not conveniently translate his fond gratitude. Walking to the little table where he had worked so many long hours, he paused for a moment then dipped his pen and slowly wrote under the name:

"I dedicate these songs which never knew life but through her artistry, and which will lose their enchanting grace if they no longer are expressed through her lips, the lips of a 'melodious fairy.' The everlastingly grateful author, C. A. Debussy."

The next morning when he awakened in the stuffy compartment meagerly illuminated by the lowered lamp, the train rolled at full speed through the plains of Provence. It was still raining and dawn, usually so luminous in this southern land, came slowly and reluctantly. Along the tracks were vineyards sheltered from the wind by lines of tall cypresses. Scattered at random among them stood rustic houses, painted white under their red roofs. Farther away one distinguished clumps of pines and myrtles, washed into soft hues by the incessant drizzle. Achille felt cold and the humidity penetrated to his bones. He was glad when the train pulled under a huge and smoky shed. "Marseille . . . Marseille . . . All out!" and the porters rushed here and there among the "welcomes" of waiting families. The connecting train for Italy would not leave till two hours later, so there was plenty of time. Achille hurried to the buffet, anxious to drink a cup of piping hot coffee to chase away his chill. He felt disappointed at the weather, as he had expected to use those two hours to visit the old city, take a stroll along the Vieux Port and its side streets so picturesque with their confusion and noise, the cries of the sailors and fishermen, the chirping of the canaries, the squawking of the parrots on the window sills and the undefinable odor of seaweed and boat hulls floating everywhere. Then there was the buzzing of the harbor itself, the bells, the whistles, the steaming engines, the creaking of the gigantic cranes. Perhaps there might have been some great transatlantic liner too, lying at anchor along the dock. At this thought all his native yearning for the sea came back strongly; but the rain, really, made the outing impossible. He stayed at his table near an enormous coal stove which purred discreetly, called the waiter and asked for pen and stationery. A note to his family . . . another one to Paul Dukas whom he had met recently at Guiraud's; finally a longer letter to M. Vasnier which he signed in florid style, intertwining the initials in a way remindful of some side comment on a Chinese print. He mailed them and boarded the train which on its way to Italy would follow the coast of the Riviera, "la Corniche," that land of flowers, sunshine, and orange blossoms sung by the poets. But the rain would not stop, and it spoiled that most beautiful part of the journey.

The border . . . Ventimiglia . . . the customhouse . . . the bersaglieri . . . one more night on the train, then finally the campagna romana and the station of Monte Rotondo. Here also it rained softly and persistently. But Achille suddenly heard friendly calls, saw hands extended toward him. The Villa Medici had come to greet him; some twenty-five young men gesticulating cheerfully, painters, sculptors, musicians, and the first one was Paul Vidal!

"Claude-Achille Debussy, we welcome you to the Villa Medici and into our Brotherhood. The sky is weeping but sunshine is in our hearts!" one of them shouted, lifting his hat in the rain. Under the amused looks of the passers-by, puzzled by that acclaim in a foreign tongue, they boarded several old jaunting cabs and began their joyous ascent toward the villa.

The concierge, dressed in a long green frock coat with gilt buttons, greeted Achille at the door and told him the director wanted to see him as soon as he got settled. Then he took him to his room, a large one with walls painted in dark green, nicknamed "the Etruscan tomb." It served as both studio and sleeping room and there was a piano and a large writing table, also a fireplace with the statue of an ox on the mantelpiece. It was the work of one of the former occupants, and another laureate in painting was the author of a large academic canvas hanging directly above. A few smaller pictures, some tapestries, a dried-out palm leaf completed the furnishings. Everything considered, it was not uncomfortable but there was something cold and forbidding to which Achille's sensitiveness reacted immediately. But the director awaited him.

He proceeded along the solemn corridor, entered a waiting room where the waxed floor, the mahogany chairs trimmed with red velvet, and several portraits of former directors were stern and formal; soon he was ushered into the directorial office.

M. Louis-Nicolas Cabat rose and shook his hand. He was a talented landscape painter and a distinguished gentleman, as Achille himself termed him later. He ran the villa rigidly and almost in military style, avoiding contact with the inmates except when it was necessary for administrative reasons. In a few measured sentences, conventionally recited, he informed the newcomer of the rules of the establishment: observance of the hours, compliance with discipline, and no disturbance of any kind. Apart from that, complete freedom. Every evening the great parlor was available for those who wanted to have music.

"All that doesn't appeal to me at all, Paul," Achille said to Vidal as he visited him a few moments later. "I am afraid the life here is going to be a mixture of cosmopolitan hotel, public high school, and military barracks. How homesick I am for Paris already."

But Vidal had completely adapted himself, and he tried to cheer up his friend by showing him the advantages that would be his: the art treasures of Rome, the opportunity of becoming acquainted in the churches with a kind of religious music impossible to hear elsewhere; and above all, no material worry, the gladdening knowledge that one can go to the dining room without thinking of the bill.

In the evening, according to tradition, Achille was invited to play his prize cantata, and when he finished he received many congratulations. Still he had played rather indifferently; the inspirational element was lacking; in mind he was hundreds of miles away, up in the petit salon of the Vasniers' apartment, where perhaps the "melodious fairy" at that same instant sang his melodies and, who knows, perhaps longed for him too. After the party he retired to his room and wrote to her. Was she not the one in whom he could confide fully, the one with whom he could share his joys and his sorrows? In phrases somewhat romantic and grandiloquent, he told her of the despair which already invaded him. Never would he get used to this sort of life, among official surroundings where one loses all pride and all individuality; much worse, he thought, than even the old stuffy loge where at least he was left alone, ate his meals without having to sit at the common table around which there was no genuine sympathy, where a lot of futile blabber was exchanged, instead of the enlightening artistic debates which could be reasonably expected from such a gathering. How he missed the intimacy of her home, the supreme refinement, the discreet elegance of her demeanor. No, he could never forget her, and he felt utterly miserable in his regret not to have resigned and remained in Paris. Once this letter written and the envelope sealed, he felt somewhat relieved, and made his preparations for the first night he was going to spend in the Etruscan tomb.

Social life occupied an important place among the activities in Rome. During the season innumerable parties, balls, dinners, musicales took place and were attended by the highest circles of fortune and nobility. Strangely enough, however, these events seldom opened their doors to the young artists of the villa. Was it because Roman society, highly polished but somewhat cool and distant, feared the contact of a youthful foreign element which perhaps they imagined bohemian, akin to the characters of *La Bohème?* Anyhow, this lack of hospitality was satisfactory to Achille, and the obligation to attend several official affairs at the French Embassy made him appreciate still more the mental quietude he found in his semiconfinement.

At least three months remained until the time when he would have to send his first envoi. So there was no hurry and he had plenty of time to adapt himself. The villa displeased him greatly, too large, too pretentious with all those columns and the statues that seemed to stare at him from every angle, wherever he went. Then, the drastic schedule; with his contrary disposition, the dinner bell always rang when he was not hungry, and when it was time to come back he invariably felt the urge to remain in town. Without being a great psychologist, his mother knew well how to handle her son: "Why don't you go out for a walk, it is so beautiful, today," she said if she wanted him to stay at home. Should she wish him to go out, on the other hand, she only had to advise him against doing so. With such a strange disposition it is natural that he was unhappy; all the more so when summer came and the thermometer rose to heights unknown in the temperate climate of Paris. At times there seemed to be no motion in the air and one felt enveloped by a cloak of moisture. Then Achille was incapable of doing any work; he remained days without going out, his mind as sluggish as his body, and it cost him great effort to write the letters which under less trying circumstances would have been an enjoyable pastime.

To be truthful, it must be admitted that in those letters he poured upon himself a considerable amount of self-pity. Some facts were magnified in order to arouse compassion. But he told the truth when once he announced the poor condition of his health. The continued stifling heat was hard on his heart; he felt so weak that sometimes he postponed the process of dressing for several hours. There were the mosquitoes too, that horrible plague! "If there is one mosquito within one square mile," he used to say, "it infallibly comes to sting me."

Unexpected relief came to him in the person of a visitor. He was Count Giuseppe Primoli, the scion of a noble family whose ancestry could be traced back for several centuries; he used florid language and had received an education of the highest order. Often he was a host to some of the young artists and to M. Cabat himself. This time Achille was singled out.

"I would be greatly honored," the count said, "if you would accept my invitation to spend a week at my house by the sea."

Achille was delighted. No more mosquitoes! Freedom, and the sea, his beloved sea!

Obtaining a leave of absence was an easy matter, since Count Primoli himself requested it from M. Cabat. So Achille took the train to Fiumiselino, and this enchanting site was all that he had pictured in his mind. But when he came to the house, built on the sea front and commanding an admirable maritime view, disappointment awaited him. The valet handed him a letter, "with the sincerest apologies on the part of Monsieur." Achille opened the message.

"Bien cher Monsieur: I have been called urgently to Paris and can hardly find words to express adequately my grief at being unable to greet you and extend to you the heartiest welcome to my home. Purposely, I did not notify you of my absence, since I wanted you to come in spite of it. Please consider that my villa is yours; orders have been given to ensure your well-being and comfort."

There are still great gentlemen in this world, Achille thought, as he stepped into the luxurious home where everything was arranged with artistry. His room upstairs opened on a balcony, and before him the sea stretched out to the horizon. Here and there the little white specks of sea gulls broke the monotony of an almost too perfect, too peaceful blue sky. From a distance came the soft music of a mandolin, so sweet that it sounded like an aeolian harp. The atmosphere was transparent and silky; the sunlit awnings, with their bright colorings, conveyed a general feeling of optimism; all was relaxation, peace, harmony.

That week meant for Achille the pacification of his troubled soul. No "military" rules prevailed here; on the contrary, the servants were instructed to comply with his wishes, and how this agreed with his taste for caprice, improvisation, luxury! Of the Italian language he knew only a few words, but enough to express his desire that the meals should be served or the carriage ordered for an excursion. However, it was on the beach that he spent most of his time. Returning from solitary wandering, his epicurean taste found satisfaction in the menus prepared by an artist-cook: rare dishes such as curried oysters, lobster, turtle soup, and also the traditional spaghetti compounded from a variety of recipes including one that made use of two dozen ingredients.

Work was not neglected. Often Achille sat for hours at the table in front of the window. No one disturbed him, not even the chef who dreaded any delays endangering the quality of his concoctions.

This was the kind of life Achille had always dreamed of, the life of a multimillionaire, and he truly reveled in it; so much so that it lasted three weeks instead of one! From Paris Count Primoli wrote and asked him to prolong his stay, since he expected to be back within a few days. But he was unable to do so, and finally Achille was recalled by a curt note from M. Cabat who thought the vacation of his pensionnaire had lasted long enough.

Back in the Etruscan tomb, Achille resumed his color-

less life. Somehow he felt, or thought he felt, an undercurrent of jealousy surrounding him. Was it because of
his three weeks' vacation? Perhaps the others, less favored,
resented what looked like partiality. Maybe this existed
only in his imagination, so fertile, so easily stirred. Anyway, he retired from the evening gatherings almost entirely, preferring to meet with Vidal and Pierné in either
of their private rooms. He discovered Shakespeare, and
his enthusiasm was not satisfied with mere reading; he
coaxed his two friends into enacting entire scenes. Thus
they forgot the heat, the mosquitoes, and the general
discomfort.

A letter came from M. Vasnier:

"I do not understand, Achille, the reason why you feel
so miserable. You never mention Rome, that glorious
city so rich in historic memories. Not a word either about
the picture galleries, the art museums. What does this
mean? Is it possible that a young man as intellectual as
you could remain in the midst of such artistic treasures
without even taking the trouble to go and look at them?
If this is the case, frankly, my young friend, I am disappointed in you, and I suggest an immediate modification
in your 'curriculum vitae.' "

Achille pondered much over this letter; there was a
shade of impatience in it, prompted perhaps by his incessant complaints. He realized how often he had written to the architect, finding fault with everything and
never satisfied. Then on several occasions he had hinted
at some material help. M. Vasnier had responded generously, but there is an end to everything and perhaps
his patience was exhausted. Achille felt that from now on
it might be advisable to "soft-pedal" his grumbling, to

M. Vasnier at least, since the epistles written by the "melodious fairy" were as discreetly affectionate as ever and showed deep concern over his real or imaginary worries.

One day M. Cabat called a general meeting.

"Gentlemen, I am going to leave you. The hour of my retirement has arrived. My successor will be M. Hébert, the painter whose name you all know. I trust you will cooperate with him as loyally as you have with me. Thank you, and good-bye."

For the first time there was a little warmth in the voice of the old director, so academic-looking with his long frock coat and his white whiskers; now he was going to enjoy his pensioned "retreat," that soft life which all Frenchmen in the employ of the state look forward to during their years of labor as the blessed culmination which brings security and peace to their old age.

Achille and the other residents felt somewhat uneasy. What kind of director would M. Hébert be? After all, there had been no trouble with M. Cabat. Would it be the same with his successor? The only thing was to wait and see, and hope for the best.

In the meantime Achille paid a visit to Sgambati, the great Italian musician, pianist, and composer, and the latter invited him to a symphony concert at which he would play Beethoven's *Emperor* concerto. On the same program was the second symphony, and Achille found its largo purely admirable. Later he gave his impressions to Vidal.

"What a pity that Beethoven didn't continue as he had started; things were going so well! Nevertheless, I also liked the slow movement of the concerto. So that makes two, instead of only one that Chopin tolerated, the adagio from the *Moonlight Sonata.*"

From his visit to the art galleries he received a tremendous impression: it was Michelangelo who elicited his greatest enthusiasm. He discussed this point with several painters at the villa and they were shocked at some of his statements; this one, for instance:

"Michelangelo . . . but to me he represents a climax of modernism. Yes, gentlemen, he was unafraid; he *dared,* almost to a point bordering on insanity! Ah, if anyone followed his example today, and I mean in music as well as in painting, he certainly would never become a member of the Institut!"

A few days passed and a second general meeting was called, this time to meet M. Hébert who had just arrived. Apprehension had been unjustified: he appeared a tractable, sociable man, not temperamental in the least and much more human than his predecessor. He had a weak spot in his heart for music, and he played the violin. It was not long before he discovered that Achille had won a prize in accompaniment.

"Perhaps we could play a sonata together, from time to time," he suggested. "I adore Mozart; his music suits my temperament better than anything else."

It is always wise to be in the good graces of one's director, Achille thought. It is like the army: if a private is friendly with the captain, he may obtain more furloughs than the ordinary rank and file. For some time, indeed, he had been thinking of taking a short vacation in Paris. He knew the difficulty of such a favor being granted. So he put himself at the entire disposal of M. Hébert, only too happy to be of service.

But there were other obstacles in the way of this projected trip; in the first place, his finances. Achille's visits to the city had meant considerable expense. The pastry shops are a great temptation in Rome; often he brought back a full bag of petits fours and they were a valuable addition to the compotes and preserves served daily at the villa. Still more dangerous to his purse was his roaming around the antique shops. He looked in at the windows, went away, came back, compared, asked prices, and it usually ended by a sudden rush to the exchange office where another bank note, perhaps two, would be converted into lire. Then furtively, as if carrying a stolen treasure, he would go back to the villa and enrich his "museum" with the new piece. His collection grew steadily and already filled one of the bureau drawers. The drain on his finances was of no consideration as compared with the joy he derived from his feeling of artistic ownership. As to the Paris trip, he would find some other way to get money; he had already written to M. Vasnier and made a casual reference to the high cost of traveling, but so far there had been no response.

The arrival in Rome of M. and Mme. Hochon afforded a new element of life at the villa. They were friends of M. Hébert, wealthy, up-to-date, sociable young people. In coming to Italy they had no other purpose than to flee from the cold dampness of a Parisian winter. They loved music and were acquainted with many personalities of the artistic world.

"We have a message for you from dear Guiraud," M. Hochon told Achille. "He sends you his most affectionate regards."

"And I want to tell you something confidentially,"

added Mme. Hochon. "He thinks you have a magnificent future; in fact, he says you are a genius!"

This marked the beginning of a social period during which a number of parties took place at the villa. The Hochons brought some friends who brought more friends, and at last there was life in that old palace, an animation it had not known for decades, perhaps had never known before. On each occasion M. Hébert took out his violin and won loud applause despite his persistent scraping and his candid disregard for time and rhythm. Achille, asked to perform some of his own compositions, gave excerpts from his cantata and also sang several songs in his grave, low voice, unplaced and untrained, but strangely impressive. Mme. Hochon seemed much impressed and listened with a sort of reverent admiration, contrasting with her usual superficial though thoroughly charming demeanor.

It was on such nights that Achille was at his best. Surrounded by sympathy, he responded readily; but when morning came his mood had once more changed and his nostalgia was worse than ever. At all costs he had to go to Paris. But how? To elude his worries he decided to go downtown and lose himself among the colorful crowd; he could hardly afford the omnibus fare now, much less do any shopping. But he could still satisfy himself by looking at the window displays, at one in particular which contained two small antique statuettes, two delicate figurines carved in ivory. They were in an old Jewish curio shop but no price was marked, so he went in to inquire; almost penniless, he could at least look at them closely, hold them in his hand.

The price mentioned (in bad French) was truly exorbitant. Achille's hopes collapsed, even for the future or in dreams. Once he thought of asking Count Primoli for a loan sufficient to cover the cost of the statuettes and his trip to Paris; but this should be done verbally and he did not have money enough to go to Fiumiselino. Besides, his friend had not been at the villa for a long time and perhaps he had gone abroad. Not knowing which way to turn, Achille made up his mind to write again to M. Vasnier.

"Please write to me very soon and tell me that you feel no resentment toward me, and that you are not forgetting *the matter you know*. My courage is about exhausted and maybe I will not have the patience to await much longer a satisfactory solution."

This would surely bring an answer, he thought rather childishly. But the days passed and nothing came. He lost his zest for everything, even his work, and began to spend his days aimlessly watching for the postman, only to be more disappointed when he had come and gone.

Several days later Vidal was still asleep when a loud rapping on the door awakened him. Jumping out of bed, he opened the door and saw Achille, pale, nervous, almost in hysterics.

"A terrible thing is happening, Paul," he exclaimed in a voice half strangled by emotion. "I have just received a wire from Paris and my poor father is gravely ill. He ought to be operated on, but he hasn't enough money."

Vidal felt the situation keenly, but he did not lose his composure and concentrated upon finding some way to help. Presently he discovered it.

"The Hochons . . . I'll go and see them at once. Wait

for me here and don't worry. I'll be back as fast as I can!"

Forgetting his breakfast, he dressed hurriedly and rushed out.

Less than an hour later he came back, all out of breath, and handed Achille a beautiful bill for a thousand francs, a small fortune in soft hues of pink and light blue with the effigy of the French Republic in the center. Achille's face brightened and he kissed his faithful comrade on both cheeks, then disappeared into the corridor.

At lunch, however, his absence was noticed. Vidal went to his room, but no one was there. Perhaps he had been detained by some red tape at the telegraph office? Perhaps he had left for Paris without even bothering to pack his valise? All suppositions were possible, and they ran through Vidal's head as the hours went by and Achille failed to return. Had he been robbed by some pickpocket downtown? Or murdered?

When he did not appear at suppertime Vidal's anxiety became serious and he decided to notify M. Hébert.

As he passed Achille's room on his way to the directorial apartment, a ray of light from the door made him stop. It was slightly ajar.

Cautiously Vidal pushed it open.

Achille was there, seated at the table in his familiar posture, with his back to the door and his head resting on his arms. The lamp was in front of him and directly under its shade the two statuettes stood, displaying their unique grace. Achille stared at them, motionless, fascinated, as if under a hypnotic spell. When he turned toward Vidal his face was illuminated by a radiant smile.

"At last . . . they are mine!" he said simply.

Vidal began to realize that Achille could not be judged by ordinary human standards. His personality defied analysis; was he, perhaps, a reincarnation of some mysterious genius transplanted from another, very old planet? Vidal was puzzled by this new incident, but it strengthened his admiration instead of lessening it. An ordinary crook steals for the lust of money; Achille had made up a story to serve an ideal . . . the idealistic impulse to possess those statuettes at all cost and regardless of the means employed. No, indeed, he could not be blamed. For Vidal, the case was settled and he dismissed it from his mind. As for the trip to Paris, it appeared necessary because of Achille's health. He was in a chronic state of fever; his strength was sapped by constant perspiration which ran down his cheeks and obliged him to change his linen several times a day. He was a northerner despite his Florentine looks, and his life in that semitropical climate was unbearable, forced as he was to take quinine and other medicine. Despite such adverse conditions, he tried to work. Often he walked back and forth in his room, then sat down and jotted ideas on any paper that was at hand, a laundry bill or the back of a letter. Afterward he went to the piano, tried what he had written and many times ended by throwing the result into the wastebasket. But the weeks had passed and soon his envoi would be due.

"It's hopeless!" he said to Vidal. "I will never be able to do it here. They sent me to Rome for that purpose; still, whatever they may expect from me will have to be done in Paris. Isn't it a joke?"

M. Hébert continued the series of receptions. On sev-

eral occasions Vidal had to substitute for Achille, who
sternly refused to leave his room. One morning the director sent for him.

"I have been wondering why you didn't attend our last
soirées, Achille. I know your health hasn't been good
lately. Still, I also know that you have spent much time
downtown. Is there any special reason for your absence?"

"Yes, M. Hébert, and it is a major reason. I ran short of
money and I had to sell my evening coat!"

The director sympathized. Achille felt this and seized
the opportunity.

"Oh, I am so ill, M. le Directeur. You don't know
how ill I feel. My brain is becoming impotent, as if paralyzed. I need a change. Will you do me an immense favor?
Please, grant me a leave of absence so I can go to Paris for
a little while."

"But you just said you had no money."

"They will send for me. I really must go, M. le Directeur; it will be my salvation. Will you give me permission?"

"But, my dear young man, you don't realize that you
are in a state institution. Rules are rules. I would like to
please you but there are certain things which I do not control, which are impossible."

Achille was a good actor; he decided to play the grande
scène. Throwing himself on his knees he stretched out
his arms toward the flustered director.

"I must go, I simply *must*. I am at the end of my rope,
desperate, heartbroken. If you refuse, I know what is left
for me to do."

His hand reached into his pocket and emerged slowly,
holding an object that was dark, glistening. A frightened

look came over M. Hébert's face. The butt of a revolver, certainly! He rushed forward, grabbed Achille's arm, picked him up.

"For heaven's sake, my boy, pull yourself together. Yes, you shall go to Paris. I will arrange it some way or other."

Anything was preferable to a scandal; a suicide in his establishment would unquestionably cause his removal and ruin his career.

Back in his room, Achille pulled the dark object out of his pocket. It was his ebony cigarette case!

While he awaited his departure, he investigated religious art. His spirits were high again and he felt in the proper receptive mood, so true is it that our reactions are governed by our frame of mind and modify themselves accordingly. Thus he received the revelation of Orlando di Lasso and Palestrina. He returned profoundly moved. from the Anima Church where he had heard their music. The temple, first, had impressed him with its architecture, so simple and pure, a happy contrast to other churches where statues, paintings, and mosaics made an almost theatrical display, where Christ himself seemed to lose some of his sublime radiance. Orlando di Lasso, Palestrina: two names he had known only through musical encyclopedias, whose mystic foresight he never suspected. What beauty they extracted from counterpoint, a form usually so dry and uninspiring! Such heavenly interweaving of melodic designs made him think of the old missals patiently colored by monks centuries ago. He was surprised, charmed, and a new musical creed revealed itself to him as he listened.

No answer had come as yet from M. Vasnier, but that mattered little and Achille knew it all could be straight-ended out amid the excitement created by his return. This silence probably amounted to no more than a temporary sulking on the part of the architect; and he had some new songs to give to the "melodious fairy."

It was a great day when M. Hébert sent for Achille and notified him that the ministerial authorization had just arrived from the Beaux-Arts. He could leave at any time for a period of two weeks. Hurriedly he went to Vidal's room, told him the good news, then packed his grip and extracted the balance of the thousand francs from the hiding place where it had rested since the purchase of the statuettes. He felt rich and had no reason to save a few pennies on his fare; so he booked a sleeping-car reservation on the Rome-Paris express.

Achille arrived in Paris the next morning. Full of expectation, he had risen early, and as the train tore through the suburban towns he looked with emotion at the familiar landscape. He felt the void of those months spent in Rome, during which he had accomplished nothing. Really, he had not climbed one step on the ladder of success. The thought of the French philosopher came to his mind: the world is like an oyster; open it who may. Words so true when applied to a young composer, ambitious, conscious of his value, yet so often unable to understand the secrets of self-promotion!

He took a cab and gave the address in the Rue Clapeyron. Paris was the same as ever: workingmen and clerks waiting for buses at the corners, housewives coming back from their shopping, their bags filled to capacity and a long, golden, crisp roll of French bread under the arm; youngsters going to school, dressed in blouses of satine and berets of the type he had worn so long himself.

Victorine and Manuel manifested great excitement at his arrival. The latter had to leave for his office, but Victorine wanted to be told all the details of the life at the villa. She was distressed when she heard of the "abominable" food. It was so awful, really. Such tasteless, impersonal cooking. No variety, either. Day after day they were fed the same stews, the same beans, the same potatoes. Ah, certainly the government would never go broke through the expense of such a miserable diet.

Victorine sympathized; she was going to outdo herself and try to make up for such misery.

In the afternoon, with a certain nervousness, Achille climbed the five flights leading to the Vasniers' apartment. What kind of reception awaited him there?

Luckily the "melodious fairy" was alone. When her husband came in she was able to break the news to him before he met Achille. There was no unpleasantness; on the contrary, the architect rather apologized for his long silence. Tired by the journey, his young friend looked pretty sick, he thought, and that was enough to soften his feelings. Of course, he had been provoked by so many complaints and had expected Achille to have more stamina.

"What would you do, my poor friend, if you actually had to serve in the army?"

Then he gave a little lecture:

"Your troubles, Achille, come from a lack of perspective. You look above, always, instead of beneath. Think of how many people go hungry, have no home, instead of thinking of millionaires. Then you will appreciate your present condition, which to many would appear a fortunate one indeed!"

The new songs were found delightful and contributed in no small measure to the restoration of former friendliness. Should his trip have no other result, this was enough to make it worth while, Achille thought.

But his two weeks were filled with many other interesting events. He asked Gounod for an appointment, and showed the master his songs and received encouraging words of approval. He went to the Conservatoire and dropped in on Guiraud, who extended to him the most affectionate welcome. He sauntered along the quays, fumbling through the bookshelves and the piles of music. Then, tired of so much walking, he landed at the Brasserie Pousset and absorbed several glasses of beer, rolling and smoking one cigarette after another and contemplating the motley crowd that streamed endlessly along the boulevard. He paid visits to the Cours Moreau-Sainti and to the Concordia, where again he met Gounod. As the two walked home the conversation turned to Wagner, but their opinions were at variance.

"I can see, Achille, that you are completely intoxicated with Wagner. I cannot understand how you, the author of such clear and charming songs, can be fascinated by an art so constantly loud, grandiloquent, foreign to our Latin ideal."

"Wagner is admirable."

"He is a great musician. I don't deny it, powerful and dramatic. But can you approve of vocal writing which treats voices as poor relations?"

"I do not think in terms of voices; only in terms of music. Wagner is admirable."

"For you . . . for you!" concluded Gounod, whose

patience was being submitted to a severe test. Luckily they were reaching the Rue de Montchanin and this put an end to the debate.

"I may see you pretty soon in Rome," Gounod added as they parted. "Hébert has invited me to visit the villa and I think I shall do so; next month, probably."

The balance of Achille's time was devoted to composition. From Rome he had brought some sketches for a symphonic piece which would constitute his envoi, and the poem by Rossetti, *The Blessed Damozel*, written some forty years before by the English poet but only recently translated into French. With his return to Paris his capacity for work had come back; again he felt in a creative mood, ideas sprang up without effort and he jotted them down feverishly, reserving the polishing process for later on.

That was the year 1886, a year notable for its artistic activities. Verlaine published *Jadis et naguère*; Berthe Morizot painted her famous canvas, *Au bain*; Degas, having at last and suddenly attained a glory delayed till his seventies, exhibited his exquisite dancing figures; pre-Raphaelitism reigned supreme in France as it did in England; impressionism, symbolism, poetic realism elicited curiosity or enthusiasm; artists from all lands began to flock to Giverny, eager to penetrate the secrets of Claude Monet. It was a happy time, during which the things of the mind passed ahead of those purely materialistic. Life was easy and enjoyable and if an artist was poor, at least he was rich in his enthusiasm, in his hopes, in his youth.

Before Achille returned to Rome with new courage, better health, and a sketchbook abundantly filled, M. Vasnier had a serious talk with him. Seeing his reluctance to leave Paris, he tried to reason with him, speaking to him as he would to a child.

"You must be sensible, Achille. I want you to promise me that from now on you are going to change your outlook. If you really wish happiness, you will find it within yourself. Think of the splendor of Rome, the beautiful trees, the sky."

"Trees . . . sky . . . they exist in Paris too."

"Promise me that you are going to be more sociable. It should be easy with such a charming man as Hébert."

"A charming man in Paris, perhaps. But in Rome I am in a prison, and he is the warden."

Hopeless, M. Vasnier thought. Nevertheless, Achille gave him his word that he would remain another year in Rome. At least he would try, and try hard.

Back at the villa it only took Achille a few days to put his sketches in order and send his symphonic number to the Institut within the proper time. Relieved of this immediate concern, he took a short trip to Milan and had an enjoyable interview with Arrigo Boïto, who advised him to pay a visit to Verdi and gave him a letter of introduction.

Achille decided to use it at once and he journeyed to the country home of the author of Aïda, whom he found in his garden, prosaically taking care of his flowers and vegetables. The meeting was cordial and Achille thoroughly enjoyed his conversation with a musician who, despite his firmly established fame, strove continually toward improvement and succeeded even during the last years of his long life.

Real friendship had also developed between Achille and Sgambati. Often this great pianist played for his young colleague in the propitious atmosphere of his softly lighted studio.

"Oh, if I could only play in public as I do here!" he remarked occasionally. But he dreaded public performances and suffered from frightful nervousness before large audiences.

Gounod's arrival caused something of a sensation, especially when it was announced that he would dine one evening with the residents of the villa, previous to a great party given in his honor by M. Hébert. Achille did not relish the idea of being with him under such conditions, since Gounod, affable and gracious, nevertheless had a certain propensity for becoming overdignified when surrounded by an admiring crowd.

"What a pity that we cannot spend the evening with him privately," he said to Vidal. "What an exchange of oversized ideas and hollow words we will have to endure at the table, between Hébert perorating and dear old Gounod being pontifical."

On the morning of the great day M. Hébert sent for Achille.

"It's important," the emissary explained without further details.

"Here is a message that concerns you," the director said as he handed Achille a letter with the heading of the Fine Arts Ministry; a cutting from the *Journal Officiel* was attached to it.

It was the report of the Academy on the symphonic work, printemps, sent recently by Achille.

"M. Debussy certainly cannot be blamed for being

commonplace or banal. To the contrary, he shows a pronounced, even too pronounced, leaning toward strange research. It is most desirable that he beware of this vague impressionism which makes him forget the importance of precision in form and contours and is one of the worst enemies of truth in works of art. The Academy hopes for, and will expect, something better from so gifted a composer as M. Debussy."

Achille stood speechless, profoundly hurt. His sensitiveness made him vulnerable to any lack of appreciation and he resented this all the more since he *knew* the judges had simply failed to understand him. His conviction remained unshaken, however; he was right, and they were wrong!

M. Hébert made an unfortunate remark:

"The last few years it seems to me that all you young musicians have deviated from logic. The influence of Wagner—"

"Wagner is admirable!" Achille interrupted.

"Wagner is not of our race; his ideals, if he has any, are strange to us. It grieves me to see—"

"Wagner is admirable!" Achille interjected more forcefully.

M. Hébert's temper flared.

"Admirable? Nonsense! Detestable, atrocious, bombastic, vulgar. I will give you a bit of advice, my dear young man—"

But Achille never knew what this advice was. Quietly he had bowed and slipped out of the room.

In the refectory preparations went on feverishly all the afternoon. Choice flowers, brought by the gardeners, decorated the tables. A replica of Gounod's portrait by

Carolus-Duran hung above the mantelpiece. A discreet squealing filtered from the director's office; it was M. Hébert toiling and laboring on his fiddle in order to offer to Gounod a performance of his *Ave Maria* that would please him.

When the author of *Faust* made his solemn entrance he was greeted by salvos of applause. Welcomes, presentations, handshakes, all the rituals were carried out according to etiquette. Then everyone sat down and the banquet started.

Gounod displayed no pomposity; he was in a genial mood and his conversation sparkled with anecdotes that were greatly enjoyed by his responsive listeners. Achille was seated at his left. On the other side was M. Hébert, attentive, unctuous, and inwardly ruminating the speech he would deliver with the champagne.

Achille felt relieved when Gounod told him that he had left Paris a week before and stopped at Nice on the way; he was not present, then, at that session of the Institut when the adverse verdict was rendered. When he heard the criticism and noticed how upset Achille was about it he threw up his arms, then clasped his hands together.

"And so you are all put out, my dear boy. You think it is terrible. You go about with a long face. Why, it is ridiculous! Let me tell you a story, my own story. Then you will feel better."

A great silence descended and the master spoke:

"My young friends, I am, unfortunately, much older than you are, and what I am going to tell you happened more than twenty-five years ago. On the night of March 19, 1859, the first performance of *Faust* was given in Paris.

I was filled with youthful enthusiasm and my hopes ran high. The next morning, however, they were shattered and I lost faith in the ultimate success of my work. When I opened the newspapers with trembling fingers, do you know what I found? I can tell you almost word for word, because I never forgot it. Listen:

" 'The only passage worth noticing in the first act is a sort of little pastoral symphony announcing the coming of dawn,' one reviewer said.

" 'The aria in which Faust endeavors to express the delight brought to him by the appearance of Marguerite shows nothing remarkable apart from a discreet accompaniment in which one distinguishes a violin solo following the outline. As to the ballad of the spinning wheel, it has absolutely no melodic character,' commented another.

"Now listen to this, which appeared in the *Revue des Deux Mondes*:

" 'The part of Mephistopheles does not stand out at all, as it should. The composer has not known how to picture this queer character, half sophist and half demon, with a few vigorous strokes. He has not succeeded any better than Spohr himself. We must say the same about the night of Walpurgis, the scene in the prison, and the final apotheosis, which are devoid of all originality and absolutely no good."

A storm of laughter followed in which Gounod himself joined, satisfied with his effect. M. Hébert's voice tried to make itself heard:

"What a shame! Insulting *Faust*, that masterpiece which made the name of our illustrious guest immortal.

Who were they, those critics who blundered so miserably and set new standards of stupidity?"

"Don't ask me. I have forgotten their names. But it never spoiled my disposition, as you realize, and *Faust* is still here!" Gounod thus concluded amid another hearty expression of approval.

When the evening was over, Achille and Vidal went outside to cool off in the balmy night air. A small group of painters were seated on the terrace. As the two friends passed they overheard their conversation.

"Here's a good one about old Gounod. Oh, surely he wouldn't have cared to tell it himself this evening. Well, do you know he extracted from Choudens, his publisher, the exorbitant sum of one hundred thousand francs for his last opera, *The Tribute of Zamora?* A regular holdup! As to the work itself, you remember it was a terrible flop. So one day, on the boulevards, Gounod met Choudens, who wore a magnificent new fur coat. 'Ah! Here is *Faust*,' he chuckled ironically, pointing to the expensive garment. But Choudens smiled sadly as he touched his shabby-looking, greasy old hat, a poor match indeed for the sumptuous fur coat. Then he replied: 'Yes, my dear master; and here is *The Tribute of Zamora!*"

"Such is glory," said Vidal.

"Such is the spirit of the villa!" Achille corrected him.

After a few months of earnest effort on his part to create an artificial world of his own from which could be banished outside interference, Achille sank again into pessimism. He simply could not accomplish anything at the villa. The whole institution was nothing but a mediocre proposition artistically, and a nest of gossip and opportunism.

"When the painters and the musicians get together they drag down the sculptors; then the sculptors get together with the musicians and drag down the painters; and so on," Achille wrote to Mme. Vasnier, preferring to complain to her and run no further risk of antagonizing her husband. "There is no sincerity of any kind here. A bunch of climbers concentrating on one sole idea: to arrive, to get there at all costs. A fine generation of politicians in the making, indeed!"

Unable himself to play politics, disgusted with the envy and the jealousy which prevailed, Achille luckily discovered something that would be a temporary diversion from his worries: a little Punch and Judy show downtown, discovered during one of his casual wanderings. He spent such an enjoyable hour that he went back and took Vidal and Pierné. He laughed heartily at the humorous pranks of the characters, and at the sight of the old brass drum player who was at the same time conductor, manager, and barker of the company. This surely interested him more than the obsolete repertoire of the Teatro Costanzi where Bellini and Donizetti reigned supreme and Verdi was represented only by his earlier works. After visiting the little theater it was not unusual to see Achille reenact some scene that had particularly caught his fancy; this he did with a sense of imitation highly diverting to his companions.

One day there was a sensation in the refectory. A startling piece of news was circulated:

"Liszt! Liszt is coming to Rome!"

The commotion created by this magic name may easily

be imagined. The great Hungarian was in the last period of his career and his reputation had taken on such fabulous proportions that he appeared in the light of a legendary character. However, he was not coming in any professional capacity; just to pay a personal visit to his former pupil, Sgambati. Achille was thrilled when the latter invited him to an informal reception at his studio.

The great man came in, affable, dignified, a trifle senile, still wearing his gray lion mane, somewhat thinned by the years. Cardinal von Hohenlohe accompanied him. When he heard the name and nationality of Achille he made a request of Liszt:

"May I suggest, my illustrious friend, that in honor of France and French art, which you love so much, you and Sgambati play the *Variations on a Theme of Beethoven* by Saint-Saëns?"

Liszt smiled and bowed in the true manner of a grand seigneur. He sat at one of the concert grands while Sgambati, terrified, took his place at the other. It was an extraordinary performance, and the swan song of Liszt in the Italian capital, since death took him a few months later.

When another long period had passed and Achille saw no progress in his own work, he felt that the time had arrived to make an important decision. How could he be bound by his promise to M. Vasnier when conditions had changed so much? In fact, they were worse than before; fever continued to burn his body and no inspiration came to his brain.

Whatever the consequences, he was going to leave, and leave at once. Other problems would be worked out later on; for the moment only one thing counted: his freedom.

Taking just enough time to get his baggage ready and to communicate to M. Hébert his decision, he shook hands with Vidal and Pierné, then boarded a train. The home voyage had started.

From the station he sent a short wire to the Vasniers. They would not have time to answer or protest. This done, a great peace filled his heart.

On the platform a passionate southern voice sang a popular song:

"Addio . . . addio!"

"Yes . . . farewell!" murmured Achille.

He had not been happy here and left without regrets. But it was with expectation and faith that he looked to the new leaf about to be turned.

3

Claude-Achille, Young Musician

"So you didn't like it at all, in Italy. Was it really as bad as all that?" Paul Dukas said as he and Achille walked along the boulevard.

It was twelve o'clock and the crowds hurried to the little restaurants for that important function in France, the noon meal. Upon his arrival Achille had gone home to salute his parents and leave his baggage, then called at the Conservatoire, for he was anxious to notify Guiraud and consult with him. Now he had accepted Dukas's invitation to lunch and they were looking for a place where there would be relative tranquillity. Achille felt happy in the company of one so congenial to him.

"Yes, indeed, it was very bad at the villa," he answered, "and I hope you can stand it better than I when your turn comes. Perhaps I am an exception. Look at the director, M. Hébert, whom I really like and appreciate, now that he no longer is my jailer; he is simply wild about Rome! When I complained about those awful mosquitoes and my face was so swollen that I couldn't open

133

my eyes, he said I was prejudiced and the mosquitoes were an invention of mine in order to break up the villa! His love for everything Roman is so great that once he told me the drunkards there always walk straight; their intoxication is heroic. Indeed, it is . . . when they fight it is not with fists, but with daggers."

They arrived at the Passage Ronceray and saw a sign advertising the excellent cooking and the moderate prices of the Restaurant Européen. The menu posted at the door looked pretty good, and the friends walked up two flights of an old stairway with badly worn stone steps, then entered a huge hall opening on courtyards and gardens, formerly part of aristocratic mansions of the old Paris now transformed into commercial warehouses.

On both sides of a central alley were rows and rows of tables symmetrically aligned and set in readiness for the invading crowd which grew every minute, an earnest-looking crowd of the lower middle class: clerks, secretaries, small shopowners, girls neatly dressed in their homemade outfits, young men with their ready-made suits from La Belle Jardinière, elderly bookkeepers with goatees, goggles, dandruff on the collar of their alpaca suits and that air of importance which never left them even when far away from desks and ledgers under the green shades of the gas lamps. They all enjoyed this respite from their routine work and ate slowly, reverently, reading the newspaper propped up in front of them against the wine bottle; each man had his napkin tucked in his collar and hanging all the way down.

Achille and Dukas took one of the smaller tables near a window, as far as possible from the incoming tide of customers. The menu was varied and offered a large list of dishes either at fixed prices or à la carte; nothing elaborate, of course, nor of the kind to be found in smart hostelries such as Tortoni or La Maison Dorée, but clean, honest food, and wine not previously submitted to "baptism," as the French humorously call the fraudulent addition of water to the original juice of the grape.

Achille was a gourmet who knew how to adapt his tastes to the particular style of the restaurant he visited; so he selected his traditional French luncheon: eggs "on the plate," lamb chops, rather rare, with fried potatoes; lettuce salad, Brie cheese, fruit and coffee. A bottle of Vouvray completed the list.

Dukas then proposed a promenade to the Bois de Boulogne, and Achille accepted with pleasure; thus his visit to the Vasniers would be delayed and he would have more time to prepare himself for what he feared would be a stormy interview. They took an omnibus to the Porte Maillot, then entered the Bois, following at times the main thoroughfares, at other times the lanes which run through the woods along the course of murmuring brooks. They arrived at the Grand Lac, stopped to watch the evolutions of the white swans gliding gracefully on the surface, smooth as a mirror. They talked music, literature, and the names of Théophile Gautier, Verlaine, Stéphane Mallarmé, Pierre Louÿs, Jules Laforgue were prominent in the conversation. Achille mentioned his recent discovery of Shakespeare and told his friend of his special enthusiasm for *As You Like It*. But it was getting late and they had to part, though reluctantly.

On the way to the Vasniers', Achille's feelings were of

a mixed order; he was glad, of course, to see once more his beautiful friend; but he dreaded the darts that would likely come from her husband's tongue.

The architect opened the door himself.

"So, here you are, Achille," he said quizzically; "we received your wire last night. Thanks for sending it. I suppose you have some interesting news to give us concerning the motive of this sudden return?"

Achille was in no mood for joking, and he answered seriously:

"There is no reason in particular. Only my desire to work; but to work where I feel free and where my brain is clear. At the villa—"

"Oh, that same refrain!" M. Vasnier interrupted angrily. "I see that decidedly you are an exception. All your schoolmates are happy there; but for you it's Paris, always Paris. What is this attraction which is so powerful as to make you jeopardize your future?"

He looked squarely into his eyes and Achille felt uneasy. Could it be that during his absence some malevolent gossip had been conveyed to M. Vasnier's ears? But he soon was reassured.

"Achille, you know we have always had the best intentions. When I gave you advice, it was with a desire to help you through my own experience. Now you want to stand on your own. What are you going to do?"

"I don't know yet. This morning I saw Guiraud and he will try and find a position for me. Perhaps I can teach. I don't want to depend upon anyone any more, either family or friends. I thank you sincerely for what you have done in the past, but from now on anything coming to me will have to be earned. If your little daughter is ready to begin her music studies, perhaps you will be kind enough to consider me for some lessons."

There was such sincerity in his voice that M. Vasnier was moved, and he agreed to the proposition.

Guiraud, on his part, had thought the matter over since Achille's visit in the morning. How could he possibly help him? It is hard to find a paying job for a young musician, for a composer especially, who knew no instrument that could make a place for him in an orchestra. There remained, of course, the alternative of playing the piano in one of those small bands operating in cafés . . . but Guiraud rejected this humiliating solution; there ought to be some other way.

Finally he succeeded. Achille's name had not been forgotten in certain musical circles; his brilliant prize for accompaniment and the sensation created by his Prix de Rome cantata had awakened the interest of publishing firms which use a staff of experts for technical work: arranging, transcribing, proofreading, and checking of orchestral parts. Durand and Schoenewerk had found the cantata so worth while that they had agreed to publish it. Guiraud approached them and his suggestion was taken up favorably. Soon he was notified that a vacancy had just occurred; his protégé could present himself and probably sign a contract. Achille went, full of hope, and when he came out he had the contract in his pocket. It called for a monthly salary of three hundred and fifty francs ($70). Of course, he was elated; this meant not only security, but an opportunity to live among hundreds of scores which he could peruse at will. Better still, he would be able to examine the new ones before even their first performance, a rare treat for a young musician eager to keep

himself informed of the very latest developments in
music. He could also increase his income through teaching, odd jobs as accompanist, and perhaps—who could
tell?—through the sale of his compositions!

The urgent thing now was to find a little apartment.
Alone, or with Dukas, he started hunting for one.

"I believe I have found just what I want," he told
Manuel and Victorine one day. "It is on the Rue de
Londres, almost at the corner of the Rue d'Amsterdam.
Oh, it isn't large: two rooms and a small kitchen. I will
use the front room as parlor and studio."

Another hunt began in the furniture stores for bar-
gains, and Victorine brought down a number of pieces
from the attic. Soon the little flat was made cozy and
reasonably comfortable.

The lessons with Mlle. Vasnier began; she displayed
a good disposition and probably could have made fine
progress under an understanding teacher. But Achille had
no patience; child psychology was an enigma to him and
he never attempted to place himself on an equal level.
Mistakes are frequent at that age and they must be accepted and corrected with leniency. Finally he gave up
the lessons, pretending an increased schedule at Durand's.

A new life began for Achille in his beloved Paris, so
romantic, so picturesque during those golden years. He
reveled in it; it was such a contrast after the dull existence
at the Villa Medici. Montmartre, at night, offered the lure
of its cabarets where chansonniers vied with one another
in joyous satire and caustic wit. Xavier Privas, Fursy,
Xanrof entertained at the Chat Noir, satirizing all the
follies of that blessed epoch and drawing to the smoky

hall of the Rue Victor-Massé crowds of visitors from the four corners of the world. Drawings of Willette, Léandre, and Steinlen decorated the walls of many cafés, while Aristide Bruant was famous for his black corduroy outfit, his red scarf, and the informal way in which he cracked jokes at the clients who entered his cabaret. In other sections Paul Delmet crooned his suave melodies and above the whole scene of Montmartre the huge wings of the Moulin Rouge seemed to set the pace for the quadrille, the French cancan, the lighthearted life free from concern and worries.

Twice a week, regularly, Achille visited Paul Dukas, who lived on the Rue des Petits-Hôtels in an old-fashioned apartment where the parlor resembled a room in a public library, with its shelves filled to the ceiling. At the side of a huge grand piano stood the cage of a parrot which squawked every now and then. Nevertheless, the two friends spent many happy evenings in those surroundings, during which they investigated much new music, including proof sheets brought by Achille from the house of Durand. Late at night Achille went home along the boulevards or by the roundabout way of Montmartre. Often he stopped at the Brasserie Pousset because its beer was supposed to be the best in Paris. He still went to the Vasniers' occasionally, but their relations were slowing down noticeably. He had a place of his own now, where he could work in peace without having to account to anyone. More and more he loved his "well-organized bohemian life." He was able to save an appreciable amount of money every month.

This enabled him to take two trips during the summer:

the first one was to London where he wanted to investigate some question relative to the rights of *The Blessed Damozel.*

His impressions of the British metropolis were mixed; he liked the red buses, the busy life of Regent Street, the misty landscapes of Hyde Park. But he criticized a general lack of comfort, above all the inhospitably hard beds with their sheets always impregnated with moisture. And all those men in checked suits and caps, such a shock to his conception of strict elegance! On the other hand, the Empire and the Alhambra appealed to him; he enjoyed the atmosphere of these music halls where attractions succeeded each other swiftly, making the spectacle colorful and varied. There were such excellent clowns, too, and he became acquainted with a comedian who called himself "General Lavine, eccentric," without suspecting that this amusing act would be the inspiration of a prelude many years later.

His greatest "find" in London, however, was tea, plain English tea. To him, it seemed that anything he had drunk in France under that name was entirely unworthy. Often he went into the inviting tearooms and relished the discreet aroma that rose from the golden beverage while he spread on his toast that other marvel, orange marmalade. Clowns, tea, marmalade, such were the impressions which embedded themselves most durably on Achille's mind.

A pilgrimage to Bayreuth constituted his second trip, and it was accomplished with reverence and devotion. For a long time he had looked forward to it with great expectation. Even the annoyance of an overcrowded city did not dampen his enthusiasm; at least he could hear on the stage, and in the most authentic fashion, the masterpieces he had so frequently read at the piano. Still his discomfort was great, assigned as he was to a small room in a private house, with a bed consisting of three square cushions placed side by side; they were hard and never remained on the same level. Then there was that funny little wedge-shaped pillow under his head, so uncomfortable for one accustomed to the sweet softness of French feather bolsters. The sheets were so small that they couldn't be tucked in; so when Achille, his nerves stirred by an exciting performance, tossed in bed for some time before being able to sleep, all the covers would get thrown off and land on the floor. The coffee was thick and tasteless, though loaded with chicory. But the beer was delicious. His pleasure was spoiled, however, when during the intermission he went to the "restauration" of the Schauspielhaus and took his place among the crowds who gobbled up with loud noises the most incredible conglomeration of sausages of all sizes and colorings. The contrast between such coarse materialism and the fervent atmosphere in the theater shocked his sense of congruity. But all was forgotten when the divine music started again, played as he had dreamed it could be played. Heavenly!

From these journeys to foreign lands Achille always came back with a greater appreciation for his home city. Was not Paris decidedly the City of Light? Where could its unique spirit be duplicated? Was there another capital in the world where noctambulism could be as delightfully satisfied as along these broad Parisian avenues brightened here and there by the illuminations of all-night cafés? What a difference between those huge German beer gardens, as impersonal as the public halls of railroad stations, with their din of band playing and roaring voices, and the comfortable intimacy of some corner in a Paris café where one could sit, read, or smoke quietly while answering one's mail on stationery furnished by the proprietor!

He thought of all that as he walked up the Boulevard Malesherbes with Gounod after a rehearsal of the Concordia. Once again they were discussing Wagner. Fresh from the Bayreuth festival, Achille raved so much that Gounod's patience came to an end. They had arrived at the Place Malesherbes. Gounod's mansion stood on the right, but before crossing the Avenue de Villiers he extended his hand:

"Good-bye, Achille. This is the point where our roads separate. Because there is a point where our roads *must* separate!"

This was the end of a long friendship which had been treasured by Achille but which he did not hesitate to sacrifice on the altar of his artistic convictions.

One night at the Brasserie Pousset he was reading *L'Illustration* when a young woman sat down at the next table; her clothes were elegant but somehow too loud, as was her make-up and the perfume which trailed behind her. Glancing sideways, he noticed her blond hair, her delicate though sensuous features and above all, her eyes, two large, almond-shaped, green eyes that shone like big drops of liquid emerald. She ordered a bock and sat there with apparently no particular purpose, humming softly now and then as a part of her pose. Then she pulled out a cigarette, stuck it between her lips, opened her bag and looked for a match. Useless fumbling was followed by the customary:

"I beg your pardon, sir, may I trouble you for a light?"

Conversation ensued, made of nothing, the weather, or

the races, during which she moved her glass to Achille's table and sat beside him.

This first contact was limited to preliminaries. Did her intuition tell her that here was a man who could not be treated like the others with her customary formulas?

Be that as it may, she remained so strictly impersonal that Achille was puzzled and could hardly figure out what her social standing was. Before leaving, he expressed the hope that they would meet again.

"We probably will if you come here often," she said. "What is your name?"

"Achille . . . Achille Debussy."

"Mine is Gaby."

Achille made another trip, this time to Vienna. It would be a splendid opportunity to meet another musician with whom, from the little he knew of his music, he had no affinity whatever. But Johannes Brahms, practically unknown in France except for a pair of *Hungarian Dances,* was unquestionably the most representative Germanic composer outside the operatic field in which Wagner was supreme.

Achille had met Verdi in Italy, Borodin in Russia, Gounod in Paris; now the conquest of Brahms would enrich his circle and supply another valuable element for psychological observation.

Without seeking any introduction he wrote to Brahms upon his arrival, asking him for a rendezvous. One day, two days passed, and no answer came. Perhaps he was out of town, or the letter had gone astray? Brahms surely would never be so discourteous as to ignore the request of a younger colleague.

With this in mind Achille went to the composer's apartment, located in the old part of Vienna.

"Herr Brahms has gone out," was the answer he received from an elderly woman, the housekeeper apparently. He left his visiting card and said he would call again. The next day he was greeted in the same manner, only the answer differed slightly:

"Herr Brahms regrets he is unable to see you. He is very busy."

"Thank you," Achille said, and went away.

The same evening, however, he dined at the house of M. de Fleury, the secretary of the French ambassador. Mme. de Fleury, a charming lady of Hungarian descent, was somewhat disturbed when she heard the story. She offered to help.

"Please, M. Debussy, do not feel hurt in the least. I know Brahms quite well and he is very likable, once you become acquainted with him. But he is shy, very shy. Often they compare him to a 'lion in his den.' One has to find the proper approach. Will you leave this to me?"

An envelope, with the address written in a feminine hand, was handed to Achille by the hotel porter the next afternoon; it was from Mme. de Fleury and contained an invitation to lunch, with the mention, "Brahms will be there."

Achille wondered how she had been able to obtain such quick results. He was unaware that the diplomat's wife often helped Brahms when he had correspondence to do in French; the social prestige of her husband also carried influence.

"Herr Brahms, this is M. Debussy, the young French composer."

Brahms grumbled something in his beard that might be taken for a polite formula, then looking straight at Achille:

"So you are the Frenchman who wrote to me and came twice. I forgive you this time, but be sure you never do it again!"

Everyone sat at the table on which several bottles of good French wine had been placed among platters of hors d'oeuvres. These included sardines, salami, celery rémoulade, potato salad, tomatoes and foie gras, all prepared and served in true French style.

Brahms started by unfolding his napkin, stretching it across his chest and under his beard and tying it at the back of his neck; then he reached for the sardines and helped himself generously; soon he had finished and took a second helping. He would have taken a third, had there been any sardines left. Nevertheless, he reached for the platter, raised it to his lips and gobbled up the oil that remained.

Achille stared in amazement, but Mme. de Fleury, who knew the informality of her famous friend, looked neither surprised nor shocked.

During the luncheon Brahms remained silent, too busy with consumption of the delicious food to bother about conversation; but the champagne, served toward the end, put him in a talkative mood.

"I want to lift my cup to the most glorious wine in the world," he began. "To the wine which our great Goethe honored with some of his immortal verses!"

This at once broke the ice. Becoming more and more expansive as additional bottles were uncorked, Brahms continued:

"Our two nations, France and Germany, hold high the flame of art, culture, and civilization."

"Aren't we in Austria?" Achille murmured to himself.

"It is such a pity, then, to think that our nations seem destined to ever-recurring warfare. We should be brothers in fact as we are brothers in art. The artistic productions of France and Germany are, and will remain, the glory of this world."

"A glory to which you are contributing in large part," Mme. de Fleury interjected with a smile.

"That is kind of you, but not quite justified," Brahms retorted. "My music is not liked everywhere; in France, for instance, where they consider me the most Germanic of contemporary composers. This shows excellent judgment on their part, and I am thankful for it. They are right; I am a German composer and feel proud of it. Any musician who willingly abandons his artistic nationalism will never leave an enduring mark on the musical history of his country. To imitate music written abroad is absolutely inexcusable. That's why I admire French literature, French art, French music. Do you want me to tell you, M. Debussy, which of your native operas I consider the best written since the Franco-Prussian War? *Carmen!* I have heard it twenty times already, and always with renewed pleasure."

"That must be a record."

"No, my friend. Bismarck, a discriminating music lover, told me he had heard it twenty-seven times; and he considered *Carmen* the all-around masterpiece of the lyric stage."

Another hour elapsed, in which coffee, liqueurs, cigars,

and aesthetic discussion played a major part. Then Brahms took his leave, but he invited everybody to dinner the next evening and a rendezvous was arranged for six o'clock at the restaurant of the Opera House.

He was again in genial mood when his guests arrived. At that early hour only a few tables were occupied.

"I thought it would be wise to come early," he explained, "because I have a surprise for you. *Carmen* is on tonight and I have taken a box."

What a delicate attention! Achille thought; decidedly the "lion" was growing tame and he really was likable despite his superficial gruffness.

The evening was greatly enjoyed and the Vienna opera lived up to Achille's expectations. It was a first-class company, excellent in all respects, disciplined, efficient, with that rare achievement: a chorus that *acted!* The hall and the building were magnificent too, perhaps second only to the Paris Opéra.

When Brahms heard that his young colleague would stay two more days he invited him to visit all the musical landmarks of the capital. So they went to the graves of Beethoven and Schubert, to the Conservatorium, to the Imperial Library where they spent a long time looking over the notable collection of manuscripts.

On the day of his departure Achille once more made his way to the little street in the old quarter, wishing to express his deep gratitude for all the attentions he had received. The same hausfrau opened the door. But this time Brahms was neither out nor busy. He received Achille in an affectionate manner and kissed him fraternally as he wished him "a pleasant trip and much success" in his career.

His large desk covered with scores at the Maison Durand, his worktable in the little flat, and the resumption of his daily tasks, awaited Achille upon his return. At Durand's, his immediate attention was needed for some transcriptions of Schumann and Saint-Saëns. At home, the sheets of *The Blessed Damozel* were already piling high. In the drawer, however, there were many other leaves covered with minute and elegant notations in pencil: the numerous songs written over a period of several years. All remained unpublished, and it was with concern that Achille realized their increasing number. What greater joy is there for a young composer than the thrill of seeing his work printed in black and white? Now, like so many others, he found himself facing a wall, the wall of indifference. He would probably have to wage a hard fight to overcome it. And at the Vasniers' there were still more songs, not counting six additional ones which he had submitted to Mme. Veuve Girod, the publisher, for examination.

Amid these depressing thoughts a sudden vision came to Achille: those eyes of soft emerald seen one evening at Pousset's and not forgotten. Why not go there? Perhaps that young woman could help him find diversion from the vicissitudes of an artist's life. He set his desk in order, took his walking stick, and went out.

There were only a few clients at Pousset's, since the real trade starts after the closing hour of the theaters, when it suddenly fills up. Sandwiches, choucroute, cold meats, onion soups gratinées are then absorbed in great quantities, all accompanied by mugs of delicious ice-cold beer.

Achille took a seat and began reading an evening paper; from where he sat he could easily see the clock and be-

tween articles he cast a glance toward it. Ten o'clock . . .
eleven o'clock . . . and Gaby didn't come. It was still
early, however, in terms of Parisian nights.

Midnight brought the usual influx, which one hour
later receded with the regularity of the tide itself. Still
Gaby did not come.

Achille was disappointed, but it was time to go home,
much as he hated to do so, fearing that Gaby might appear precisely at the moment he turned the corner.

As he called the waiter to settle his bill, the door opened
and she came in, unescorted.

"Bonsoir, mademoiselle."

"Bonsoir, M. Debussy."

So she remembered his name! She took off her coat,
laid it in the rack and without waiting for an invitation
sat down beside him.

"It's a long time since you were here last. Two weeks,
at least. It seems long, anyway; I had been looking for
you."

Was she making advances to him or just being polite?
Achille was again puzzled by this young creature whose
manners were informal but not vulgar, whose language
was slightly plebeian but not slangy. A true Parisian, of
course, born and educated in the faubourgs. What was
her status in life? He could not tell and he did not care;
he enjoyed her presence and she seemed to enjoy his company; that was enough for the time being. She lived on
the Rue Fontaine, at Montmartre, and he walked with
her as far as the door. When they parted they made a
date to attend a night festival announced for the Bois de
Boulogne later in the week.

For some time Achille had not called on the Vasniers

and he had received no word from them. Evidently their relations were suffering a setback. There was no particular reason for this save a secret resentment on the part of the architect for the way his advice had been disregarded, and some weariness felt by Achille at the decidedly bourgeois ways of his friends. Perhaps a minute investigation of his feelings would have disclosed a certain lassitude, a vague ennui born of monotony inherent in long-standing habits. Gaby certainly was a factor in the modification that was taking place, and she injected a new element of youth and novelty into Achille's life.

The fete in the Bois de Boulogne drew an enormous crowd from all districts of Paris. The smart set occupied the de luxe pavilions and restaurants while the plain folk monopolized the lawns facing the spot at Longchamps where the fireworks would be displayed. Soft music floated in the air, interrupted at times by the blare of the bands. On the lakes the rowboats drifted, their course lighted by dim reflections of pink and green lanterns.

Gaby and Achille sat under a network of green branches and in the distance they could see the movement of the dancers in the ballroom of the Cascade restaurant. She was close to him and they hardly spoke until the first sky-rockets began to fly upward. Then the commonplace in her flared up. Eagerly she watched the thrilling spectacle, joining the multitude in spontaneous applause.

"Look . . . the beautiful blue! Look . . . the beautiful red!" she exclaimed as more rockets, bombs, and pyrotechnics of all kinds filled the night with dazzling light. Finally a "bouquet" was fired, and its immense glare drew huge clamor from the throng.

At last it was over. As Achille and Gaby walked back,

the distant sound of bugles became audible; it increased steadily and a parade approached, marching along the Avenue des Acacias. The drum major headed it and flourished his stick; some of the soldiers carried torches trailing in their wake a black, acrid smoke; a youthful mob followed, boys and girls arm in arm, joyous, singing, happy.

The couple reached the Porte Maillot and Achille hailed a cab.

"Rue de Londres," he told the driver.

Was this intentional or was he so absorbed by the beauty of this unusual night that he overlooked the presence of his companion?

In any case, Gaby did not protest and for them both the end of the festival marked the initial hour of a new idyl.

Paris was awaiting with tremendous interest the opening of a great International Exposition. For two years the preparations had upset several quarters along the Seine; a strange structure grew on the Champ-de-Mars, a tall tower of iron and steel devised by the engineer, Eiffel. Looking down from the heights of the Trocadéro one could see at one's feet an immense workshop in feverish activity: lumber, piles of sand, narrow-gauge tracks, canvas, stucco. Pavilions of all nations, attractions of all kinds, were being erected on the banks of the river. That year of 1889 was a great one for all Parisians, when visitors flocked to the exposition by millions. Achille, like everyone else, visited it with much curiosity, but neither the exhibits nor the park of attractions aroused his interest. The colonial section disappointed him greatly; he hated its falsified atmosphere, its tin-pan displays, the rattle and the tumult

of music supposedly picturesque. To him it was like cheap
prints of Egypt or Arabia, faked for the enjoyment of
gullible tourists who knew no better and admired everything confidently; faked in the same manner as the novels
of Pierre Loti which he could not read beyond the tenth
page! But he found compensation in the little Annamese
theater. In its exotic performances, imported directly
from the Far East, he discovered more than a colorful
setting: there was a strange relation between these em-
bryonic dramas, obviously under Chinese influence, and
the formula used by Richard Wagner in the Tetralogy.
Only there were more gods, and less scenery. A shrill little
clarinet led the pathos and a tam-tam came in to spread
terror. That was all. No need, here, of a specially con-
structed theater with a hidden orchestra! No other need
than an instinctive craving for art and a sense of fulfilling
it ingeniously without deviating from exquisite taste.

It was, however, in the section of the Low Countries
that Achille received his greatest revelation. There, to the
rhythms of the gamelang and an orchestra composed
chiefly of percussion instruments, the bedoyos from Java
swayed gracefully. At times their flexible bodies undulated
like a wheatfield in the breeze; at other times they swayed
like so many flexible reeds, or took hieratic postures that
turned them into a cortege of ancient idols. Then, swiftly,
they glided along the surface of a river of dreams. A clang
from the gong . . . a sudden stop . . . and they were
transmuted into mermaids and flower maidens floating
gracefully among garlands of color.

There was a strange intensity in Achille's eyes as he
watched those heads crowned with wreaths of luxuriant
flowers, the glossy luster of jet-black hair, the somber sen-

suousness of expressive eyes contrasting with glittering costumes.

Musically, he was perplexed and confused. New horizons opened before him and he realized the tremendous advancement that this form of art, apparently primitive, might mean for one who could assimilate certain of its principles and apply them tactfully.

This Achille accomplished later through the magical instinct of his God-given genius. What other French musicians failed to understand, he was able to fathom to its depth. And it was with full knowledge of their significance that he expressed his enthusiasm in the following words:

"Even Palestrina's counterpoint is child's play when compared with the one we find in Javanese music. If we can listen to the charm of its percussion without any European prejudice we are forced to acknowledge that our music, in comparison, is merely the echo of some barbaric circus noise."

Another period of intense activity began for Achille. He was at work on new songs and a *Fantaisie* for piano and orchestra. Encouragement had come to him in the form of a proposition from Mme. Girod. Her "examination" completed, she had decided to risk the venture of publishing the six songs submitted. "Oh," she hastened to explain, "it was an artistic move, not a financial investment; what music lover could be expected to purchase with actual cash an album of songs by an unknown composer?" Achille knew well that in offering a co-operative arrangement the kind old lady was doing her best. She was known as an idealist and persistent in her desire to help struggling young artists, a noble aim which she was able to achieve through the small but certain editorial fund inherited from her husband.

The songs did appear, but alas, there were few sales and the months went by.

Meanwhile, Gaby's first outings with Achille had developed into what seemed to be a permanent and sincere friendship. From her modest origin she had derived a fine sense of the practical: she was a good cook, and when she came to the apartment, which was almost every day, she assumed control of the kitchen. From London, Achille had brought back several packages of tea and the resolution to learn how to make it; but heretofore they had remained stored in a corner of the cupboard. Gaby taught him the secret of preparing the perfumed drink as well as a few elementary principles of cooking which enabled him to prepare light meals. When his work was finished it was not a rare sight to see Achille take two fresh eggs from the food-box bulging outside the kitchen window, light the gas stove and fry them appetizingly in butter, while a kettle stood in readiness for the tea.

Gaby continued to live at her apartment, and this agreed with Achille's taste for an isolation which permitted him to work unhindered. Not that secretly he did not long for the day when he would have a real home and share it with the beloved but still undiscovered elect of his heart. But Gaby obviously could not pretend to play such a part, and probably did not care to. So everything was for the best and no clouds came to darken the clear horizon of their fantasy.

Often Achille took her to concerts, and he was pleased to see that without any musical education she made intelligent remarks; above all, her attitude was unobtrusive, and her clothes had become more conservative.

The Société Nationale de Musique was then the most important channel open to the production of new music; its public was the most intelligent in all Paris, formed mostly of professional musicians and discriminating amateurs. Achille missed few of its concerts, held fortnightly and alternating between the Salle Pleyel and the Salle Érard. There he became further acquainted with leading musicians and interpreters, and one night a group of his own songs was introduced by a tenor friend, the initial step in a long line of first presentations which would extend throughout his career.

A great loss of his illusions awaited Achille in Bayreuth, where he went for the second time during the summer. Still, *Tristan und Isolde* was on the bill, that beloved *Tristan* for which he had fought with undaunted spirit, defying official wrath during his years at the Conservatoire and with Gounod himself more recently. What had happened in but a few months to modify his taste to the extent of changing his whole attitude toward Wagner?

Possibly, and probably, his visits to the Javanese theater. In listening now to the colossal production of Bayreuth he realized what an abyss separated those gigantic conceptions from the conciseness, the refinement, and the discretion representative of the French spirit in art. He saw what a danger Wagner's influence represented for musicians who fell helplessly under its powerful spell. A sense of reaction began to manifest itself within him. On his return to Paris he referred to it in many intimate talks with Dukas and with Guiraud. Perhaps it would be his mission to maintain the music of his land within the path of clarity and distinction from which it never should be allowed to deviate.

On the Rue de la Chaussée-d'Antin, near the Opéra and almost across from the corner house where Rossini lived, there was a small bookstore with a sign reading "Librairie de l'Art Indépendant."

In the show windows on either side of the entrance door books were displayed, together with paintings and etchings of an evident symbolism which disclosed the tendencies of the owner. This store could boast of a literary past: previously it had sheltered the offices of the *Revue Indépendante,* often visited by Verlaine, Villiers de l'Isle-Adam, Mallarmé, and Jules Laforgue. The magazine went into bankruptcy, however, and its offices remained closed until M. Léon Bailly, publisher, dilettante, art collector, and promoter of young but still obscure geniuses, reopened it and tried to give it new life. He was a short man, with a goatee and a pair of gold-rimmed spectacles. His wife officiated at the cashier's desk, while the pet of the house, a plump black cat answering to the name of Aziza, snoozed comfortably at her side.

M. Bailly was more than a dilettante: he composed music of uncertain value, practiced occultism, and published a scientific bulletin devoted to esoterics. Besides all that, he claimed to be a poet. According to certain rumors, he had been active in the artillery during the communist revolution of 1871; but twenty years had passed and if anything revolutionary remained in him it was only so far as music and poetry were concerned.

Under such leadership it was not long before the store

became a center for the vanguard of the young generation. There were periodic reunions at which recent literary productions were introduced and discussed. Then it was not uncommon to hear M. Bailly declare that he felt the presence of spirits; all would sit around a small three-legged table while the publisher questioned the immaterial callers from beyond. Occasionally the séance was interrupted by the entrance of a customer in quest of some rare opus.

"Have you got the *Upanishad* of the great Aranyaka translated from the Sanskrit by Ferdinand Hérold? No? . . . Then what about *The Cavern of the Nymphs,* translated from ancient Greek by Pierre Quillard?"

M. Bailly would adjust his glasses, climb his ladder, look through records, and usually unearth the precious piece. In fact, his store was known all over Paris as the only one where such rarities could be obtained.

Such was the setting into which Achille stepped casually one day when he was loitering in the neighborhood. At once a bond of mutual sympathy established itself between him and the proprietor, who introduced him to several poets who happened to drop in, Henri de Régnier among them.

Whenever he had an opportunity to meet this distinguished circle, Achille listened attentively to their artistic discussions. If these turned to musical matters he took part in them and his statements were usually severe, almost merciless, except in the case of Ernest Chausson and Vincent d'Indy whom he respected and admired. Despite his lack of a solid literary background, the theories which he propounded and the language he used in defending them were always individual and precise. Whatever the subject, he seemed to be moved by a mysterious instinct: invariably the correct sentence came to him at the right time. His reserved attitude was also appreciated by M. Bailly and his friends, and they liked his discretion, contrasting it with the arrogance of so many young artists anxious to "push themselves."

Everything was progressing auspiciously when a serious illness interrupted the course of Achille's activities. Attacked by a high fever and various other ominous symptoms, he was laid up for many days. The doctor looked concerned, as he feared it might be typhus; luckily, it was only pneumonia of a rather mild form.

Thanks to the attentive care of his mother and of Gaby, he soon became convalescent, and in his first letter to a friend he commented humorously on the dark period just past "when one single soft boiled egg assumes a significance which is really stupendous!"

Ernest Chausson occupied a place of prominence in the musical life of Paris. He was related to high political circles through his wife, who was a sister of City Councilor Escudier, and was wealthy in his own name. His mansion at 22, Boulevard de Courcelles was the center of many artistic and social activities. When he came to Paris Eugène Ysaye always stayed there. Malicious tongues contended that the reason why the Belgian violinist performed Chausson's *Poème* so persistently was his desire to repay his friend not so much for the dedication of the work as for the number of hotel bills he helped him save.

The drawing rooms, giving directly on the boulevard, were a sort of private temple of art in which many chamber music works, now well known, were first played before an intimate circle made up of the initiate. When this took place during the late spring the windows often were left open, and a small crowd gathered outside, listening attentively to the strains that poured out into the night.

Being exceedingly receptive, Achille's personality was much influenced by the distinguished atmosphere prevailing there. Chausson, it is known, was a fervent disciple of César Franck. Recognition had finally come to the latter after many years of waiting, and he was considered the leader of a school comprising several promising composers, among others Vincent d'Indy. Although Achille had no special regard for the general aesthetics of "the old Belgian angel," as he sometimes called Franck, he respected him, and that was sufficient to keep the frequent discussions within the scope of courteous eclecticism.

Chausson, a delightful man of the world, cultured and refined, was endowed with a great sense of altruism; his generosity was proverbial and he was always ready to help a fellow artist. On several occasions he noticed the recurring financial troubles that befell Achille; then he found the proper approach to help his friend without hurting his sensibility. He knew well the reason why Achille's purse became depleted so repeatedly. Sometimes, perhaps on the very day Achille received his salary, they left M. Bailly's bookstore together and took a stroll along the boulevards. They passed before windows full of tantalizing frivolities: tiny objects made of crystal, shimmering under the bright lights from beneath; miniature animals delicately carved in ivory; canes of precious wood imported from Malacca; fancy pen-holders; umbrellas with elaborate handles and streamlined in their needlelike slenderness; cigarette cases adorned with vivid flashes of enamel

—all that the Parisian instinct for good taste and luxury can suggest to those skilled artisans whose creations are justly famed the world over.

Achille, fascinated, lingered in front of these marvels so artfully and attractively laid out. Sometimes Chausson succeeded in drawing him away; but at other times he succumbed to temptation. History repeated itself, or in this instance, the episode of the Roman statuettes came to pass again, though with less drama.

Regulations governing state and official institutions are something of an enigma; so it appeared to Achille when one day he received a visit from an emissary of the Ministry of Fine Arts. The object of this call was to inform him that it was his turn to be granted a whole program by the Institut as a further result of his capture of the Prix de Rome. This concert was to be given with orchestra, soloists, and even chorus if required.

At first Achille was puzzled and thought there must be some mistake. Hadn't he run away from the villa, handed in his official resignation?

But when assured that this gesture had nothing to do with the routine of these periodic presentations, he was elated; not because of the publicity, but because of the opportunity to present his major works. He expressed his thanks:

"So there is going to be a Debussy Festival? I appreciate it very much indeed."

"Yes; and the secretary of the Institut has instructed me to ask you for your program. He wants it as soon as possible."

Achille went to his table and picked up a pencil. Better, he thought, to attend to this at once and get it over with.

Suddenly a sardonic smile came to his lips. He remembered his symphonic work sent from the Villa Medici, the verdict of the Institut, the sharp condemnation of the *Journal Officiel*. Now was the time to get even with them. "Revenge is a dish which must be eaten cold," the French saying goes; how sweet it would taste to him!

At the top of the page he wrote:

"No. 1. *Printemps*, symphonic suite for orchestra and chorus."

Then he completed the program, placed it in an envelope, and handed it to his visitor.

Achille and Gaby were having their dinner, made more elaborate in celebration of the happy event, when the bell rang. Once more it was the representative from the Beaux-Arts.

"I am very sorry to disturb you again, but there must be a change in your program."

"Why is that?"

"You have featured *Printemps*. It is not acceptable to the Institut. The secretary told me to ask you for another composition."

Achille turned pale, then red. His artistic integrity was at stake! Calmly but firmly he gave his answer:

"I will give no other title. Please tell the gentleman that the Debussy Festival is called off!"

Among recently written works Achille had in his files a series of songs founded on poems by Baudelaire; he thought a great deal of them and was anxious to see them published. Guiraud liked them very much, and Achille also had shown them to Gabriel Fauré, the young organist of the Cathedral of Rennes in Brittany. The latter expressed his admiration in unequivocal terms and called the poems "a work of genius." Guiraud, however, warned Achille against too much optimism: some puritanically inclined people, including even the publishers themselves, might object to Baudelaire's verses; and their vocal range was liable to frighten the average singer. Why not try, instead, to publish some of the easier songs?

"I can do that," Achille said, "but the *Poèmes* must also be printed; and they will be, even if I have to do it myself!"

An idea came to him: Would not M. Bailly be interested in them? With his tastes, they might be just the thing he would like . . .

At first M. Bailly was receptive; but his ardor cooled somewhat when he saw the length of the manuscript and thought of the expense such a publication would involve. Philanthropy is a fine feeling; but it ought not to upset the commercial equilibrium of accounts already leaning dangerously toward the red side. But he made an equitable proposition: the *Poèmes* would be published by subscription to the extent of one hundred and sixty copies printed on fine paper, worthy of Achille's tastes and of M. Bailly's reputation. At twelve francs a copy the total made seventeen hundred and twenty francs.

The subscription lagged lamentably, however, and few application blanks were sent in. But suddenly things took a different aspect . . . the whole amount was covered!

Achille was delighted, of course, and he never knew that Chausson and another musically inclined philanthropist, Ernest Dupin, had intervened and secretly signed their names to the balance that remained unsold.

His relations with the Vasniers continued to wane and one day he called on them to collect his manuscripts.

What changes can occur in a short time! Even the "melodious fairy" appeared to him in a new light, somewhat haughty, distant, supercilious; the type of the Parisian high-class bourgeoise. Perhaps she had heard of his new friendship with Gaby and this was responsible for her attitude. They had moved, too, and the new apartment they occupied was too formal to be friendly. All in all, the interview was correct and conventional, with a frigid touch brought about by the realization that their feelings once had soared so high and now had ebbed to a level of polite indifference.

Meanwhile Achille continued to compose. He completed a suite of piano pieces begun at Ville d'Avray, which included the *Clair de lune*. Probably the stars were with him, since the pieces had the good fortune to find favor with M. Fromont, the discreet publisher who had his place of business at 40, Rue d'Anjou, a quiet street off the Boulevard Malesherbes. Discreet is the correct word, since he often purchased compositions and advanced a little cash, then became frightened at the risks involved; at that stage the manuscripts gained admission to his shelves and began a slumber that might well be long, if not eternal. The musty odor which emanated from those piles of forgotten music testified eloquently to this.

As a diversion, Achille sometimes called on Guiraud with whom he maintained the friendliest relations. At his home he met the Hochons again. They were delighted at this renewal of their acquaintance and Mme. Hochon in particular seemed to look at him with more than casual interest. As to Guiraud, he had just been proposed for a vacant seat at the Institut and had every chance of being elected, but this did not alter his simplicity nor his taste for cigarettes and billiards. He and Achille still discussed things musical and occasionally it became a caloric dialogue.

"I still cannot see, Achille, how you can get away with certain of your theories. Now that you are free you can do whatever you please, of course. I even admit that some of the results are lovely; but theoretically it's absurd!"

"I don't believe in theory," Achille declared vehemently; "there's no such things as theory. One must listen, one must hear, and that's enough. The pleasure of my ear is my rule!"

"I agree to that . . . if the one who indulges happens to be a naturally gifted personality, in short, one like you, Achille. But what about the others; how will you teach them music?"

"Music is something one does not learn."

"Nonsense! You are forgetting, young man, that you spent ten years of your life studying at the Conservatoire."

With this Guiraud scored his point, and Achille had to admit that, after all, there may well be a doctrine of music.

"Yes," he conceded, "I see that perhaps what I said was idiotic. Although the question is a difficult one and it seems impossible to reconcile all its aspects, I admit positively that if I feel so free it is because I went through the mill, and if I can get away from the fugue it is because I know how to write one."

Once a year the Société Nationale went to great expense; it hired a full orchestra for the presentation of symphonic works. There was always great demand for a place on that program, which was the crowning event of the season. Achille had no difficulty in this respect: Vincent d'Indy was to conduct and spontaneously he chose the *Fantaisie* for piano and orchestra. Unable to pay for the services of a professional copyist, Achille had to attend to that tedious work himself. But one morning his joy was great as he went to the Salle Érard for the rehearsal. He sat in a dark corner of the second gallery. To Vincent d'Indy and the members of the orchestra, the *Fantaisie* appeared fine work, well planned, cleverly instrumented, and pianistically very brilliant.

But Achille's impression was different, and he was not satisfied. He was sorry he had agreed to this performance. The defects of his *Fantaisie* were so obvious to him. In fact, he found in it everything against which he was beginning to rebel: too much form and structure; too much traditionalism in the developments; too much scholastic atmosphere. It was heavy, labored, stilted. When the rehearsal was over he felt ashamed of himself and refrained from going backstage. Instead he went downstairs to the piano pedal-board studio from which he could watch the exit of the musicians. An idea had come to his mind. The *Fantaisie* simply could not be played.

At noon everyone left, including Vincent d'Indy.

Making his way across the salesroom filled with grand pianos, Achille opened the door of the winding staircase leading to the artists' room and furtively climbed the steps. There wasn't a soul around. The parts had been left on the music stands, in readiness for the concert.

Achille collected every one of them, placed them in his brief case, and deliberately walked out. The concierge was enjoying his noon meal with his family and did not see him. From the post office at La Bourse Achille sent a telegram-letter to d'Indy:

"I am sorry, my dear friend, to be obliged to withdraw my *Fantaisie* from tonight's program, and more so when I realize that this is against the rules of the Société. However, this move is dictated by my conscience and I am sure you will understand. Please accept my excuses, and I do hope it will create no particular disturbance."

There was no resentment among the committee, and at another concert the *Poèmes de Baudelaire* were presented. They were courteously received by the public; but Achille happened to read a short review in the *Echo de Paris*, signed "L'Ouvreuse" (the Usher):

"M. Debussy has thrown the manure of his music upon the *Flowers* of Baudelaire."

This needs an explanation. L'Ouvreuse was the nom de plume used for his musical criticisms by a witty writer, Henry Gauthier-Villars, the author of a series of popular books centering on a striking type of young Frenchwoman, "Claudine." There were *Claudine at School, Claudine in Paris, Claudine Married,* and a few others, all full of humor, sarcasm, raillery, and badinage. Gauthier-Villars was helped in his reviews by several musical ghost writers, but whatever their advice, what guided him most was the possibility of making a pun or a "bon mot." For years he occupied an important position and wielded great influence. His unique turn of mind can best be illustrated by recounting two incidents which stirred the musical world and amused Achille greatly.

Once, in an article, he had maligned a pianist who happened to be an athlete. The pianist waited for him outside the Nouveau Théâtre where a concert was in progress, and when Gauthier-Villars came out he was given a pair of well-adjusted and sonorous slaps. But Gauthier-Villars's version read as follows: "Nothing much to report about the Concert Lamoureux of last Sunday, except that in the corridor I saw my friend Willy breaking his cane on the back of Monsieur X, an obscure 'gobble-notes' who well deserved this thrashing as punishment for so many tortures imposed by him upon his unfortunate listeners." The article was signed "L'Ouvreuse" as usual, and "Willy" was another of his noms de plume, known by everyone in the musical world. Few people had actually seen the incident, but the article was read by thousands, and those who knew the truth chuckled most.

The other affair came as a phase of a feud that had arisen between Gauthier-Villars and Auguste Mangeot, the editor of the *Monde Musical*. No one knew what this feud was about, but both were on the warpath and all kinds of epithets were hurled back and forth in their respective columns. One day a sonnet appeared in the *Monde Musical*; its title was *Ode to Music*. A note written by Mangeot accompanied it, in which he highly praised the verses sent by an "anonymous writer" and expressed his joy at having been able to publish them. Next followed an article by L'Ouvreuse: "M. Mangeot claims that I have no brains. He must have thought differently when in his last issue he published a sonnet of which I am the author. To identify my authorship may I ask my readers to read the sonnet as an acrostic." Everyone did, and it produced the motto: "Mangeot is a jackass."

It may be said in passing that Auguste Mangeot was and still is a fine character and the defender of whatever represents, musically, a worthy cause.

As to the "manure" criticism, Achille felt hurt by it but did not bear a grudge. This was fortunate, since Gauthier-

Villars soon came to a better understanding and turned out to be one of his supporters.

The atmosphere of musical Paris during the last twenty years of the nineteenth century is interesting. It was the formative period for Achille, and during the last decade the composition of his capital work, *Pelléas et Mélisande* was completed. From 1880 to 1890 the three prominent conductors who guided public taste were Colonne, Lamoureux, and Pasdeloup. They had to accomplish the work of pioneers. Wagner, and even Berlioz, could be presented only in small doses; otherwise there were likely to be noisy manifestations. Then all at once, around 1890, conditions abruptly changed; the public accepted quite readily what it had rejected shortly before and it was, paradoxically, in the very halls where the opposition had been loudest that sudden enthusiasm climbed to greatest heights. Colonne, at the Châtelet, gave repeated presentations of *The Damnation of Faust* and Lamoureux reaped outstanding success with his Wagner Festivals. Many French musicians, young or old, fell under the Wagnerian spell: César Franck showed signs of Tristanesque chromaticism, and Vincent d'Indy wrote his "Trilogy of Wallenstein." Some critics discovered similar symptoms in Achille's *Poèmes de Baudelaire.*

Precisely at that time when he began to dream of new methods of expression Achille came across a recently published play by Maurice Maeterlinck: *Pelléas et Mélisande.* He bought it and read it. Immediately it dawned upon him that he had laid his hand on an ideal subject: a mysterious tragedy which knew no age, no race, no particular setting; which was true a thousand years ago as it is true today and will remain true through the years to come.

A few months earlier he had made the acquaintance of Pierre Louÿs, a young poet upon whom initiates founded great hopes. Louÿs lived in an old house on the Rue Grétry, and he had taken the place of M. Vasnier as Achille's literary mentor. One day the latter went to Louÿs's apartment and pulled the bell-knob on the side of the thickly padded door, wishing to consult his friend about his project. At first the reaction was unfavorable; Louÿs thought that no decent libretto could be built on such a story; besides, there were no opportunities for vocal ensembles or choruses. Nevertheless, he gave Achille all the information he wanted regarding Maeterlinck, who at that time lived in Ghent. Then a short dialogue took place:

"Do you know Maeterlinck personally?"

"Yes, quite well."

"May I ask a favor of you? Will you come to Ghent with me, so I can ask him for authorization to use his work?"

With this Louÿs realized how futile it would be to try to sway Achille from a resolution already made. He admired him too much to feel offended.

"All right," he said, "I'll go with you."

The pair took the train and a few hours later landed in the old Flemish-speaking city.

Maeterlinck was a tall gentleman, somewhat heavy, quite cordial, with something in his make-up that reminded one of an actor. Having been introduced, Achille declared his project to him and the reaction was gratifying.

"I am not a musician," Maeterlinck declared, "not even a dilettante, and I know nothing of music; but judging from what our friend Louÿs thinks of you, I augur much from our eventual collaboration. It may be that you are just the right man to do justice to my work and I feel honored that you selected it."

When he accepted the offer formally, Achille was delighted and full of gratitude to Pierre Louÿs whose timely assistance had made it possible.

On the way home they stopped over in Brussels, went to Ysaye's house on the Avenue Brugman, and broke the big news to him.

"I am going to start at once on a new work and I think it will be a capital one!" Achille told Gaby upon his return. Immediately he began a minute study of *Pelléas* in view of the adaptation of the play to music. Maeterlinck had authorized him to make whatever changes might be needed. As he proceeded his conviction grew that in *Pelléas* he had hit upon a perfect subject. Never mind if there could be no chorus, or rather, so much the better! Were not choruses antiquated anyway? He smiled as visions came to him of so many traditional operatic scenes in which harmless warriors brandish their cardboard spears: "Forward . . . forward!" or sing "Let's drink . . . let's drink" while raising empty glasses; and last but not least the unavoidable climax: "Revenge . . . revenge!" Ridiculous, melodramatic, Meyerbeerish, Rossiniesque!

Soon one entire scene was written; not the initial one in the forest, but that other one, most beautiful of all, when Mélisande's hair flows down from the balcony upon Pelléas, and she falls under the fervor of his caresses. Other scenes followed without any preconceived plan but according to the inspiration of the moment.

Pierre Louÿs was the first to hear these sketches. In his apartment filled with bookshelves, paintings, autographed pictures, tapestries, curtains of embroidery and gold, deep divans and couches, there stood also two musical instruments, a piano and an harmonium of old vintage. It was on these relics that much of the new score was revealed! Louÿs was overcome and his rapturous comments aroused much curiosity among his friends, Henri de Règnier, Albert Samain, Maurice Barrès, Jean Moréas, Paul Valéry, and others, including Georges Hartmann, the publisher, a man of clear intelligence. Of foreign birth but naturalized French, Hartmann was the representative in France of the Wagner family. His interest in *Pelléas* was instantaneous and he visualized the possibility of becoming its publisher.

At the little flat Achille's life had become a busy one. The visits of Gaby, their evening walks to Pousset's or on the boulevards, an occasional concert, were the only diversions in which he indulged. From time to time some minor incident broke the routine.

One morning there was a knock at the door and Achille opened it. On the landing stood a tall gentleman of military bearing, florid complexion, with gray hair; he wore a tweed suit and the odor of tobacco that came from his pipe transported one immediately to Piccadilly Circus and Trafalgar Square.

"Monsieur Day-boussy?"

"Himself."

"My name is Read; General Meredith Read."

They shook hands, ending the verbal exchange: the distinguished Scotsman knew no French and Achille knew no English!

The general smiled and Achille smiled. They tried to communicate by signs but the result was negative. Finally the general, who held a piece of manuscript paper in his hand, pointed downstairs and said:

"Whisky-soda."

Amused, Achille followed him into a tavern on the Rue d'Amsterdam, directly in front of the post office. The paper was unfolded and it contained, as far as Achille could guess, a popular song of Scotland. The general pointed to the manuscript, then to Achille, but all he could say was:

"Music!"

At that point a jovial-looking man entered the bar: it was Alphonse Allais, the humorist. Speaking some English, he volunteered as interpreter. The theme submitted was the *Song of the Ancient Earls of Ross*, a noble family whose origin went far back into history. In the olden days the chief of the Rosshire Clan had a private band of bagpipers who played this tune on gala days and also before and during battles. General Meredith Read was a direct descendant of these earls and he wanted to commission Achille to compose a real march.

Another whisky-soda was absorbed, followed by another and still another. Then the general pulled out his wallet, extracted a fifty-pound note and presented it to Achille with the promise that another one would be forwarded upon receipt of the composition. Congratulations, handshakes and an ultimate whisky-soda sealed the deal. That night Gaby and Achille did not dine at home; they went to Pousset's and celebrated with a de luxe meal!

The march was soon completed in the form of a piano

duet and mailed to the colorful nobleman, who promptly acknowledged it by sending the other fifty pounds.

This should have made Achille's life easy for some time. But his spending propensities made it impossible. Time after time he got into financial straits. Because of the great work in the making, he had given up much of his work as an arranger. It is true that at times he received money for the sale of some composition; but how much? For his string quartet he was paid the measly sum of two hundred and fifty francs, and still this seemed considerable when he thought of certain colleagues who were unable to get their chamber music productions printed, even by giving them away!

For some time Achille had been disturbed by Guiraud's failing health. Each time he went to see him there was a change for the worse. So he was not surprised when a message came announcing that his teacher and friend had passed away. Achille himself had caught cold and was confined to his bed, but the services were to be held two days later and he hoped to feel well enough to attend. Victorine came every morning and stayed till lunchtime and Gaby arrived shortly afterward; so he was well taken care of.

As Achille woke on the day of the funeral, the rain was coming down in torrents and it was so dark that he had to light his lamp.

"Never mind my fever," he mumbled to himself, "I will go anyway. Dear old Guiraud, who has always been so nice to me. What weather . . . what weather! But I will be there."

Victorine came in, bringing his clothes carefully brushed and his shoes neatly polished. At that moment the storm

took on the proportions of a cyclone. Hail fell so heavily
that it was like a thousand drums beating fiercely on the
zinc of the roof.

"Achille," she cried with evident fear, "this shower is
terrible! Isn't it imprudent to go out? You still have a
fever."

"I don't care. I simply must pay my last tribute to
Guiraud."

"Yes, I understand how you feel. And, of course, you
must be seen there."

At these words Achille's face changed suddenly.

"Is that so? I *must be seen*. Well, that settles it. I am
not going! I will go to the cemetery, by myself, after that
crowd of hypocrites has gone away."

He did as he had said. In the afternoon he went to a
florist's, bought a bunch of roses and entered the deserted
necropolis. After laying his floral offering he stood pen-
sively, remembering long years of deep friendship as twilight enveloped the grave freed at last from banal con-
dolences and official oratory.

As summer advanced Chausson and his family moved
to Luzancy, north of Paris, where they had rented a propriété luxuriously furnished and surrounded by a park.
When he received a package from Russia containing the
score of *Boris Godunov*, he lost no time in notifying
Achille, who came over immediately. Both were tremendously eager to read that score. There was only an upright piano, but it proved quite sufficient. The whole afternoon Achille sat at the keyboard while Chausson turned
the pages. To both, the music appeared unbelievably modern, considering the date of its composition. The day was
warm and Achille took off his coat; then he continued

and never stopped until the last chord sounded, leaving them amazed at such dramatic and epic grandeur.

Another interesting event for Achille was the performance of *Pelléas et Mélisande* at the Maison de l'Oeuvre, a suburban theater, in the original dramatic version. He loved the play on the stage as much as he had loved it in book form. But on the stairway he overheard some scathing words coming from a group of critics:

"Really awful . . . obscure, incomprehensible. Ah! how good it feels to breathe this fresh air. I am through with this Maeterlinck. No more of his plays for me!"

The man who spoke was Francisque Sarcey, the omnipotent dean of the Parisian critics.

"Old idiot!" Achille murmured disdainfully but loud enough to be heard.

Meanwhile the news of his activities was making its way from mouth to mouth, and attracted attention among the musicians. There was considerable talk about *Pelléas* but the opinions were contradictory. It will be sensational, it will astonish the world, said one side. There's nothing to it, claimed the opposition. All this increased expectation. Then came the splendid publication of *The Blessed Damozel*, turned out by M. Bailly under an artistic cover by Maurice Denis. Dupin and Chausson sent all their copies to the musical world and soon the presentation took place at the Société Nationale under the baton of Gabriel Marie, with the assistance of Julia Robert and Thérèse Roger. The latter was the daughter of a society woman who had become a singing teacher. Chausson appreciated her talent and often used her for the interpretation of his songs. She did full justice to the part, as she was an intelligent, cultured, and musical young lady. She also

studied some of Achille's songs and he coached and accompanied her. A friendship grew between singer and
composer, which Chausson and his wife noticed. They
looked upon it favorably; it seemed to them that their
friend was too sensible to adhere eternally to his bohemian
life and they came to the conclusion that perhaps this
recent encounter might mean much for Achille's future.
They were convinced that, deep down, he had a desire
for a normal life shared with a companion who could be
a help and an inspiration.

"Achille is a conservative bohemian," Chausson often
said of him.

He and his wife decided to follow up the matter, multi-
plying the opportunities for the pair to meet. Of course,
they knew of the relationship between Achille and Gaby,
but they were convinced that he had no serious intentions regarding the green-eyed beauty; just a caprice, a
passing fancy.

Their efforts apparently were crowned with success and
an unofficial engagement was quickly settled. This would
be announced publicly as soon as Achille could straighten
out his situation and liberate himself.

In the meantime his string quartet was played at the
Nationale by Ysaye and his musicians, who came from
Brussels especially for the occasion.

"Fine work, my brother!" Ysaye commented as he
tapped Achille's shoulder affectionately. "Now we must
give it in Brussels, and very soon."

Back home, he immediately took steps toward a Debussy Festival. The participants would all be Belgians,
with the exception of Thérèse Roger who would come
from Paris with Achille and the Chaussons.

What happened then . . . and how did Gaby's jealousy suddenly become aroused? She felt that something was in the air. When Achille told her of his plans she interrupted him:

"I'll go with you."

In vain he tried to appease her.

"I will go with you," she repeated.

So he was obliged to find an excuse in order not to travel with the Chaussons but leave on an earlier train. In Brussels he stopped at a different hotel.

The concert was a success; Ysaye had prepared it with infinite care. All the notables of Brussels were there: musicians, painters, and writers sat next to members of the royal family, high officials, and social luminaries. This was due to the violinist's prestige and not to the program of works by an unknown composer. Ysaye had been particularly insistent that Félix Gevaert and Maurice Kufferath should be there; the former was the dean of Belgian music and director of the Royal Conservatory; the latter, the editor of the magazine, *Le Guide Musical*. Two seats in the front row were reserved for them.

At nine o'clock the hall was completely filled, but Gevaert was not there. Ysaye decided to wait. The minutes passed and Gevaert did not appear; every now and then Ysaye's face turned discreetly toward the door and each time it revealed growing anger. By nine-fifteen the audience became impatient. He had to begin.

The quartet had been under way for a few minutes when Gevaert made his belated entrance and walked majestically down the center aisle. Ysaye almost burst with indignation: a flick of his bow stopped his partners and he turned on his chair, looking fiercely at the intruder.

Director or no director, could he not have a little consideration and wait till the first movement was over?
When Gevaert was seated Ysaye once more lifted his bow,
and the performance was resumed from the very first bar.

Achille appeared in person as accompanist. His phys-
ique interested the painters, while the poets' attention was
focused on the verses of two songs written by the musician
himself:

"On the sea, twilight is falling . . ."

The sea, still and always his friend, in words and in
sound.

After the concert Ysaye, faithful to his habit, invited
a few friends to a stag supper. Very democratic in his
tastes, he disliked elegant restaurants and preferred the
cozy atmosphere of some plain brasserie with marble
tables, leather-covered benches, and sand on the floor.
For a long time they sat, reviewing the program while
the steaming choucroute and native beer brought their
spirits to a high pitch. Achille received many congratulations and the evening was unanimously pronounced a
success.

The critics, however, thought differently.

"An artificial art, the product of a somewhat deranged
brain . . . Plagiarism of Borodin, of Grieg, of Wagner
. . . Songs that are unsingable . . . Complete absence
of tonality." Such were some of the comments. As to Kufferath, even Ysaye's influence had failed to awaken his
comprehension and he wrote these amazing lines:

"At times it was pure cacophony. If it was not a joke
being played on the public, we fear that the composer's
sense of hearing is gravely diseased in a way similar to the
distorted vision of some painters." And Achille was clas-

sified as an apostle of "musical pointillism," a victim of
"universal amorphism," and other such extravagances.

"Sit down, and don't look so crestfallen!"

It was the next day in Ysaye's studio. Achille had come
to say good-bye. He had just read the articles.

"Oh . . . those critics . . . those critics!" he repeated
dismally.

Ysaye lit his pipe, rose from his big chair and came to
him. He put his arm around his shoulder.

"Don't worry, my friend. You are all right, take it from
me. As to *them* . . . If I had listened to *them* I would
have stopped playing the violin many years ago. Courage,
and confidence!"

The return trip was rather gloomy. Even Gaby had lost
her cheerful disposition. In addition, her presence had
been noticed and reported to the Chaussons and to their
friend. As a result, Achille's engagement was broken off.

Nevertheless he continued to work with renewed ardor,
and soon he came to Chausson triumphantly.

"I have just finished the great scene of the fourth act,
'A Fountain in the Park.' "

He played it, then left immediately, as he was in a good
writing mood and wanted to take advantage of it. The
next day, however, he called again.

"I tore up everything," he said. "Yes, when I got home
and played it once more, it didn't sound right at all. A
conventional old duet. There was even in one corner a
shadow of Klingsor, alias Richard Wagner! Now I am
doing a little chemical work in order to find a more personal formula. And do you know, I have discovered the
most wonderful means of expression. It is *silence*. What
emotion silence brings into a phrase, when used tactfully!"

He really was in a fine composing spell, and another work was in the making. Pierre Louÿs had revealed to him the poems of Stéphane Mallarmé and since then he had been haunted by one of the eclogues, *The Afternoon of a Faun*. More than ever the desire to "open windows," musically speaking, was present in his mind; could there be a lovelier tableau than Mallarmé's evocation of "the various scenes through which the desires and dreams of the faun evolve, in the heat of a summer afternoon"?

He visualized lawns of green, rustling fountains, sunlight coming through dark foliage, nymphs at play on the edge of a mirror lake, while the faun awakened and watched lustfully the enticing scene.

Here also he could assert his faithfulness to the esprit français, to the pure Gallic tradition.

There was much expectation at the Salle d'Harcourt, located on the steep Rue Rochechouart a few steps from the Salle Pleyel, when this *Prélude* was presented on a program of the Nationale. Its acoustics were mediocre and not favorable to a good perception of orchestral finesse. But the public was intelligent and spontaneous; for the first time in its history the Nationale opened its doors to nonmembers who cared to buy tickets.

At the end of the *Prélude*, when the faun, tired of vainly pursuing the elusive nymphs and mermaids, gives himself up to the intoxication of slumber filled with longings at last realized in dreams, there were a few seconds of silence, a short pause that permitted the intense charm to effect its grip. Then the applause broke out, thunderous, formidable. From all sides came loud cries of "Encore! Bis! . . . Bis!" The exquisite pagan poem was repeated; the public had understood!

Stéphane Mallarmé was in the audience. After the concert he wrote a short letter to Achille in his peculiar style, translated here almost word for word:

"I have just come out of the concert, deeply moved. The marvel! Your illustration of the *Afternoon of a Faun,* which presents a dissonance with my text only by going much further, really, into nostalgia and into light, with finesse, with sensuality, with richness. I press your hand admiringly, Debussy. Yours, Mallarmé."

Several times Achille read these precious lines; they filled him with new courage and were the best recompense for his efforts.

Toward the end of the century a queer figure appeared in the musical circles of Paris: Erik Satie. He was a native of Honfleur, the picturesque Norman fishing port from which the early settlers of Canada started out on their great adventure. Composer, writer, polemist, epicurean, humorist, his appearance was as bizarre as his character, reminding one somewhat of Don Quixote. The music he wrote was strange and almost of childish simplicity, but he was clever enough to dress it up with odd titles that ensured its sale: *Pieces in Form of a Pear, The Woman Who Talks too Much, Genuine Flabby Preludes for a Dog* are a few typical examples.

Satie lived at Arcueil, just outside Paris, in a single room. Devoted to the pleasures of the table but of modest means, he only ate a meal a day so he could make that a real one. In order to save his money for that purpose, he never took a streetcar but walked to Paris and back. A faithful member of the Société Nationale, it was there that Achille met him. They struck up an immediate friendship and soon Satie became a regular caller at the little apartment, one of the privileged few who made up the intimate circle to which Achille sometimes turned for consultation on his problems. Among Satie's works the latter noticed a suite of three pieces, called *Gymnopédies*, which he liked so well that he decided to orchestrate one of them. This meant much for the author who had never been taken seriously by anyone but himself. His admiration for Achille rose to the point of fanaticism and he became his voluntary press agent. Every now and then he also helped his friend by running some of his errands.

When Achille, tired of living in the noisy district of the Gare Saint-Lazare, made up his mind to move to quieter surroundings, Satie offered to go apartment hunting. He quickly found one, on the fourth floor of a recently built house on the Rue Gustave-Doré, a new street off the Avenue Wagram. There were plenty of trees in that quarter and the air was purer than in central Paris. Achille was much pleased with this new flat. The rental was higher than on the Rue de Londres but he could afford it, since he had started a new activity which proved successful: the presentation of "Wagnerian hours" at the piano, with verbal comments, in the salons of distinguished music lovers. This had nothing to do with his personal conviction which separated him from Wagner more and more; but the Titan of Bayreuth had been adopted by the snobs and Achille took advantage of the opportunity.

Sometimes, when he thought of the status of his compositions, he was somewhat concerned about the *Ariettes* printed by Mme. Girod; they seemed to have sunk into oblivion. As to his piano pieces, including the *Clair de lune,* they were entering their fifth consecutive year of unmolested slumber on Fromont's shelves. He was hurt and worried by this neglect and eventually consulted Satie on what ought to be done.

"Why don't you try somewhere else?" the latter advised. "You ought to go to London and see if anything can be done there. You could probably obtain a release from Fromont and others. If they refuse, they can be threatened with a lawsuit for the recovery of your rights."

The idea was agreeable to Achille and he went to London. As the steamer sailed out of Boulogne he noticed a short man with aquiline nose and grayish beard, walking up and down on deck. He wore a heavy scarf around his neck and looked at some distant fishing boats through a pair of powerful field glasses. It was Camille Saint-Saëns. He was already the dean of French music and, though Achille had no special regard for his conservatism, he walked up to him and paid his respects. Saint-Saëns happened to be in a good mood and the conversation was pleasant. He was always glad to go to England where he was greatly appreciated and received many attentions: bestowal of honorary degrees, receptions at the universities, command performances before royalty, all were much enjoyed by the great man who always had a weakness for official honors.

For some time the train had been rolling between rows and rows of brick houses all built on the same pattern and extending as far as the eye could see; then it slowed down, crossed a bridge over the Thames and entered a covered depot. Achille leaned out and saw a big white and blue sign, an exact replica of those used in France to indicate the names of the stations.

"This is London," said Saint-Saëns.

"Not yet . . . this is Bovril," Achille corrected him, much to the amusement of the master.

The great city had not changed at all since Achille's first visit. It was the same gigantic agglomeration, cut here and there by the green patches of parks and drowned in an eternal mist through which floated vague odors of tea and tobacco.

From his hotel in Russell Square to the music house was only a short walk. Achille sent up his card and after a few minutes' waiting he was led upstairs and shown into a conservative office where a bust of George Frederick Handel stood proudly on the mantelpiece; the rug on the floor was about an inch thick and the chairs were deep and comfortable.

"What can I do for you, monsieur?" asked the publisher, who had a smattering of French.

Achille extracted his manuscripts from his brief case and presented them to the important personage, who looked at the titles with Olympian indifference. Without waiting for an invitation Achille went to the piano and proceeded to play his suite, while the publisher, anxious not to lose any of his valuable time, fumbled through a pile of mail and made notes on his memorandum pad.

"Very nice . . . very good," he commented when the audition was over, "but I see no reason why our firm should become interested in these pieces."

Seeing the disappointed look on Achille's face, he hastened to explain:

"Our public is very, very peculiar . . . They go mostly by names. You are a Prix de Rome winner, I know, and that is very fine, but of no commercial value here. You see, my dear young man, you are not known in England."

With this Achille realized the failure of his interview. He murmured a few courteous words, bowed and walked out with his brief case under his arm. Inside were the manuscripts. Among them was his *Clair de lune*.

More disappointment awaited him in Paris. At Durand's he heard that the string organizations to which complimentary copies of his quartet had been presented declined to perform it on the ground that it was "unplayable!" Still, it had been played by Ysaye! Not stopping to think that all violinists were not of Ysaye's caliber, Achille's imagination at once began to build up a pessimistic picture in which professional jealousy came under strong suspicion. There must have been intrigue somewhere. Again "his soul took on the color of iron gray, and bats flew ominously around the steeple of his dreams." He was totally incapable of adapting himself to the ups and downs of artistic life; the slightest variations of luck or mischance made him rise to tremendous optimism or sink into despair.

It was during such depressed periods that Achille felt most keenly the absence of such friends as Ernest Chausson, who was at Arcachon with his family. But he found compensation in Satie, whose jocularity and wit were a great comfort. Every Saturday afternoon, regardless of weather or temperature, Satie walked from Arcueil and arrived at the Rue Gustave-Doré about four o'clock. While Achille prepared tea Satie went to the piano and tried out the latest of his extravagant concoctions, a thing he was unable to do in his own room for lack of an instrument. Then they sat at the table, ate cakes and drank their tea. The afternoon always ended with the playing of the latest additions to *Pelléas*.

The pile of manuscript sheets was steadily growing, and one day when Satie came in he was greeted with a big piece of news.

"*Pelléas* is finished!"

The announcement was premature; the following week it was completely reversed.

"I have started all over again," Achille declared. "When I read it over I wasn't satisfied at all. It needs complete remodeling . . . a few more years of work probably. But I'm only thirty-three and the future is mine!"

A letter came from Maeterlinck, reiterating his assent to any decision that Achille might take:

"I want to assure you again that *Pelléas* belongs to you entirely and that you may have it performed when and where it will be agreeable to you. I expected to come to Paris in August; unfortunately I have been unable to do so, for very humble reasons. I hope these reasons will soon vanish so I can see you, shake your hand and talk of 'our *Pelléas*.'"

Once more Achille was "on his horse," full of stamina and patience, that blessed patience without which no permanent work of art can be conceived.

One Sunday afternoon he went to the Concerts Lamoureux to hear *Tamara* by Balakirev, the successor to Glinka as leader of the group called "The Five." He came out profoundly moved by the impressive eloquence and glowing instrumentation of this work. Balakirev, however, was still practically unknown and his name carried no particular prestige; because of this the reaction of some cautious, or rather ignorant, critics was extremely mild. In the foyer Achille encountered one of them, M. Cappelle, who was in charge of the music department at *Le Gaulois*, newspaper of the nobility and aristocracy. Cappelle was a perfect picture of what was jokingly called a "pontiff": elderly, stout, with long, broad, gray whiskers, he wore an overcoat with extra cape and a top hat. As Achille excitedly proclaimed aloud the wonders of Balakirev's composition, Cappelle interrupted with:

"Is that what you think? Well, *I* do not care for *Tamara.*"

"It would be too bad if you did!" Achille retorted slashingly.

This met with the approval of a young man of short stature, apparently eighteen or nineteen years old, extremely frail and of slender, almost angular figure; yet obviously full of stamina, with his prominent nose and a pair of brilliant eyes dotting two thin cheeks.

"Bravo, monsieur!" he bravely interjected.

It was Maurice Ravel, piano student of Charles de Bériot, who also was making his first attempts at composition, jotting down sketches in his spare time for some *Auricular Sites* and an overture for *Schéhérazade.* Like Achille, he never missed a chance to hear something new.

A few months later Ysaye came to Paris for one of his famous series of piano and violin sonatas with Raoul Pugno, and Achille saw much of him at Chausson's home. Ysaye had already endorsed *Pelléas* unreservedly, but when Achille let him hear some excerpts from the revised version, his enthusiasm became vehement. Shortly before he had approached the directors in Ghent and Brussels about a presentation, but without success. Of course, he kept this to himself; but he knew how difficult it would be to convince theatrical promoters, who surely would consider *Pelléas* unoperatic and impractical. So he mentioned to Achille the possibility of offering some fragments at one of his symphony concerts in the Alhambra. Perhaps this would attract the directors' attention.

Achille didn't at all approve of this suggestion, and an animated discussion took place between him and the violinist, who spoke as colorfully and temperamentally as ever.

"I am not of your opinion, my dear brother. Certainly, I would prefer telling you, 'we put on your work in a theater.' But I realize how impossible this is without the 'sinews of war,' not to speak of other considerations. Sooner or later, of course, some director will open his doors wide to *Pelléas*. But when will that be?"

"I don't care . . . I am willing to wait."

"All right; but if you wait too long the presentation may only occur after your style has changed. Youthful productions should be presented at the time and in the atmosphere in which they were born. If your dream can't be realized, I think it's a good move to accept a partial concert performance."

"A partial performance would do credit neither to my work nor to myself."

"You are wrong, my friend. It's a great help. It brings a work out of the obscurity where it lies whining, aging, shriveling, withering until it has lost its teeth! Only one thing could harm your work: a bad performance. But played by a youthful and vibrant orchestra, con amore, with intelligent singers, I contend that the attention of those who 'hold the wires' will be aroused."

"Perhaps, if the character of my work permitted this mutilation. But it cannot be done with *Pelléas*. Its music flows like a river; can one interrupt its course?"

"Why not? Look at Wagner! May I remind you that his theater started in the concert halls? Who could contend seriously that it ever hurt Wagner's prestige? These fragments, repeated over and over, finally turned the tide."

Ysaye put his arms around him, kissed him and gave him new assurances that his orchestra was a young institution, daring and forward-looking, known for its willingness to dedicate itself to worth-while discoveries and for the spirit of curiosity demonstrated in its programs. If the public saw that *Pelléas* attracted them—*them*—it would mean much; and whether it turned out to be a triumph or a fiasco would not matter in the least.

The months passed. *Pelléas* progressed steadily, though without any hurry. This time Achille polished every measure until he was sure that each note was exactly right. His financial situation became materially improved when Georges Hartmann came to him with a proposition. If Achille would agree to give him exclusive publishing rights to his future production, he would be paid five hundred francs a month. Six thousand francs a year! That was a pretty good income, not counting the extras, and many a family lived decently on even a smaller one. Of course, the agreement was signed at once.

While working hard, Achille continued his visits to

Pierre Loüys, Chausson, and a few others who belonged to the "intellectual minority." He also called often on Manuel and Victorine. Everything was still in the same place; the butterflies and the colored prints still decorated his former room and he enjoyed sitting at the old table for a tasty meal. Manuel continued to work at the Fives-Lille company, and became excited at the idea that soon perhaps he would hear, at the Opéra-Comique, a work composed by his son; to that excellent man, this represented the climax of glory.

The Opéra-Comique at that time was under the artistic leadership of a distinguished composer and conductor, André Messager, on whom the director, Albert Carré, relied greatly for anything pertaining to musical matters. Messager already knew Achille through *The Blessed Damozel,* so when Hartmann approached him his reaction was favorable. A ray of hope came to Achille: perhaps his dream of a stage performance would materialize, after all.

His activity on the score slowed down for a few days when an intimate drama occurred. Though he had kept Gaby in the dark about his visits with Thérèse Roger, before their break, and lately with Mme. Hochon, whose admiration was taking a more personal turn, a vague intuition made her sense that something was wrong, very wrong.

One day as she brushed one of his suits she found a letter which fully confirmed her suspicions. When Achille came in there was a violent scene; Gaby's green eyes shone fiercely, like those of an infuriated tigress. She screamed so loud that all the neighbors came out of their apartments; and she threatened to "shoot him like a rabbit" with a revolver that was real, not an ebony cigarette case.

Despite his greater strength Achille could hardly subdue her and his life would have been in danger had not the concierge got hold of her, pulled her out of the flat and said he would take her to the police unless she stopped disturbing the peace. So another friendship, this one of long standing, came to an abrupt end.

There is one spot in Paris which perhaps has no equal at sunset on a lovely, bright day: the Place de la Madeleine, where the boulevards converge into the Rue Royale in front of the imposing structure which once was Napoléon's "Temple of Glory." At its side the flower market displays its vivid colors, while on the Rue Royale the terraces of the cafés are filled with elegant customers, important politicians, clubmen, tourists, comedians, and mannequins. In those years it was called "l'heure verte," the green hour, because of the absinthe, since prohibited, which filled the glasses. Its aroma floated in the air, mixed with the odor of Havana cigars. Bits of gossip were passed from table to table, together with the latest theatrical and race-course news. On the pavement carriages rolled by in a long parade as they returned from the Bois de Boulogne. It was truly a "Parisian hour," an hour of relaxation and lingering.

The silhouette of a man dressed in black, with a wide-brimmed hat of the same color, emerged from a corner of the boulevard. He carried a brief case under his arm, looked excited, and walked fast. As he passed along the terrace of the Taverne Royale in whirlwind fashion he heard someone call him by name. The voice came from a group of men who had recognized Achille.

"*Pelléas* is finished! This very morning at eleven o'clock, to be historical!" he cried to his friends without stopping. But two long arms seized him and seated him under the awning; he made no resistance, glad to have this respite imposed upon him. Pierre Louÿs, J. P. Toulet, Mallarmé, and a few others formed the group, and they were delighted to hear the good news. Congratulations followed and glasses were lifted to a prompt première and a great success.

During the conversation, Achille was asked if he would take part in a competition which had just been announced. Organized by the City Board, it was open to French composers only; the prize was five thousand francs and the work to be submitted must be a cantata for soli, chorus, and orchestra. Achille shook his head:

"No, my friends, I will not take part. Perhaps I would, but only on one condition."

"And that is?"

"First of all I should be allowed to . . . examine the examiners!"

Before the party broke up they agreed to meet again the following Friday afternoon at La Bodinière, a tiny theater in a courtyard of the Rue Saint-Lazare where a disinterested young pianist, Jules Berny, gave fortnightly matinees devoted to the music of contemporary composers. Vincent d'Indy had been featured, and also Gabriel Fauré, who had left Rennes and was now successor to Théodore Dubois at the organ of La Madeleine. The next program of the "Matinées Berny" would be devoted to Ernest Chausson, and he would appear personally in the rendition of the slow movement from his piano quartet.

Pelléas being completed, Georges Hartmann decided

that the time was ripe to speak more precisely to Messager. Just at that moment Achille was once more in the process of moving, as he could no longer bear the discredit in which he was held by his neighbors since the regrettable incident with Gaby. He had found an apartment at 58, Rue Cardinet, at the corner of the Avenue de Villiers. It was larger than the other and along the front there was a balcony from which the view spread out over the Lycée Carnot and the treetops lining the avenue on both sides. One morning a big van arrived, the furniture was unloaded, and with the help of Satie, Achille took possession of his new home. Then followed for both the pleasure of installing everything, taking measurements, the shouts or the laughter at discovering that despite all precautions some pieces would not fit where they were intended to go. Achille manifested almost childish joy as he contemplated a double door with beveled glass, then considered quite a luxury. The faithful little upright was placed directly on its side!

Why was it that during the months which followed Achille underwent such a fit of depression? Often he remained for days and days without writing, his brain clad in an armor of weariness. Was it the excessive number of projects he had in mind and his doubts about some of them?

For twelve years he had been thinking of incidental music for *As You Like It*. There was also an idea for an opera with Pierre Louÿs.

"You know what we ought to do, Achille," the latter said to him, "if we both had a little more nerve? We ought to do *Hamlet*, because that's exactly what you would do best."

"But there is one already, by Ambroise Thomas."

"I insist. And we don't care a damn about M. Thomas."

Of course, nothing came of this, nor from *Aphrodite*, *Daphnis and Chloe*, and several other subjects. Perhaps what held his attention most was a book of short stories by Edgar Allan Poe. Immensely impressed by some of them, he seriously thought of starting work at once on the librettos. But he felt sluggish, low-spirited, and sometimes sat on the sofa, thoughtful and mysterious, watching the smoke that ascended in blue spirals from his cigarette. Was it music alone that absorbed him so much, or a shade of longing for the green-eyed friend who had brought him so much cheer? The break was final and he saw her no more; but perhaps in memory he fancied the whiteness of her skin against the silk of the sofa as he sat beside her, holding her hand and gently patting her bare arm.

He became so introspective that even his own works seemed to lose interest for him. Once Pierre Louÿs asked him to give three recently written *Chansons de Bilitis* as an illustration for a lecture. Achille declined and wrote:

"Can you tell me what my poor little music would add to the pure and simple reading of your text? Absolutely nothing. It would even disturb the emotion of your listeners, and most untactfully so. You may ask me why I write music? This, old friend, is another question. My ultimate hope lies in *Pelléas*, and God only knows if this hope is anything but a dream."

Soon his mind sank into still greater gloom and he wrote to Pierre Louÿs again, begging him for moral support.

"I am very much in need of your affection, I can assure you. I am so terribly lonely and upset. No change in the drab sky which is the setting of my life and I hardly know which way to turn except perhaps toward the great beyond. Have I really come to that through my lassitude in fighting against impossible odds? Perhaps my work and I deserved a kinder fate. You know me, dear friend, better than anyone, and only *you* perhaps can come and assure me that I am not entirely a lunatic."

His visits to his friends became rare and already he had withdrawn into the retirement which caused him to be called "le grand solitaire."

One day on the boulevard a hand came down on his shoulder:

"Debussy!"

It was Henri de Régnier.

"I never see you any more," the poet pursued. "We miss you so much and we preserve such a vivid recollection of the afternoons at Louÿs's studio when you played *Pelléas* for us. Why don't you come? What are you doing with yourself and what news have you about *Pelléas?*"

"A little hope, if nothing else. We may have an audition at the Opéra-Comique, but who can tell?"

"Do not worry; a man like you cannot be kept in the background."

Achille shook de Régnier's hand affectionately; a word of encouragement from such a man was more precious to him than loud applause from thousands. For crowds he felt nothing but disdain; according to him, an artist in modern civilization will always be a human being whose usefulness is realized by the public only after his death. So why mingle with your contemporaries? So few of them are able to participate in the same joys.

Achille was convinced that the highest form of art is not for the masses, and he favored the creation of a society for "musical esoterism" instead of any attempt at popular diffusion.

If there was one musician in Paris whose personal attributes predisposed him to a clear understanding of *Pelléas* it was André Messager, the author of delicate works rich in Gallic virtues. At a time when Wagnerian influence was so strong, he had the great merit to remain himself; to be discreet, tender, witty, instead of inflating himself in bombastic platitudes.

The audition took place and Messager was conquered. Then they sat around a table on which Achille, who knew his visitor's tastes, had placed some whisky and a bottle of Perrier. As for Georges Hartmann, he was beaming.

"Carré must hear this score," Messager said. "I'll speak to him at once and arrange another appointment."

Then they discussed the important question of the cast.

"Do you know that Maeterlinck recently married Georgette Leblanc, the artist who acted the part of Mélisande when it was produced at the Bouffes?"

"Yes; and I saw that performance. She's an admirable actress," Achille answered.

Hartmann, publisher and psychologist, added this conclusion:

"And she also sings. So we will have to consider her. Maeterlinck would probably insist on it anyway."

It was a thrilling interview for Achille and he now saw the future in more rosy shades.

The new apartment offered many advantages: street cars and buses at the door, and at the corner of the Rue Fortuny, a mere hundred yards away, one of the best pastry shops in Paris, Les Délices. Quite near, too, were the popular market of the Rue Lévis, a tobacconist's shop, and the drugstore of M. Pradel.

In France a druggist is more than just a distributor of medicine; he knows his customers individually and often helps them with a little medical advice. Sometimes, if he happens to be talkative, his store becomes a club where politics and other topics are discussed by friendly neighbors who occasionally drop in.

M. Pradel was not much interested in politics, less still in the Dreyfus case which then shook Paris to its foundations; but he loved fishing and never tired of talking about it. Every Sunday he rose before dawn and spent the whole day watching his lines from some shady nook along the Marne or the Seine. Then for a few days the drugstore would be filled with stories of wonderful catches. Sometimes the sound of a piano streamed down the winding stairway: it was Mme. Pradel. She had a good taste for music and often attended concerts in company with a young lady friend who lived in the neighborhood, Lily Texier.

Achille already traded there while on the Rue Gustave-Doré and he continued to do so now that he lived nearer. The druggist and his wife knew that he was a musician, but without any further particulars, since Achille never talked much about himself.

Going back now to the days which followed the Festival Chausson, one afternoon Achille entered the drugstore on a casual errand. M. Pradel was reading *Le Petit Journal*. At the sound of the call bell he raised his head.

"Did you see, monsieur, that awful accident which happened yesterday?"

"No. What was it?"

"A musician . . . a composer who was learning to ride a bicycle. Perhaps you know him," and he handed the paper across his counter.

Achille's face turned frightfully pale.

"Chausson is dead!" he cried.

Grief-stricken, haggard, he dropped the paper and rushed out without saying good-bye. At the Chausson home the doorkeeper gave him all the details.

"Terrible . . . really terrible! After the concert last Friday afternoon Monsieur and Madame went to Limay, near Mantes, to spend the week end in the propriété they have rented for the summer. There is a big garden that runs downhill. Recently Monsieur had taken bicycle lessons in the Bois de Boulogne. So he took his bicycle to Limay; and yesterday, Sunday afternoon—"

His voice broke in a sob; he coughed, wiped his eyes, then continued:

"It happened about five o'clock, after tea. Monsieur started riding in the park. But he came to one spot that was dangerous because of the sharp incline. He lost control . . . the brake didn't work. Finally he crashed, head on, right into the stone wall at the bottom. Madame was in the house with some friends and when Monsieur didn't come back they became worried and went to look for him. They found him with his head crushed beyond recognition. It's a terrible blow for his family, his friends, and all of us. Monsieur was so good, so kind. Fate is unjust, really very unjust!"

Achille hurried to the nearest post office and sent a wire of sincere condolence. Yes, the concierge was right. Was there any justice in this world? Chausson . . . such a fine character, talented, happy in his home life, kind to his friends, wealthy, still young—only in his forties . . . It was indeed hard to accept and even to realize.

André Messager, too, was a man of high character who never made a promise lightly. When he asked M. Carré to hear *Pelléas*, the director knew that it must be an unusual score.

Achille again sang his work with that strange, deep voice; a voice that was warm but hollow, resonant but muffled; a "composer's voice," to use musical vernacular. Carré was moved by its persuasive inflections and *Pelléas* was immediately accepted.

"Now let us see how we are going to stage this work," he said.

Acceptance is one thing, but actual performance is another; between them stand all kinds of negotiations, difficulties, compromises, and they must be overcome if the curtain is going to be raised and the footlights turned on. The work was so unusual that at first they thought of organizing some special presentations apart from the regular series of performances. But this idea was abandoned as Carré preferred to have it follow the normal course. There was plenty of time anyway, since the orchestration was not even begun and the theater had a list of works already scheduled. It would be at least a year or two before rehearsals could begin. But the three men agreed that all announcements would be made under the name "Claude Debussy." "Achille" was definitely dropped and henceforth even his old friends should call him by his other name.

4

The Great Claude Debussy

WHEN Maeterlinck's "humble reasons" for not traveling disappeared he came to Paris with his wife. Both were anxious to see Claude and to confer with him. Of course, the author fully expected that Georgette Leblanc would be cast for the title role. She was impatient to hear a work which it would be her part to promote and defend.

Claude played several scenes and her enthusiasm ran high.

"Admirable!" she exclaimed. "I feel I am going to fall in love passionately with this work. It realizes all my dreams!"

As Claude almost apologized for the way in which he used his voice, so different from anything done before, she made some intelligent remarks.

"This also is admirable. It leaves to the interpreter such wide scope for dramatic expression! It allows more color and more life. What is your impression, Maurice?"

"Why ask *me?* You know I completely lack musical perception; it has even been said that I dislike music!"

"Never mind. These words were written by *you.* I want to know how they sound to you, in their musical form."

200

"Well, I find them really more effective!"

Georgette Leblanc turned to Claude:

"Did you hear that? It is the triumph of your logic!"

As the turn of the century drew closer, Paris once more made its preparations for another Exposition. Many musical plans were under way: Saint-Saëns was writing a cantata, *Le Feu du Ciel*, for the inauguration, and Claude was asked to contribute a program. Now that the fate of *Pelléas* was settled he had more time to himself, so he renewed his regular meetings with his faithful friends, Louÿs, Vidal, Dukas, and others. But the longing that he felt deep in his soul was becoming more urgent. He needed more than a friend: secretly he craved for the perfect mate who would understand him and perpetuate his name. Sometimes it seemed to him that Chausson's voice, from the grave, came to him and brought gentle words of advice as in the past.

Recently Claude had been introduced to Lily Texier, a friend of Mme. Pradel. She was an attractive brunette, gay, vivacious, intelligent. Occasionally he met her on the avenue, at the drugstore, or on the streetcar; each time was an occasion for conversation which her quickness at repartee always made pleasant. Her friends described her as a bright and practical woman who knew how to bargain and for whom a household held no secrets. In short, she was just the opposite of Claude, who knew nothing of arithmetic and was unable to walk out of a store without buying something. The difference was still greater when it came to music: she knew nothing of it whatever.

Nevertheless, extremes often meet, and Claude began to think of her in a serious way. Whenever she came she brought cheer and sunshine, and he needed nothing more than that. She was simple and unaffected, not one of those terrible "bluestockings!"

But how in the world could he ever broach the matter to her; he, the supershy man par excellence? At the mere thought he felt fainthearted, pusillanimous, almost cowardly.

The greatest problems are often the most easily solved, however. Lily's parents owned a little country home at Bichain in the Département de l'Yonne near Burgundy. Claude was invited once to spend the day, then a week end, and after a few visits he and Lily became engaged. They planned to be married after the summer ended.

With all this Hartmann was getting little music from Claude; but he continued to pay him five hundred francs every month. He had to leave Paris for some time and go to Germany to consult with the Wagner family; so he went personally to the Rue Cardinet, to see how the *Nocturnes* were progressing.

"Is M. Debussy at home?" he asked the concierge.

"I haven't seen him go out," the concierge answered in the usual way.

But if the concierge had not seen him, Claude had seen Hartmann from his balcony, and fearing some reproaches he did not open the door. A letter came the next day:

"What has become of you and why do you leave me so long without news? You were to send me the score of the *Nocturnes*. You did not, and here we are at the end of September at the same point as a year ago, with the renewed prospect of an empty winter. You are a terrible man! Affectionately, Hartmann."

Upon the publisher's return, Claude called on him.

"You asked what was the matter with me? It's quite simple. I am going to be married in a month!"

That was a valid excuse, and Hartmann regained his good humor. Claude invited him to the little stag banquet at which, according to French custom, he was going to "bury his bachelor's life." Unfortunately, this took place on the fifteenth of October, which in France is also rent day. So many expenses combined again left his purse completely flat.

Claude had a lesson scheduled on the morning of the nineteenth, his wedding day. He decided not to postpone it and this was a happy move, since the fee enabled him to pay for the luncheon he had, according to Lily's wishes, alone with her after the ceremony at the City Hall.

At a concert of the Société Nationale a young man came in and sat in the last seat of the last row. He wore a high stiff collar, a "Lamartine" tie, and his sidewhiskers made him look like an Austrian diplomat. It was the same young man who had so spontaneously applauded when Claude deflated the conceit of a critic. One of his works, *Les Sites auriculaires* for two pianos, was featured on the program. It was Maurice Ravel.

The second of these numbers drew considerable attention because of a novel formula: harmonies revolving around one basic note.

Claude was in the audience and after the concert, amid the din of discussions and comments that filled the artists' room, he walked up to Ravel.

"I enjoyed your suite very much and I sincerely congratulate you. Would you let me have your manuscript for a few days? There is one point that I would like so much to examine."

Ravel consented with pleasure and that night Claude walked home with the *Sites auriculaires* under his arm, not suspecting in the least the consequences that this simple act would bring.

Georges Hartmann, in the meantime, continued to prove a most serviceable and understanding publisher. For Claude he often became a banker who furnished extra funds when needed. Now he had purchased Mme. Girod's stock and had become an associate of Fromont, where he was the power behind the throne. On several occasions Claude secured loans from him. Some expenses connected with his wedding still had to be paid, and he considered buying a little house of his own at Bichain, moved by the characteristic French instinct for landownership. He enjoyed the days he and Lily spent at the house of his father-in-law, of course; but those stones, those flowers did not belong to him, and how much more would he appreciate the lovely azure sky if the wicker chair in which he sat were his own!

While Paris was experiencing another influx of visitors coming to the new Exposition, Claude put the final touches to the *Nocturnes*. Hartmann had arranged for the first performance at the Concerts Lamoureux under the direction of Camille Chevillard, son-in-law and successor to Charles Lamoureux. Claude had the whole summer before him, and it was with delight that he polished and repolished his work. As he did so he recalled the circumstances under which they had been inspired. "Clouds" . . . one day as he crossed the bridge of La Concorde he had watched the gray clouds drifting endlessly among gusts of raw wind; down below the horn of a tug blew hoarsely on the Seine. "Festivals" . . . the musical transposition of that fete night in the Bois de Boulogne during the early days of his friendship with Gaby.

The Javanese dancers were not at the Exposition this time, and this was a disappointment. But Claude heard many interesting concerts and at one of them Dukas's *Sorcerer's Apprentice* was played by the Société des Concerts du Conservatoire. The two men met afterward.

"How are you, Claude?"

"Fine, always, since I have heard the *Sorcerer*."

"Thanks . . . and congratulations."

"What for?"

"I just heard some talk among the musicians of the orchestra. One of them is the librarian of the Opéra-Comique. It seems that *Pelléas* is going to be put on next season!"

Soon the rumor was confirmed. When Claude got home the concierge handed him a note scribbled on his table by "a man who came all excited." It was Hartmann, and the letter read:

"Big news! Carré is all set for next winter. Messager just told me so. Now I urge you to give me the piano score at once. Two months for engraving, another month for printing; we must be ready to distribute the score to the artists in October. Remember: we must not put ourselves in wrong. I count on you without fail!"

Unfortunately the generous publisher was not intended to see the result of his efforts. A few weeks later he passed away suddenly, to the profound grief of his friends. Claude felt this loss deeply.

He started working feverishly on his orchestration. At night he reviewed what he had accomplished during the day and it was a labor of love, done quietly when all noises had died down and the big city had sunk into slumber. Sometimes dawn surprised him by creeping discreetly through the shutters. He went out on the balcony, leaned on the railing, took a few breaths of fresh air, then lit a cigarette and watched the awakening of Paris; the faint glimmer coming from the windows of the early risers, the carts filled with vegetables going to Les Halles, and the man with a black cap and a blue blouse who walked from one side of the street to the other with a long pole in his hands, putting out the gaslights.

Messager's visits or telegrams kept Claude keyed up. Lily managed everything concerning the house and did it remarkably well. She kept out intruders and admitted only a few friends she had learned to know.

Soon came the problem of copying the orchestral material. This is always a difficult question for a young composer who cannot, like the older "glories," mobilize a small army of professional copyists. Claude had heard of a young musician who did beautiful work. He had no experience in extracting parts from a score, but he assured Claude that with a little explanation he would be able to do it quite well.

In spite of all that was done, when Claude and Lily came back from their vacation at Bichain it became obvious that no one would be ready for the season just opening. Hartmann's death had wrought havoc in the schedule of the Maison Fromont, and the copy did not progress as fast as had been expected. But neither Claude nor Messager was disturbed, knowing that time is a chief factor in success.

Claude's attention was momentarily focused on his *Nocturnes*, the first performance of which was only a few weeks off. One morning Camille Chevillard sent for him as he wanted to get the tempi and some other details of interpretation. The conductor was then in his middle thirties; an affable man to those who knew him, he cloaked himself in a mantle of gruffness when he was in the office of the Concerts Lamoureux. In reality, he was a timid man who put on a ferocious look in order to reassure himself. But he was an object of terror for any soloist who appeared under his baton. With all that, a great conductor, accurate, dynamic, and unsurpassable in Schumann, Wagner, and the Russian school. Claude had known him in Conservatoire days, and twice they had been fellow contestants; but since then their careers had gone in different directions and they had hardly seen each other.

"Bonjour. Sit down and play your music," said Chevillard, who never spoke more than was necessary.

The noise from the street was loud, since the office was on the ground floor and the grand piano was shaken by the jolting vans and buses. Nevertheless, Claude began the first measures of "Clouds."

"Stop!" Chevillard suddenly exclaimed. "Do you know the songs of Moussorgsky?"

Claude didn't see the point.

"There's one called *Sans soleil;* your first measure is exactly its first measure!"

He went to the shelves, pulled out an album and showed him the song. Certainly this man knew his authors: the same intervals, the same "motion" were there. But it was of no consequence; perhaps Claude, unconsciously, had been haunted by that formula so much that it came back to him as part of his own inspiration as he watched the clouds from the bridge over the Seine. But from the second measure the atmosphere differed and, reminiscent or not, the matter appeared to Chevillard so insignificant that he advised against modification of the text.

The *Nocturnes* were well received by a majority of the press, but on that occasion various musicians acted as guest critics at the request of the newspaper editors; so Claude didn't have to suffer from judgments handed down by incompetents. The articles of Alfred Bruneau and Paul Dukas, especially, made a great impression in musical circles and delighted Claude because of their intelligent insight.

"You see, Lily," he commented, "I wouldn't mind any criticism if it came from someone I respect musically. But it is unacceptable when it comes from those improvised amateur critics, doctors without patients, architects without houses to build, lawyers without cases to plead, who invade the field mostly for the sake of gaining free admission to concerts and theaters. What hurts me beyond words is the authority with which those ignoramuses judge things they don't understand."

By an amusing coincidence Claude, a few weeks later, received a visit from the secretary of the *Revue Blanche* who asked him to become its music critic. He would have complete freedom and could review concerts, opera, or write any kind of technical articles that would appeal to him.

So Claude, who often suffered from the critics, became one of them! Of course, the *Revue Blanche* did not have the same importance as a daily newspaper, but it was read by an élite following and the mere fact of contributing to it carried unquestioned prestige. For Claude it was a safety valve for the expression of his feelings toward the stupidity or the ignominy of certain conditions; also a weapon which might avert attacks and eventually help him to retaliate. But he did not want to be taken for one of those "inflated pontiffs" whose lucubrations made him exhaust all his profane expletives, so he assumed his duties in a light spirit and his first contributions took the name of "Interviews with Mr. Quarter-Note."

The time arrived when the copied material was delivered to André Messager. After a delay of one year *Pelléas* was definitely billed for the next spring and rehearsals were about to begin. But something happened, one of those incidents unavoidable in the life of a big theater. One day Messager appeared.

"I must talk to you at once about a thing of great importance," he said to Claude, who instantly feared some catastrophe. "I have thought over the matter of the cast. Georgette Leblanc is a splendid comedienne, a supreme artist in many ways, and even Maeterlinck's wife. But she is not Mélisande!"

"What is your suggestion?"

"Recently a foreign singer applied for an audition and I was much impressed by her artistry. She is young, intelligent, lovely to look at. Her name is Mary Garden. I don't think she has had any experience on the stage, but she seems to have extraordinary intuition. In short, she *is* Mélisande. I want you to meet her."

Claude had an interview with her in Messager's studio. He soon shared the opinion of his friend and agreed to the change in the cast. Considering the matter from a purely artistic angle, he never thought of any possible repercussions.

Maeterlinck at that time had left Ghent and lived in Paris on the quiet Rue Raynouard, formerly the main street of the village of Passy. He and his wife occupied a ground-floor apartment at No. 65, in an old mansion of graceful Italian architecture. It wasn't long before malicious tongues set to work, and before Messager had a chance to use his diplomacy, word was conveyed to the Belgian poet that, owing to intrigues, the part was being withdrawn from his wife and given to a young and unknown singer.

The news made him so furious that he grasped his strong walking stick and, jumping out of his apartment window, yelled at the top of his voice:

"I'm going to give Debussy a thrashing that he will remember for the rest of his life!"

Georgette Leblanc stood there, terrified, unable to do or say anything.

At the Rue Cardinet he climbed the stairs three steps at a time and, disregarding the bell, pounded terrifically on the door with his cane. Claude himself opened it.

"Infamous, what you did! Scandalous!"

Maeterlinck pushed Claude into the drawing room while the latter tried to make himself heard and to assure him that he was not responsible, that it was the Opéra-Comique. At that point the cane was brandished so threateningly over Claude's head that he turned pale and, feeling faint, collapsed on the divan. From the kitchen, where she was ironing, Lily came in.

"Get out!" she cried in a voice that permitted no reply.

As Maeterlinck continued his ravings and paid no attention to her order, she grew fiercely angry.

"Get out of here! Get out at once! Or—"

She ran to the cupboard and pulled out a drawer. But Maeterlinck, afraid, was already on the stairway.

When he recovered Claude went to his room and looked for a letter kept carefully in his files. He found it and, as his eyes came to a certain passage, a smile of satisfaction showed on his face.

"I want to assure you again that *Pelléas* belongs to you entirely and that you may have it performed when and where it will be agreeable to you."

With this he was safe, and all Maeterlinck's threats were of no avail. When the poet proclaimed all over Paris that he was going to challenge Claude to a duel, Messager and Albert Carré offered to substitute for him because they deemed him physically unfit for such a fight.

Much of the winter was taken up with all kinds of preparations and it was an exciting one for Claude: coaching the singers; conferring with the costumier and with Jusseaume, who was painting the scenery. There also came more work when Carré stated that there was not sufficient time to change the settings between tableaux and some additional interludes had to be written. But Claude kept calm, acceded to all demands, so that no more trouble arose until the day when Messager ascended the conductor's stand for the first orchestral rehearsal.

Soon, however, all seemed to go wrong; the musicians did not know where they were and neither did they understand Messager's beat. Then it was discovered that the copyist, in his inexperience, had forgotten to mark the changes of beat or signature in the silent measures. This caused no end of trouble, of course, and correction after correction had to be made, causing great loss of time. Messager was furious and the pitch of his voice rose all the time. He also had difficulty with many badly written incidentals in the orchestral score. Finally, he crossed his arms:

"Ask the composer, he is back there."

A shower of questions were hurled at Claude. "Is it a sharp at measure seven from letter K?" asked the flutist. "Is it a three per four beat at letter L?" asked the bassoonist. Submerged under the flood, Claude naturally could not figure out what they meant, and when he answered, "I honestly can't tell you," they scoffed and pandemonium increased.

Just the same, when the corrections were done with the patience of pioneers clearing a jungle and Messager lifted his baton for an ensemble rehearsal of several scenes, the atmosphere changed completely. The majority of the musicians were suddenly seized with a sort of sacred frenzy.

Harmonies so new . . . Colorings unheard before . . . Surprise . . . Enchantment . . .

No longer did they mind the length of extra time; they were under a spell and their spirits were high. Never mind a small opposition: exception confirms the rule and it was laughed at. After that rehearsal the first trombonist came to Messager:

"We, the brasses, haven't much to do in this score. But what we have to say is wonderful. When Arkel sings, 'If I were God I would have pity upon the hearts of men,' well . . . I don't know what your impression is, but for us down there it is beautiful. Oh, so beautiful!"

The end of April brought the great day of the répétition générale. In French theaters, including the Opéra and the Opéra-Comique, the general rehearsal is, in reality, the première; critics come and have ample time to write their articles, which appear immediately after the official first performance a few days later. The invited audience consists of the press, many musicians, some social lights, a few politicians, and a large number of people who always attend those events, though no one can tell why or how they manage to get there. It is, in short, the same gathering that is on hand at every affair of the brand qualified by social reporters as "bien Parisien." Premières, Grand Prix at Longchamp, a wedding or a funeral, it matters not so long as the attendance is made up of that crowd prone to sarcasm, caustic comment, skepticism, gibe and cynicism, to enumerate a few "very Parisian" characteristics, at least among that queer set.

The day can still be remembered as a beautiful one. Spring had come prematurely and in the parks the lilacs were already in bloom. Around the Opéra-Comique there was much agitation; never in the past had a new work aroused such expectation. On the streets outside the theater some young men distributed a brochure called "Select Program"; it contained a synopsis which turned the libretto into ridicule, made fun of the characters, and did its best to throw discredit and suspicion upon *Pelléas*. There was also a reprint of Maeterlinck's letter, published in the papers a few days before, in which he repudiated the work and declared solemnly his ardent wish for its complete failure. Obviously written with an attempt at witticism, this pamphlet failed miserably; it was trite, vulgar, with a undertone of jealousy and blackmail.

Certain persons hinted that Maeterlinck might well have inspired it, if he had not written it himself; this was a mean lie, but picked up and peddled by those in search of sensationalism.

The curtain went up in an atmosphere of suspense. Lily was in the audience, but Claude, like Bizet at the opening of *Carmen*, remained behind the stage, pacing the floor with apparent calm that concealed great nervousness.

It was not long before reactions began to manifest themselves; slight murmurs here and there, accompanied by derisive coughing so descriptive of mounting irritation and impatience. When this happened, however, the youthful element in the upper galleries countered strongly.

"Sh! . . . Sh! . . ." This and other compelling exclamations, mixed at times with more precise epithets, began to sound ominously. The conflict on the opening of *Namouna* at the Opéra in Claude's student days was being re-enacted, but this time he was not the actor; one of his own works was at stake!

When the first act was over the public poured into the corridors where skirmishes began between opposing camps.

"This kind of music cannot live; it has no form."

"Admirable . . . wonderful . . . so young, so fresh, so subtle!"

"No rhythm, no coloring, no sense, no life. No good!"

"Debussy is a revelation . . . the greatest genius of today!"

"They can say all they please. In this *Pelléas* there's nothing so far that can touch the quartet of *Rigoletto!*"

The last comment came from a much-decorated elderly

gentleman; he repeated his statement complacently, convinced that he had found an original formula!

During the balance of the performance excitement rose
to a new pitch. When Mary Garden, with a strong English accent, pronounced the words, "Oh! oh! . . . je ne
suis pas heureuse," a storm of laughter swept the audience.
But it changed to a clamor of protest when Golaud, seiz-
ing little Yniold in his arms, lifted him up to the window
and asked him to report on what was taking place inside.

"And the bed . . . are they near the bed?"

"The bed, little father? I cannot see the bed."

It was like a hurricane suddenly sweeping through the
theater.

"Shocking! . . . Disgusting! . . . Immoral! . . . Stop
that! Cut it out!"

The faithful followers upstairs reacted sharply, and it
turned into general confusion, while Messager at the conductor's stand tried to continue and waved his free hand
in an effort to restore peace.

When again the public walked out for the intermission their quarrels shifted from purely artistic grounds to
more personal ones. Some of the youthful element had
made their way into the lower foyer and contact with the
conservatives brought many lively exchanges.

"You old fossil!"

"You impudent brat!"

"Fool!"

"Ignoramus!"

These and other epithets were hurled by both sides. But
the battle remained verbal and never went so far as the
fist fights invented later by overworked imaginations.

After the performance Albert Carré appeared and spoke to Claude:

"There is something that must be settled immediately. The Secretary of State for Fine Arts has just asked me to tell you that he disapproves of the 'bed scene.' He requests that you suppress it."

"But—" Claude began.

"There is no but. We have a success; I am positive of it. You cannot afford to antagonize an official who, on the other hand, seems to be quite an admirer of yours."

A rendezvous had been arranged by Claude to meet Pierre Louÿs, Satie, and a few others at Weber's on the Rue Royale. It was already late, and when they all arrived night had fallen. Fromont's store was only a few hundred yards distant and the publisher awaited him. Claude excused himself and hurried there; with a pencil he noted the cut and made necessary adjustments; then he went back, relieved, and sat with his friends while they reviewed the events of the afternoon and drew conclusions of a most optimistic nature.

They lingered for a long time, basking in the softness of the Parisian night and the cheering thought that all was over.

Finally everyone decided to accompany Claude to his home. When they reached the Rue Cardinet he extended a general invitation to come up and have tea, tea made by himself.

As they sat in the parlor, around the steaming cups and a plate of petits fours from Les Délices, Claude took the floor:

"You know, my friends, there comes a time when something happens in art which changes the course of accepted ideas. It needn't be anything of tremendous size or apparent importance."

Everyone nodded approvingly, thinking he was referring to himself.

"But if it comes from the heart it goes straight to the heart," Claude continued. "This afternoon during the battle, the horn of Oberon came to visit me secretly. I cannot tell you what those three notes meant to me as I waited anxiously for the outcome. In our epoch which is so strange, our epoch when humanity follows so willingly those who don't even know how to walk, the call of that distant horn takes on fuller significance than ever before!"

Soon Claude and his wife left for Bichain, anxious to get away from the big city and to find in the smiling country the relaxation they needed after a long season of high mental pressure. There, among the orchards and the wheatfields, along country lanes and river bends, he could ponder at length over projects which would soon absorb his activities. From the many he had in mind, which would be selected first? Would he turn to *As You Like It* or to *The Fall of the House of Usher*? In the meantime, he lived peaceful days and gave himself up to his great love of nature.

All would have gone smoothly if the finances of the household could have been kept at a higher level; this unfortunately was not the case, despite Lily's superhuman efforts to balance her budget. In Paris it was not rare for her to come back from the market on the Rue Lévis and tell Claude that she was going right out again.

"I heard some women talking," she explained, "and they said steaks were five cents cheaper at the other market on the Rue Poncelet. I'm going there now. I just came up to let you know, so you wouldn't get nervous at my being away so long." In spite of these measures her treasure chest continually ran low or even became empty; then it would mean the annoyance of borrowing small amounts from her family or from some friends, which she repaid as soon as money came in. No one, however, seemed to understand how a man who had leaped so fast into prominence could be in such perpetual financial straits. But, sad as it was, there continued to be no relation between artistic successes and material returns.

About midwinter a great piece of news was brought to Claude: a promotion in the Legion of Honor included his name! Lily was overwhelmed with joy; for her the little red ribbon still retained its prestige. Claude was less enthusiastic; like Alain, the great philosopher, he disapproved of decorations, thinking that "those toys of vanity give a government too powerful a hold over the individual. There was even a taint of bribery about them. How can a person who passionately desires a ribbon which the Minister of State alone can bestow live freely, uninhibited in action or judgment?"

His first reaction was to refuse the distinction, as Maurice Ravel did years later; but when told that it had been granted at the special request of Jules Combarieu, secretary of the Minister of Education, a fine man and a highly cultured music lover, he refrained from doing so.

Claude continued his activities as a critic; they even were enlarged when he relinquished his "Interviews with Mr. Quarter-Note" and became the regular critic of *Gil Blas*, a daily newspaper of importance. Once they commissioned him to go to London and report on the opera

season at Covent Garden. It was June, which in London is
the most delectable of all months. The idea of this trip
appealed to him: he would again ride on top of the red
buses, smell the hay-flavored tobacco, linger in Hyde
Park. But on second thought, would he be able to do
that? He was asked to send a daily article of at least one
whole column; how in the world would he be able to ful-
fill such an obligation, being the slow writer that he was?

Claude, indeed, experienced enormous difficulty in putting into clear language ideas which presented themselves
spontaneously to his mind; it took him sometimes one
hour to negotiate a sentence. He wrote it, rewrote it,
changed the syntax, read it over and found a better wording, until after many experiments he finally hit upon a
satisfactory version. Never would he consent to sign his
name to articles of the current journalistic, harebrained
type, written hurriedly on the corner of a café table. Nevertheless, he accepted the commission and went to London
where he spent most of his days in the correspondence
room of the Savoy Hotel, hardly having time to complete
his review and mail it before it was time to attend the
next performance. What Claude really enjoyed most of
the whole journey was the ride through Normandy man-
tled in the white canopy of appleblossoms and the crossing of the Channel; it was upon his return that the idea of
La Mer began to materialize.

In July his critical duties required his presence at the
Institut where the Prix de Rome cantatas were to be
heard. Almost twenty years had passed since the day when
he awaited the verdict so tranquilly, admiring the pan-
orama from the Pont des Arts. He had never attended a
competition since then; but as he crossed the courtyard

his memories were revived and he recognized the spot where Gounod had come to him and predicted his brilliant future.

How would Claude find musical conditions now, and what were they writing, those young men separated from him by the span of one generation? It was with expectation and curiosity that he climbed the wide granite steps and stood in the hall under the cupola. But what was that he heard? Could it be the work of supposedly talented contestants? No, that was impossible!

His indignation grew until, during the recess, he met Messager.

"I am horrified," he said to him; "simply horrified! Twenty years ago the old gentlemen of the jury loved to dispense their favors to anything that was stupidly old-fashioned and bombastic. Now all is changed, and they apparently appreciate music that's 'dramatic.' So the young composers imitate Signor Leoncavallo. Heavens, what music! What are they? Musicians or butchers?"

A circle had gathered around the two notables.

"Be careful," Messager warned, "this is the Institut. You ought to watch your words. You . . . one of its future members!"

But Claude and musical politics were irreconcilable.

"A member of the Institut! I? A place where such incredible artistic business is perpetrated? A place that succeeds in making one feel disgust for music? A place—"

He probably would have gone on for a long time had not Messager, catching his arm, dragged him away to a more private spot.

He recovered from all that bad music the next day when, at the invitation of Jacques Durand, he went to

Fontainebleau to spend the day at Bel-Ébat. This was the name of the estate owned in the royal city by the wealthy publisher and musician. From the entrance gate one could see a small army of gardeners constantly at work on lawns as smooth as velvet, on trees and ivy carefully clipped, on flower beds full of a gorgeous and colorful fragrance.

"Look at that, Lillo!" he said to his wife. "Isn't it really a magnificent domain? When I think of the royalties it would take to buy a similar one I feel panic-stricken!"

This visit had more than one purpose; Jacques Durand was desirous of coming to an agreement with Claude about the *Pelléas* property which the composer had jealously preserved, not so much through speculative spirit as for sentimental reasons.

When after lunch, and in the propitious atmosphere created by fine liqueurs and Havana cigars, Jacques Durand broached the subject, he found Claude unresponsive; neither the hint of a high figure nor the prospect of a possible guaranteed income had any effect on his determination.

"Never mind in the least," Durand concluded; "we will resume this talk whenever you wish. If you change your mind, please let me know."

On the train coming back Claude and Lily discussed the matter.

"Why didn't you at least go into details?" she reproached him. "He never named a real figure . . . only hinted. Suppose he had offered you more than you dreamed?"

"Even then I wouldn't sell *Pelléas*. It means everything to me."

"We have only fifty francs left in the box. Doesn't that mean anything to you?"

The next day there was a ring at the bell, brief and imperative. It announced a man dressed in a frock coat and carrying a brief case. He said to Lily:

"Is M. Debussy at home? I want to see him on a very important matter."

"May I ask who you are and who sent you here?"

"Certainly. I am a clerk from Maître Rouillé, the bailiff, who sent me here at the request of Général Bourgeat."

This was too much for Lily. She decided to call Claude, who probably would know something about it.

"M. Debussy," the man of law began ceremoniously, "I am under obligation to ask you to state your intentions regarding a refund of the money advanced to you. Général Bourgeat desires an immediate settlement."

"What does this mean? I don't know any general by that name."

"Perhaps so. But the general knows you very well. He is the heir of Georges Hartmann. In the latter's papers he found some notes signed by you. Mr. Hartmann never enforced them. But the general thinks differently. Are you disposed to repay in whole, or at least partially?"

Claude had turned pale and Lily's lips were drawn together. Both thought of that little box, back there in the kitchen, and of the fifty francs that it contained.

"I am sorry . . . very sorry," Claude finally uttered in tremulous voice, "but for the present I don't see my way to pay anything at all."

Meanwhile Lily had recovered and joined in:

"Permit me to tell you that such a claim is all wrong.

My husband gave his music in return for the extra money he may have received."

"Have you any written agreement to that effect?" continued the merciless lawyer. Of course, they hadn't, and he knew it. He smiled sardonically and gave Claude one month's grace to come and straighten out the situation.

Left alone, Claude and Lily gave way to their deep anxiety.

"What are we going to do?" Lily said. "We can't afford disgrace. You know what those bailiffs are up to. They might come and attach the furniture, then auction it off on the sidewalk."

"I will go at once and see Dr. Desjardins. I met him at Chausson's. His wife is Mme. Chausson's sister. Through their father, a city councilor, I think I can get some help or at least the name of a reliable lawyer."

This visit was successful and brought temporary relief.

That same summer a celebration took place at the Villa Medici in Rome. It was the centennial anniversary of its founding and the newspapers gave it ample notice. Claude's resentment, however, had not been lessened by the years; he sat at his desk and had no trouble in wording some twenty lines. The conclusion was slashing:

"It is to be hoped that on this occasion, and in the future, some improvement will be made in the food served at the Prix de Rome table. In my time, I remember, the diet came very close to slow poisoning; still, dyspepsia is not an obligatory contribution to the aesthetics of an artist!"

Once more Claude and Lily spent the summer at Bichain. His time was divided between his worktable, the wicker chair in the garden, and the long walks he loved to take under the shady trees. Sometimes he brought out a large folder containing press reviews of *Pelléas* and read them over. There was unanimous praise from the musicians, sneers and sarcasm from the others. But one article irritated him more than any other. It was signed by Jean Lorrain and contained an attack on the neophytes of "Debussyism." This is how they were described:

"I see one there in the first tier boxes . . . a blond maiden too frail, too white, and too fair. She evidently strove hard to make herself look like Mary Garden. Slowly, indolently, her languid long hands turn over the pages of the score placed before her on the velvet sill.

"In the orchestra seats the clan of handsome young men has gathered. Almost all of these Debussy fans are young, very young; slender lads with long hair artfully brushed down on the forehead, rosy cheeks touched up with a shade of rouge and delicate powdering; thin purple lips, dark penetrating eyes, coats with velvet collars, sleeves too wide, waists too tight, floating silk ties. . . . They are in a trance. To them the gestures of Mary Garden, the scenery of Jusseaume, the lighting effects of Carré are like an intoxicating philter which they drink in ecstasy. From time to time they lean over and whisper into one another's ear some secret thought that touches the uttermost depths of their soul. They are the 'Pelléastres'!"

It was this last word which made Claude abandon his usual forbearance; the unsavory pun, untranslatable into English, aroused his indignation; and as a climax its author was Jean Lorrain, a despicable character known all over Paris as the most notorious representative of that strange species of degenerates. Each time Claude thought of this article it made his blood boil!

There were a few others, too, which compared his music to "the squeaking of a door hinge" . . . "the noise of furniture being dragged along the floor" . . . "the distant whining of a peevish baby"; his art was termed nihilistic, diseased, negative, unwholesome.

From such nonsense he found relief in a few lines written by a young musician, Émile Vuillermoz, who had just been dismissed from the Conservatoire because of his admiration for *Pelléas,* expressed to his professor in defiant terms. The following warmed Claude's heart:

"There will be great fun in the halls of the National Library on that day when our great-grandchildren discover, among the dusty old collections of newspapers, some of the articles published after the première of *Pelléas.* Indeed, there will be fun . . . but there will also be horror and shame."

One day when Claude was in Paris doing some errands, a gentleman called on him at Durand's. It was Robert de Flers, nobleman, playwright, socialite, and one of the outstanding feature writers for *Le Figaro.*

"M. Debussy, the object of my visit will probably surprise you. We have read every article published about *Pelléas.* You certainly must have had interesting reactions concerning them. *Le Figaro* would consider itself highly honored if you will give it your own 'criticism of the critics.' "

"I accept with great pleasure, monsieur. For ten years of my life *Pelléas* has been my faithful companion. I make no complaint about those long years of labor from which I derived much joy, an intimate contentment which stands far above any words of censure. I have tried to obey a law of beauty and make my characters sing like normal persons. Perhaps this has seemed incomprehensible, but one must not forget that in art any new attempt is taken by many as a personal offense. I will write the article and hope it will help me to become better understood."

Point by point Claude refuted the arguments of his opponents, when he felt that their judgment had been sincere. But he refrained from lowering himself by even mentioning the worst of them all: Jean Lorrain's name was dropped like some refuse that one pushes, with the toe of one's shoe, out of the way into the sewer.

To be in the country presented more than one advantage: Claude was out of the bailiff's reach, since his concierge in Paris had been instructed not to give his address to anyone; besides, he had secured the services of a competent lawyer who would know how to resist the general's threats. The cost of living was comparatively inexpensive and Lily managed to make both ends meet, though not without difficulty, or, as she put it, "cutting the pennies in four." Through it all she retained her lively disposition, bustling about, laughing and singing.

Claude, at times, found it rather hard to concentrate on his work and inwardly wished that Lily could be less superficial. Her artistic tastes inclined toward the popular variety. There was in Paris at that time a vaudeville artist named Dranem who had gained some reputation through singing an idiotic, though funny, repertoire. Lily often went to hear him and his ditties lingered in her memory.

Sometimes Claude, deeply involved in rare harmonies, suddenly became aware of a feminine voice warbling:

"Ah, the green peas, the green peas, the little peas!
It's a tender, very tender vegetable . . ."

At the time of his marriage Claude had hoped gradually to educate Lily and bring her to a higher standard of musical appreciation; but he realized that without any background this would be impossible.

The presence of Lily's parents on their continual visits also made work difficult. They were nice, plain folk, but did not understand how hard it is for a musician to pick up the thread of inspiration, once it is broken. So Claude was thinking of moving to another location, not too far, but far enough to allow more privacy.

There was a lot for sale in the charming city of Montereau and he went to investigate; it would be best to build something to his own liking, he thought, instead of buying a ready-made house of the suburban type. The owner was an old peasant, smooth, crafty, stubborn; as soon as he realized that Claude was interested in his property the price went sky-high. Then he became undecided about selling, changing his mind every minute until Claude gave up his building dream, fearing the whole affair would be another source of worry.

One day he was seated in the garden and while looking through the music column of the *Petit Journal* a paragraph caught his eye: *"The Fall of the House of Usher,* after Edgar Allan Poe, music by Claude Debussy, is mentioned prominently among novelties to be presented at the Opéra-Comique during the coming season." This announcement shocked him at first. Then he remembered that once, while talking with Albert Carré, he had mentioned his special interest in this story from which he could extract a libretto of his own. That was all. And already the newspapers magnified the news! Was his name so important, his prestige so great? Claude was by no means modest and he knew the value of his talent, but he was inclined to be pessimistic where a proper appreciation of his genius was concerned. In this case, the announcement produced a favorable reaction in him.

A few weeks were devoted to final reviewing of a new suite about to be sent to his publisher, the *Estampes*. He dreamed of an elaborate publication, a light-blue cover in "papier Ingres" with his monogram in letters of pale gold, and he had just drawn a sketch for it when his wife came in.

"Lily, for the *Estampes* I think we should have a soft shade of blue."

"That's fine. How d'you want your potatoes; fried or mashed?"

She returned to the kitchen and Claude went out. It was the hour of twilight and the peaceful landscape reflected some of his own thoughts. Once more, amid a countryside filled with the melancholy of autumn, he felt the nostalgia of ancient forests, falling leaves heralding the glorious death of the trees. The faint pealing of the distant Angelus reminded the fields that their day's work was over.

The Nationale concert at the Salle Érard was over and the *Estampes* had been a great success. But what was this excitement and hasty gestures in the groups that gathered in the courtyard? A small crowd surrounded Maurice

Ravel, who looked disturbed yet dignified. Questions were flung at him:

"It's pure plagiarism. Aren't you going to protest?"

"It's more than that . . . a deliberate steal!"

"It's not the first time that Debussy has done that! Remember 'Clouds'?"

"That's right! And as the proverb goes, 'He who has drunk, will drink again.'"

The uproar was caused by the second number of the suite, "An Evening in Granada." The Spanish rhythm was treated in exactly the same manner as Ravel had used in the "Habanera" of his *Sites auriculaires,* heard six years before. It had been considered a find, then; hadn't Claude himself been so charmed with it that he had borrowed the manuscript from the composer? This naturally brought suspicion into the mind of Ravel himself and he began to think of some way to assert his artistic rights.

The conflict, however, was of small consequence when compared with Claude's ever-growing fame. The demand for his music increased steadily, and of this he had ample proof when he received a package from Fromont. To his surprise, it contained those old piano pieces which had slept so long on the shelves of the publisher. He had almost forgotten their existence and felt profoundly hurt by their publication without consulting him. These compositions had been acceptable fourteen years earlier, but now he found them thin, obvious, primitive. But what could he do? Protest, if nothing else, and about one of them in particular. He sat down at his desk and wrote:

"I regret very much your decision to publish the *Rêverie* . . . I wrote it in a hurry years ago, purely for material considerations. It is a work of no consequence and I frankly consider it absolutely no good."

Few musicians are likely to agree with him on that, and the *Rêverie* remains a graceful and charming composition. What would Claude have thought if some clairvoyant had told him that thirty-five years later this same *Rêverie* would be taken up as popular music and earn in one winter enough royalties to buy the domain of Bel-Ébat?

Around the New Year, Claude receive a letter from the Royal Conservatory in Brussels, asking him to write a competition number for the students of chromatic harp, latest invention from the fertile brain of Gustave Lyon, director of the Maison Pleyel. Claude accepted because of his friendly connections with the latter. But time was pressing and both Claude and his publisher received a shower of letters and telegrams. Finally the harp professor came to Paris to investigate the situation.

"M. Debussy, our director has sent me to tell you that he must have printed copies of the *Dances* in ten days without fail."

"But I just gave my manuscript to Durand. From a letter I received I understood copies wouldn't be needed until two weeks from today."

"Yes; but before copies are distributed to the students, they must be examined by M. Gevaert."

"What?"

"That is the custom at the Royal Conservatory. New music must be presented to him."

Only Claude's friendship with M. Lyon prevented trouble. His pride had been hurt and the incident was still in his mind when he commented to Durand:

"It is incredible, really. Does M. Gevaert imagine that my music speaks profane language and doesn't know how to behave in public? Perhaps now it will have to be presented to Mlle. Cléo de Mérode, favorite dancer of His Majesty Léopold II, King of the Belgians. If they are not satisfied, let them go and get their competition pieces written in the prisons!"

Lily's reaction had been different: Why had he agreed to put in so much work solely for the sake of art? Once more the rent had created a hole in the family bank roll and the same old worries had returned.

Shortly after this Claude received a letter from Dr. Desjardins seeking his advice on the purchase of two grand pianos. His wife wanted a Bechstein but both wanted Claude to help in selecting them.

After trying out and comparing a dozen instruments, Claude decided on two which were immediately delivered and paid for.

"How much did Dr. Desjardins give you for your time?" Lily inquired.

"Oh, nothing! I just did it to oblige him."

"Your time is as valuable as his. You spent at least three hours, so it ought to be worth at least one hundred francs. Sit down and write him a letter."

"But haven't you forgotten that two or three times during the past year Desjardins visited me when I felt ill? He never charged anything."

"That's different. Are *you* forgetting that Desjardins is a rich man? He can buy two grand pianos . . . and all those Van Dongen pictures, which certainly he doesn't get for nothing. But *we* are as poor as church mice! You must be sensible. Write that letter at once."

The matter was still on Lily's mind next day, when she asked him this question:

"Claude, how much did the Bechstein people give you as your commission?"

Decidedly Claude had no practical sense. He hadn't thought of that!

"So you mean to tell me that before going there with the Desjardins you didn't stop at Bechstein's to arrange your commission? Too bad. Now that they have paid, it may be too late."

She urged him to go at once and he did so; but as the streetcar carried him along the Boulevard Malesherbes he became more and more uneasy. Would he ever dare to ask for that commission?

Probably he passed ten times in front of the Bechstein store on the Rue Saint-Honoré before he took his courage in both hands and stepped inside. The clerk, a businesslike German in an impeccable cutaway, received him at the door. Claude gave his name and explained what he wanted as best he could, whereupon the clerk asked him to wait and went to a private desk in a corner where the director was seated.

On hearing the name, the latter raised his eyes, then got up and walked toward Claude who was in fear and trembling lest he be asked to leave. Instead, it was with a broad smile and an extended hand that the director approached him.

"M. Debussy . . . cher maître . . . such an honor for the house of Bechstein to see you again! Won't you please come and sit down. Your commission? Well, of course, cher maître, of course! We are only too glad!"

Promptly he figured out the percentage, called the

cashier and whispered a few words: one minute later Claude took possession of a neat little roll of bank notes and the director saw him to the door with renewed manifestations of courtesy.

Lily awaited his return anxiously. When she learned of his success she burst into song:

"I'm the son of a shoemaker . . . a shoemaker . . .
A shoemaker that makes shoes!"

That week was marked by a new offensive from the general. He did not come himself, of course, but sent a bailiff who left with the concierge some kind of green paper. This is the way in France: if you ever have trouble about the settlement of any bill, your opponent never bothers about it personally. He turns the case over to the bailiff who begins circling around his victim like a mosquito or a gadfly; it is impossible to shake him, to keep him away. At least once a week he comes back with a paper of a different color, a command, a summons, a threat, or whatever his imagination may invent. It is a war of nerves though which the bailiff hopes to break the morale of his enemy. The worst of it is that in France such notices do not have to be handed over personally. In Claude's case, for instance, it was addressed to "M. Claude Debussy or any person speaking in his name"; since the law accepts the concierge as such a person Claude had a constant fear of seeing a little corner of pink, green, yellow, or blue stick out from between the letters in each mail.

5

"A . l . p . M ."

Iₙ the midst of this uncertain atmosphere, and when Claude was troubled in mind, a tremendous thing happened.

Sometimes, invited by a friend, he attended a musicale or an evening party; this he did more willingly when his interest was aroused by the promise of a musical revelation of some kind. Such was the case when one evening he proceeded to an aristocratic home on the Faubourg Saint-Honoré. Works of Gabriel Fauré were to be featured, including a cycle of songs, *La Bonne Chanson*, written ten years before by the young organist of La Madeleine. Strangely enough, Claude and Fauré had hardly ever come in contact and no friendship had been, or would be, established between these two great modernists so purely French and similar in attributes, yet so far apart psychologically.

La Bonne Chanson was to be sung by Mme. Sigismond Bardac, recipient of the dedication and the wife of a Russian financier who had left his native Odessa to come to Paris and build up a successful banking concern. Gabriel Fauré in person was to play the accompaniment.

The program opened with a piano quartet and *La*

Bonne Chanson followed. Mme. Sigismond Bardac, nèe Emma Moyse, stood in the curve of the grand piano. She was rather short, dainty, and frail in appearance, with the exquisite refinement of a porcelain doll; still one felt an intense artistic flame burning within her and as she began to sing her voice, crystalline and golden at the same time, took on extraordinary tonal qualities. Intuitively she understood how to blend it into the rare modulations which poured forth from the composer's fingers. Of Jewish birth, she carried into her music the inborn artistry and the nostalgic accents of her race. The aristocracy of Fauré and the melancholy of Verlaine found in her an ideal interpreter, the needed link between their aesthetics.

Claude listened with deep attention; never before had he heard such singing!

When it was over and the guests began to spread through the salons he found himself suddenly in front of her. A friend took his arm, pushed him forward:

"Mme. Bardac, may I introduce M. Claude Debussy."

She looked at him; her eyes met his eyes. A few seconds of silence; then she spoke:

"At the hour of my death, monsieur, I want to hear the slow movement of your string quartet."

Claude walked home leisurely, unaware of earthly surroundings. His mind was filled with ecstatic joy, joy caused by the fulfillment of artistic yearnings mingled with a vague hope that perhaps, one day, his own music would be the medium through which that heavenly artistry could be expressed.

A new phase began in his life, one of alternating reverie, resolution, depression or inactivity. He seemingly had lost the thread of his ideas and however hard he tried to work, nothing worth while resulted. Everything around him, even his home, appeared unattractive and commonplace. His mind was elsewhere and he suffered immensely from a secret to which he was bound. How he would have loved to proclaim that secret! But this was impossible. He felt an urge to ascend, to climb summits, to lose himself in something mightier than anything he had created before. He knew that his admirers expected it from him. And *she*, perhaps, with them!

They met again after that memorable night, here or there, at a concert or at a party, and each time both felt more and more driven by an irresistible power that filled their hearts with happiness when they met, and left them forlorn after parting.

They sometimes met more privately at the elegant and discreet lounge bar of the Élysée Palace on the Champs-Élysées, where they listened to intoxicating soft music while sipping a rare port. They talked music, literature, art . . .

Then one day he brought to her, fresh from the press, a copy of his first edition of *Fêtes galantes*.

In the confidential atmosphere of the dimly lighted lounge he stood before her, holding the music in his hands and presenting it reverently. She took the proffered gift and as they remained silent they could feel the tremor of their fingers through the pages that united them. They looked at each other with infinite tenderness. It was at this supreme moment that the course of their lives was changed.

This torrent once unleashed and their resistance at an end, they were at the mercy of its resistless force. They could think no further, only follow their impulse.

When night came they found themselves on a train,
free to live and love, liberated at last!

The fourteenth of July is France's national day; when
the tricolor flags are taken down, when the popular balls
on the streets have ended and the echo of the fireworks
has died out, the Grande Saison is over. The capital is
then invaded by the periodic influx of tourists from the
provinces and abroad. For the smart set, it becomes inele-
gant to be seen on the boulevards or along the Avenue des
Acacias in the Bois de Boulogne. An exodus takes place
either to the seaside, the châteaux, or the country estates.
In the better districts of Paris, rows of apartment houses
can be seen with their shutters drawn.

In the Rue Cardinet, the little flat with the balcony was
one of them. But its occupants were far apart: Lily, heartbroken, had sought refuge at Bichain in the house that
had seen her childhood. As soon as she realized that
Claude had gone, that the drawers of his worktable no
longer contained his manuscripts, she packed her bags
and went to her parents' home. The Opéra-Comique
was closed for the summer; Messager, Pierre Louÿs, and
Claude's other friends were all away. Besides, what solace
for her grief could she expect from them, save the usual
conventional sympathy? Her instinct told her clearly the
motive for his absence and Claude's attitude, recently, was
an explanation in itself.

Meanwhile, on the green island of Jersey, Emma and
Claude spent probably the happiest hours of their lives,
in one of nature's beauty spots and in a peaceful atmosphere exempt from all social or professional obligations.
No one knew of their abode; there were no letters, no visits.

Claude, relaxed after the strain of his momentous decision, was able to give himself fully to the newly found miracle in which his soul discovered unsuspected horizons. From this complete fusion and understanding he derived new courage, new resolution.

A table was installed near the window of his room at the Grand Hotel of Saint-Hélier. Below, his eyes saw the old roofs stretched out in a gentle slope and reaching to the harbor, with the sea beyond. Plumes of bluish smoke ascended peacefully from the chimneys and lost themselves in the sky. On stormy days he could watch the sweep of the clouds and hear the onrush of the waves against the breakwater. An ideal setting for the completion of a work begun several years before, a work that his friends and his detractors awaited with equal expectation, but which he had been unable to conclude because of an accumulation of material and psychological complications.

At once he resumed his daily task and the sheets of *La Mer* were the first to be placed on this table.

Each day Emma and he, walked down to the little harbor and watched the evolutions of the fishing boats coming back from their night at sea; or they went inland, along the shady lanes winding among the apple trees and lined with hedges fragrant with the perfume of hawthorn. Back at home, Emma would retire to her own quarters, leaving him to his musical labors.

Soon his goal was achieved, the composition of *La Mer* was brought to an end, and nothing remained to be done but the orchestration, a work of relaxation and pleasure.

Before his sudden exit from Paris, Claude had called at the Maison Durand and asked the chief of the manufacturing department if he could still make an addition to the proofs of his second edition of *Fêtes galantes*. Luckily they had not yet gone to press.

"I want to add a dedication," he explained. "Here it is: 'To thank the month of June, 1904; A. l. p. M.'"

Puzzled, the man adjusted his glasses as he looked at the words written on a scrap of paper.

"What does that mean?"

"Never mind. Print it as it is. It may look mysterious . . . but isn't it necessary to do something from time to time for the sake of the record?"

Before leaving, he emphasized again the great importance of the text.

This was still on his mind at Jersey and he sent a short note to Jacques Durand himself, requesting him to make sure that the wording of the dedication was correct.

Claude was right when he thought that the moment had come to declare himself through an important work. In spite of his retreat from Paris the movement around his name went on unabated. More, it gained momentum all the time: already there was a legion of young "Debussyists" who announced themselves his devoted champions. Most of them were composers; naturally, they had assimilated his discoveries and exploited them cleverly in their own works. This musical group had been joined by snobbish circles, always ready to admire blindly anything considered "highbrow," even though they are unable to understand it.

In the face of the rising tide of these supporters, before their inopportune and exaggerated zeal, Claude began to suffer deeply. Indeed, they were too aggressively enthusiastic; they could not fail to arouse resentment and antagonism. And how he hated polemics, debates, fights, he who only dreamed of some far-off land where he would be involved in no disputes, where he could pursue unhampered his recreation, where he could get away from the exacting and tyrannical devotion of the "Debussyists"!

He was further disturbed by certain articles which appeared in the press and particularly in some musical magazines, accusing him of being a "one-work composer" and criticizing his near-impotence since *Pelléas.*

"Let the master find in the works of his disciples food for thought," one of these writers advised, "and he will be struck with fright at discovering the danger which increases around him. If, through a new effort, he does not seize again the leadership of the contemporaneous musical movement, Claude Debussy will soon realize that the parasitic young generation which is developing around him 'writes debussy' better than Debussy himself!"

From the enchanting island of Jersey Emma and Claude returned to Paris, but only for a few hours, since they were going to Dieppe for another stay of several weeks. He liked that old Norman fishing town, so picturesque with its narrow streets, its open-air markets, and the imposing structure of its medieval castle towering from the high cliff over the city. There was also the animation of the harbor, the arrival and departure of boats and trains filled with English tourists. The Casino had an excellent orchestra and there were many concerts of symphonic and chamber music which Claude attended incognito and enjoyed very much. His daily walks along the sea front brought him new ideas for the instrumental coloring of *La Mer,* now nearing completion.

It often happens in France that September turns out to be the most beautiful summer month; everything is more mellow, more subdued, more mature. So it happened toward the end of their sojourn. They lived intensely then, counting the days that separated them from the dreaded return when they would have to face the situation squarely. In the meantime they extracted from each hour all the bliss that it contained.

But everything comes to an end. One day the baggage was hauled atop the hotel omnibus and they proceeded to the station, jolting along on the cobblestones. A few hours later they descended at the Gare Saint-Lazare. Emma went to the home of a trusted friend while Claude, pending the liquidation of his married life, established his quarters in a residential hotel on the Rue Washington.

The first consideration facing him was of a financial order. His recent expenses had been considerable and his slim reserves were almost exhausted. It was necessary to find a solution; but what could it be?

A thought suddenly flashed through his mind. His salvation was at hand: *Pelléas!* Unfalteringly so far he had refused to discuss the cession of his author's rights. But he remembered the words of Jacques Durand. At the prospect, however, he felt a tug at his heart.

Claude waited a few days longer, like a gambler staking himself to his last penny. Then one morning he went to the Place de la Madeleine.

In a low voice, embarrassed as ever by this kind of situation, Claude reminded Durand of his offer. Was he still in the same frame of mind? He didn't have to wait long for the answer.

"Certainly, my dear friend, certainly. And if agreeable

to you, I wish we could discuss an arrangement covering your entire production from now on."

Soon the firm's lawyer was called in and a formal contract drawn up concerning the rights of *Pelléas* for which Claude would receive an immediate cash payment of twenty-five thousand francs, or five thousand dollars. Moreover, and in return for his future production, another contract was signed calling for monthly payments of one thousand francs. Nothing was specified as to the amount of music to be supplied by Claude.

"Of course, I trust that you will give us as much copy as possible," commented Durand-the-businessman. But it was to Durand-the-musician that Claude made his answer:

"I promise one thing. I will give you all I can, as soon as my artistic conscience is satisfied."

Between the two foremost symphonic organizations in Paris there was great rivalry. During the summer months the Concerts Lamoureux tried to learn the program of the Concerts Colonne for the forthcoming season; of course, the Concerts Colonne did the same with regard to the Concerts Lamoureux, and it was amusing to watch the efforts of each director to outwit the other. The result was often gratifying because of the competition created. Should the Colonne announce a Wagner Festival with distinguished soloists from Germany, then Chevillard also announced one, but with more famous names. Similar conditions prevailed regarding novelties, and the composers were often placed in the delicate position of having to straddle the fence. Handling such a situation was more the work of an astute diplomat than a musician; and

Claude was absolutely incapable of playing that part. Luckily, Jacques Durand stood by his side; he was an expert for whom those peculiar byways held no secrets. When the moment came to decide who should be selected to present *La Mer*, he handled the matter with such tact that no ill feeling was aroused. It went to Camille Chevillard, who several years before had likewise given the initial performance of *Nocturnes*.

In the meantime, the consequences of the new situation created by the events of the past summer began to be noticeable. Lily had yielded to the advice of her parents and put her case in the hands of an able lawyer who began divorce proceedings on the ground of desertion. Claude, whose abode had become known, was submerged under another flood of multicolored notifications. He decided to submit to the lawsuit without waging a counterfight in which he would have stood no chance whatever. The inception of the legal proceedings brought him at least one advantage: he was able to reinstall himself in the apartment on the Rue Cardinet without any fear of personal demonstrations on the part of his wife, and he appreciated this tremendously after several months of "camping" in anonymous and uninspiring surroundings. But before long he noticed that most of his friends ignored him. With the exception of Erik Satie and one or two more, he did not hear from anyone and was afraid to try to renew relations with others, fearing unpleasantness and humiliating rebuffs.

Once more springtime had come and the weary earth renewed itself. The trees below his balcony were in full bloom. Leaning on the railing with his eternal cigarette between his fingers, Claude one afternoon saw a cab stop in front of the house. A lady stepped out, dressed loudly in a pink gown, her head covered by a wide straw hat adorned with a bunch of varicolored flowers. Obviously she was a foreigner. She looked up to verify the number, then disappeared into the hall. One minute later the bell rang and Claude opened the door.

"M. Debussy, I am Mrs. Hall, president of the Orchestral Club of Boston."

Claude bowed deeply.

"Three months ago our club presented your *Afternoon of a Faun* for the first time in America, conducted by M. Longy, your countryman. Beautiful, very beautiful. Now I wonder if you would write a piece especially for me."

"For you?"

"Yes. I play the saxophone. Oh, just as an amateur. In fact, my doctor has prescribed it in order to exercise my lungs. But I don't want to play what everybody plays. I want my own reportoire, composed for me by the leading musicians of the world. I have already seen M. d'Indy and he has accepted a commission. Won't you do the same? Please!"

"But, madame, I am afraid the saxophone is an instrument unknown to me."

"What of it? A genius like you can write anything."

At the sound of the word "commission" Claude's ear had been pleasantly tickled. The mention of five thousand francs conquered his last hesitation. Mrs. Hall opened her bag, took out five large bank notes and handed them to him with the request that the piece should be ready before her return to America in the fall.

In the meantime Emma and Claude made their plans for the summer. Happy memories of their stay at Saint-

Hélier induced them to go once more to the seaside, but they wanted to make a change and perhaps cross the Channel to one of the English South Coast resorts. Both hoped that soon their respective matrimonial ties would be severed. Lily's action against Claude was following its normal course; his disregard of a summons to attend a meeting of "tentative conciliation" had caused the judge to decide against him. The final decree was only a matter of a few days. Emma also had taken the customary legal steps; but her husband, being more business-minded, had made it possible, through friendly intervention, to arrange a settlement by mutual agreement out of court, thus eliminating many otherwise unavoidable delays.

There was a reason for their mutual impatience for freedom, and it was one of great significance. Emma one day had come to Claude and taken his hands in hers. Then, as he leaned toward her, she whispered a few faint words. He seized her and held her close to his heart. He had learned that their great love was going to be consecrated. The secretly cherished aspiration of a lifetime would soon be realized: Emma would be the mother of his child.

They decided to go to Eastbourne. There would be few chances of meeting anyone they knew in that international resort where everyone is lost among the multitude from all lands. Toward the end of July they crossed the Channel in fair weather and arrived at Eastbourne where they installed themselves at the Grand Hotel. At first Claude liked the surroundings very much. It was still early in the season and the atmosphere of tranquillity permitted him to work on a number of manuscripts, mostly piano pieces, which he had brought with him. How pleasant it was not to hear any noise, except when he went for a walk and the distant sound of those delightful player pianos came to him, replete with fantastic arpeggios, trills, and embellishments of all kinds! No danger of being annoyed by musicians talking painting or painters talking music! One felt in everything the correctness of British tradition. In front of the hotel was a lawn on which "little sprouts of important and imperialistic Englishmen gamboled." In short, a delightful place to work, a lovely spot to cultivate egoism. And along that immense sea front there was only one beggar, comfortable looking at that!

One of the first things they did was to go to the music house and rent a piano. Claude's choice fell on a Blüthner parlor grand which had a lovely liquid tone well suited to his taste. Thus the stage was set once more for a period of productive activity. Unfortunately it was interrupted by a combination of annoyances. With August a tidal wave of excursionists began to pour into Eastbourne. Cockneys invaded the promenade, picnickers took possession of the beach, and the streets were filled with barrel organs, accordions, and other noises of every description. As a climax there came a series of hot days, all the windows of the hotel were opened, and drafts raced merrily through halls and corridors. Claude, sensitive to such conditions, began to suffer from facial neuralgia.

Early in September they left and decided to spend the rest of the month at the Palace Hotel of Bellevue, just outside Paris. Recently built on the hill overlooking Paris, the Seine, and the Bois de Boulogne, it had all modern conveniences and, above all, that of being only a few minutes from the city. Before leaving Eastbourne, however, Claude

had fallen in love with his piano, bought it and arranged to
have it shipped to Paris.

It happened that the Palace Hotel was almost entirely
empty, owing perhaps to the alarm of July, when war with
Germany had threatened dangerously. A few Americans,
several Russians "forgotten by the Japanese," and Claude
and Emma were about the only clients of the sumptuous
hostelry.

Their tranquillity was interrupted by only one visit. Mrs.
Hall, the "saxophone lady," had discovered the hiding
place of her composer. One afternoon she made her appearance on the terrace, went straight to Claude and asked
him for news of the promised manuscript. Of course he
had forgotten all about it and not one note was written.
But he dared not acknowledge this. Being in a jovial mood,
he got out of the situation by explaining that all summer
he had tried to investigate the saxophone and its possi-
bilities.

"I can assure you, madame, that soon your fantaisie
will be done. With the exception of Rameses II, it is the
matter which most occupies my thoughts."

Mrs. Hall accepted this explanation and went away
quite satisfied. Claude's little joke, however did not make
him forget his obligation: he resolved to get to work and,
first, to consult various treaties on instrumentation. But
at that time the saxophone knew none of the tremendous
popularity it acquired later through jazz music. No mention of it was even made in these books, and Claude wondered where he could get this information when one day,
by chance, a band came to play in the square. What an
opportunity! The program concluded, Claude climbed the

steps of the little kiosk and walked up to the leader, an elderly and affable man.

"My dear colleague, I am a musician myself and much in need of some enlightenment regarding the saxophone. Would you be kind enough to permit one of your musicians to give me a little demonstration?"

"Certainly, my dear colleague, certainly."

The solo saxophonist was called, and for Emma, who had remained down below, it was a rare spectacle to watch Claude listening intently to the alternating low grunts and high nasal squeals of the queer-looking instrument. As for the band leader, he probably would have collapsed with emotion, had he been told that his "dear colleague" was Claude Debussy, the famous composer of *Pelléas!*

It was a great day for Claude when he heard that the decree had been granted in his divorce case. Naturally, it was against him and he would have to pay alimony. But he was free! And when Emma's agreement with her husband was confirmed by judgment, they felt that nothing stood in their way any longer and they could make public their decision to wipe out the past and rebuild their lives.

They went to Paris to look for a place where they could live peacefully and comfortably. Avoiding the noise of the busy avenues and streets of the Champs-Élysées district, they discovered a stately mansion at the end of a private square opening into the Avenue du Bois de Boulogne, close to the Porte Dauphine and the entrance gate to the Bois itself. There was a small garden in front, with a circular lawn on which three trees flourished; a walk of fine pebbles surrounded it, and a sculptured bowl stood in the center. Everything gave an impression of solid and lux-

urious refinement. The rental price, of course, was high;
but what did it matter, since Claude's name was becoming universally known and returns from his music would
soon be increased accordingly? Besides, the settlement
reached between Emma and her husband provided for an
income of around three hundred thousand francs. With
all that, they sincerely hoped to keep material worries from
their path.

Anxious to have the house ready by the end of September, they began the always interesting work of furnishing
and decorating. Much time was devoted to shopping.
They went to Maple's, to Waring and Gillow's, to elegant
bookstores where rare editions could be obtained; color
schemes were discussed, special bookshelves built in, curtains and rugs minutely examined. Finally everything was
in readiness. Little did they suspect that the scene was set
for a few joys and a long tragedy.

With October came the reopening of the Paris season
and also the resumption of social activities among which
the slanderous gossip of spiteful tongues holds such a
prominent part. It was not long before Emma and Claude
occupied a place of honor in the list of scandals whispered
around. In the world of music, there was an outbreak of
indignation. Strong words were used. "Claude? A gold
digger who had flatly dropped a perfectly good woman
whose only fault was her poverty. . . . A fortune hunter
who in cold blood disrupted another man's home. . . .
A schemer whose only thought was to marry again, this
time a rich woman. . . . A social climber of the worst
kind . . ."

One day as he walked along the boulevards Claude saw

a friend coming toward him. He stopped and extended his hand, but the friend looked him straight in the eyes, put his own hand in his pocket and walked away.

Gossip, like bad news, travels fast. It soon reached Lily in her retreat, and it was the last crushing blow to her hope, a hope she did not care to admit even to herself, but which dwelt secretly in her heart. Perhaps Claude was only the prey of a passing fancy; perhaps someday he would come back to her. With the announcement of his new marriage this dream was definitely shattered.

Lily opened a cupboard, unlocked a wooden chest, took out a few papers and also another object which she concealed at the bottom of her bag. Then she walked to the station and took the train for Paris. What she would do there she did not know. But the solitude of Bichain, with the return of autumn and the death of nature, was more than she could bear.

At the Gare de Lyon she took a cab but gave no address. While the driver waited she suddenly made up her mind.

"To the Porte Dauphine!"

Through the bustling, swarming streets the cab proceeded, while Lily's brain became more excited and more feverish. Her hand went inside her bag and her fingers fumbled with the object that lay at the bottom. Would she dare do it? Would she find the strength to take the law into her own hands and inflict punishment on the man who had betrayed her so heartlessly?

The cab now left the Rue de Rivoli and came to the Place de la Concorde, to the exact spot where Marie-Antoinette, before a maddened revolutionary mob, saw her last hour. Lily looked at the magnificent buildings, silent witnesses of France's history, and an immense feel-

ing of despair invaded her soul. What was she, after all?
Music needed him, but what did her grief mean to anyone? She felt the great burden of her poverty closing down
upon her, pushing her against an impassable wall. Her
fingers grasped the object and brought it out; she raised
it to her chest.

At the sharp report the driver stopped with a sudden
twitch of his arms, jumped from his seat. Inside, his pas-
senger's head lolled to one side; her face was livid and a
bloodstain began to show on her bosom. The revolver had
fallen to the floor.

A few moments of suspense, then the cab was surrounded by an excited, yelling crowd:

"A doctor! . . . A policeman!"

Carriages stopped; people stepped out, anxious to learn
the cause of the uproar. Two gendarmes came running
from the near-by Navy Ministry. An ambulance appeared
and Lily was rushed to the emergency hospital.

Claude took infinite care in the arrangement of his
studio. He selected a room at the far end of the mansion,
away from the entrance door. It was by no means a large
one, but every object in it showed taste and refinement.
In a corner, between high windows protected by awnings
against excessive light, there stood a small Bechstein upright. On the large desk a few diminutive animals of
carved wood or ivory had been placed, together with a
crystal bowl in which goldfish swam about. The books
included some of his favorite authors: Ronsard, François
Villon, Banville, Baudelaire, Verlaine, Mallarmé. There
were other books selected because of their attractive bind-
ings. A few delicate water colors and etchings adorned the

walls. The color scheme was subdued and suggestive of discreet comfort.

In this setting Claude started his new life. The break with the past was consummated; he regretted nothing and was willing to pay the price for the happiness that lay ahead. His sense of perception, however, made him aware of the hostility that increased around him and made him the target of disparaging and unjust remarks. This strengthened his determination to isolate himself still more, to live his home life under the protection of his "ivory tower." When the eagerly awaited event happened and he became a father, he felt within him a sublime sensation of fulfillment, the perfect joy of heaven.

Soon his new work, *La Mer*, would be presented to the public. Already he had rehearsed it on the piano with Camille Chevillard. Then came the first orchestral reading, that always feared hour of test. Seated in one of the baignoires concealed under the balcony, Claude listened to the actual playing of the music he had hitherto heard only in dreams. As the music went on, some themes evoked actual moments, brought vivid recollections of his last months at Bichain, of the enchanted hours at Jersey, of many dark days too, which now seemed to have vanished before the rising of a new dawn. It seemed to him that he had succeeded in renewing himself, that this music was more powerful than anything he had written before; and it was with confidence that he awaited the concert on the following Sunday afternoon.

When Chevillard raised his baton the Nouveau Théâtre was crowded. Among the public, as before, one felt two conflicting currents. When it was over, the applause was mingled with strong opposition, each faction trying to

overcome the other. There was clamorous approval and
strident hisses (the latter being considered in France a
supreme insult). But something unexpected happened:
from the upper promenade the trumpetlike note of a shrill
voice called:

"I am sick . . . I am 'Sea' sick!"

The Gallic sense of humor asserted itself and the strife
ended in a general burst of laughter.

Claude was painfully surprised at several of the press
reviews. Some critics who had fought his battle so courage-
ously in former years evidently failed to understand the
transformation which was taking place in his manière.
They censured precisely the very points on which he be-
lieved himself entitled to praise. A few of the articles were
insulting and one of them, accusing him of "being finished," was a definite outrage.

His feelings were again hurt by this new incomprehension, but he suffered still more when anonymous letters
began to appear in his mail. Who the guilty coward was,
he could not figure out. The worst articles were carefully
enclosed, accompanied by slashing side notes of sneering
sarcasm. One envelope contained a clipping from a small
magazine called *Paris Musical* which Claude had not
read. It bristled with base jealousy, trying to throw ridicule on the composer and those who played his music: here and there appeared personal attacks expressed
through words of contemptible double meaning. At first
he thought he would conceal such things from Emma;
but would it not be wiser to seek solace in her devoted
understanding?

Emma read the review without any trace of anger. But
later on, when Claude had returned to the privacy of his

studio, she ordered her carriage and drove to a book-store.

Before going to sleep that night, Claude read from a book that had been placed on his bedside table. A special passage had been marked:

"One thing which is certain and easy of demonstration to those who might doubt its existence is the natural antipathy of the critic to the creator, of him who makes nothing to him who makes something, of the drone to the bee, of the gelding to the stallion.

"You do not become a critic until it has been completely established to your own satisfaction that you cannot be a creator. Before descending to the melancholy office of taking care of the cloaks, and noting the strokes like a billiard-marker or a servant at the tennis court, you long courted the Muse and sought to win her virginity; but you had not sufficient vigor to do so, your breath failed you, and you fell back, pale and worn, to the foot of the holy mountain.

"I can understand this hatred. It is painful to see an-other sit down at a banquet to which you have not been invited, and sleep with a woman who would have nothing to say to you. With all my heart, I pity the poor eunuch who is obliged to be present at the diversions of the Grand Seigneur. He is admitted into the most secret depths of the Oda; he conducts the Sultanas to the bath; he sees their beautiful bodies glistening beneath the silver water of the great reservoirs, streaming with pearls and smoother than agates; the most hidden beauties are unveiled to him. His presence is no restraint—he is a eunuch! The Sultan caresses his favorite before him, and kisses her on her pomegranate lips. His position is, in truth, a very false one, and he must feel greatly embarrassed.

"It is the same with the critic who sees the poet or the musician walk in the flower garden with nine fair odalisques, and disporting idly in the shade of large green laurels. It is difficult for him not to pick up the stones on the highway to cast them at him, and, if he be skillful enough to do so, wound him behind his own wall.

"The critic who has produced nothing is a coward, like a priest who courts the wife of a layman: the latter can neither retaliate nor fight with him.

"The critic advances this or that. He lords it, and makes a great display. Absurd, detestable, monstrous; it is like nothing; it is like everything. An opera is produced, and the critic goes to hear it; he finds that it corresponds in no respect to the opera which he had fabricated in his head on the suggestion of the title; and so, in his review, he substitutes his own opera for the author's. He gives large doses of erudition; he unburdens himself of all the knowledge he has obtained the day before in some library, and treats like dirt people to whom he should go to school, and the least of whom might teach men more able than he.

"Authors endure this with a magnanimity and forbearance that is really inconceivable. What, after all, are these critics whose tones are so peremptory and words so short that one might take them for true sons of the gods? They are simply men who have been at school with us, and who have evidently profited less by their studies than we, since they have never produced a work, and can do nothing but bespatter and spoil the words of others, like veritable stymphalian vampires.

"Would it not be something to 'criticize the critics'?

For these fastidious grandees, who make such an affecta-
tion of being haughty and hard to please, are far from
possessing the infallibility of our Holy Father. There
would be enough to fill a daily paper of the largest size.
Their blunders, historical or otherwise, their forged quo-
tations, their grammatical mistakes, their plagiarisms, their
dotage, their trite and ill-mannered pleasantries, their
poverty of ideas, their want of intelligence and tact, their
ignorance of the simplest things which makes them ready
to take the Piraeus for a man and Monsieur Auber for a
musician, would provide authors with ample material for
taking their revenge, without involving any work but that
of underlining the passages with pencil and reproducing
them word for word; for the critic's patent is not accompanied by that of a great writer, and mistakes in language
or taste are not to be avoided merely by reproving such
in others. The critics prove this every day. It would be good
to have a police regulation forbidding certain names from
jostling with others. It is true that a rat may look at a
thoroughbred, and that St. Peter of Rome, giant as he is,
cannot prevent drunkards from polluting him in strange
fashion below; but I none the less believe that it would
be advisable to write beside certain reputations: 'Commit
no nuisance here.' "

These memorable lines, extracted from the book bought
by Emma in the afternoon, were read by Claude with
special emotion, and it was with a sincere and joyous
heart that he bowed reverently to the great memory of
their author, Théophile Gautier.

After the dramatic episode of the Place de la Concorde,
Lily had been taken to a hospital and attended by the

interns until the arrival of Dr. Desjardins. When he came, her condition was serious, and for a few days she hovered between life and death. But the skill of this great surgeon and the excellent care with which she was surrounded finally succeeded in warding off the danger. After a few weeks she was permitted to leave for Bichain.

The newspapers had carried extensive stories of this Parisian drama, because of Claude's prominence in the musical world and his new wife's social standing. Naturally, these aroused new feeling against him. His name continued to be conspicuously mentioned in the potins of Paris, and anonymous letters continued coming to his home. Presently there also came a new summons from Lily's lawyer; some of her friends had discovered that the settlement should not be considered satisfactory. They advised her to question certain matters connected with the liquidation of their "common property" marriage contract, and on this the lawyer went diligently to work. Emma did her best to keep these annoying developments from him, and she also tried to detect the suspicious envelopes mailed by the anonymous senders. But the latter were tricky and constantly altered their handwriting; so detection was difficult without risking invading the privacy of Claude's mail.

Refusing to let himself be handicapped, he resumed work on an idea, already several years old, of setting to music the story by Edgar Allan Poe entitled *The Fall of the House of Usher*. This matter had been constantly on his mind and though only a few sketches had been written, the outline of the scenario had become more and more clear. As he had done for *Pelléas*, he intended to adapt the text himself without having recourse to the service of a scenario writer. Thus he would attain greater unity between words and music.

Frequently, at night, passers-by on the boulevard could see a faint ray of light filtering between the long gray curtains of his studio. Sometimes it burned until the stars grew faint and the dawn began to appear in the east. Claude was at his desk, with his fetish, Arkel-the-toad, in front of him and his fancy penholder in his hand. For long stretches at a time he pondered, deeply absorbed. Then the image became clear and his pen would race across the paper:

"Madeline! . . . Madeline! . . . Was someone there? . . . Who was there? . . . No . . . 'Twas that horrible dream, always the same and which I have had for so many long days. . . . Ah, old stones, bleak stones, gray walls, you weighed upon my childhood so that no thought could liberate itself which wasn't dark and gloomy. My soul must have your own color. My thoughts oppress my heart as you oppress my eyes. What is your mysterious power, you who took all my beloved ones, one after the other, without any chance for a single one to escape your grip? Ah, you know it well; I cannot leave you! You know that soon you will take my sweet Madeline, the only one who sometimes could smile in spite of your shadow; and you will leave me; me, the frail, the desperate, the last scion of the ancient race of the Ushers.

"Can you not understand me? It is not in vain that all of my race suffered and loved in this house. Through them was slowly formed the strange and despotic soul of the stones to which I, the last of this condemned race, could do nothing but submit. Where shall I find the strength to combat their silent influence, importunate and terrible, which for centuries has controlled the destinies of my family and has made me such as I am? (*To his friend*) Come! . . . Look at this great gaping rent which made its way through the wall and loses itself in the fatal waters of the pond. . . . This rent which grows wider every day; it dwells within me like a wound through which I feel my life and my reason leaving me at the same time. . . . 'Tis also through this rent that fear has entered, that hideous ghost which every night comes to visit me. A time is near when nothing can shield me in this unequal struggle, not even you, poor Madeline, poor sister so tenderly loved. I will die from this rent . . . I will die in this struggle . . . The past of the house of Usher will kill me!"

Satisfied with these lines which had cost him a night of work, Claude laid down his pen, bade good night to Arkel and retired. As his weary steps ascended the stairway, he could already perceive the strange resonance of new harmonies, of queer formulas with which he would accompany Roderick's fantastic monologue.

That winter was marked by the première of *Pelléas* at the Théâtre de la Monnaie in Brussels. For one as fond of souvenirs as Claude was, this new visit to the Belgian capital proved rich in opportunities.

The "petit Paris of Belgium" looked exactly the same as years before. French fried potatoes were still an institution and equally delicious whether you ate them in the grill of the Métropole or bought a nickel's worth at one of the popular friture stands. The cafés with their lights aglow and their small orchestras were still used as a meeting place, a club, an after-supper lounge by the whole population; placid, old-fashioned geniality prevailed everywhere.

Claude remembered: Here, at this corner café, he and Pierre Louÿs had stopped for a glass of beer upon their return from Ghent and their successful visit to Maeterlinck; there, in that tobacco store, he had bought several packages of native cigarettes to be smuggled discreetly into France. The news-kiosk still stood at the side of La Bourse, where he had bought the first gazettes carrying such adverse notices of his Festival.

But how conditions had changed now! He was famous, the Monnaie received him with high honors, and Ysaye beamed at the realization of his prediction.

"Didn't I tell you, my brother? Here is *Pelléas*, in Brussels after Paris. You were right not to accept a concert performance." And he tapped Claude's shoulder more affectionately than ever before.

The première was a success . . . but Claude had already left for Paris! His little daughter, Claude-Emma, or Chouchou as he familiarly called her, was slightly ill. Besides, the final rehearsal had made him nervous.

"It was better for me to leave," he commented to Emma. "I was too much in fear of an imperfect performance. Imagine! There was a bell, indeed, but by some spirit of contradiction it was in C instead of G. When it rang, it sounded like a dinner call at the castle! Perhaps it made Mélisande's death less heart-rending? Honestly, it is better for a composer to be dead, so they may do whatever they please with his music. Probably the singers and the orchestra wished I was, since they complained so much about my being crabbed and impossible to please."

Spring was near and Emma reminded Claude of his

promise to Mrs. Hall. Surely she would soon arrive with the flood of tourists.

"You are right," he said. "I would really like to satisfy her; she certainly deserves a reward for her patience."

At once he started sketching the fantaisie, but despite the demonstration on the village square he still remained uncertain in handling the resources of the "aquatic instrument," as he called the saxophone. He thought something in the Oriental style would probably be the most adequate thing. A few nights were spent looking for tonal combinations that might be new and original. With a few pages written he felt better. His sense of duty was appeased and he expressed his satisfaction to Emma:

"You don't know how glad I am that I finally have done something on that fantaisie. I really had delayed too much, for let's not forget that it is over a year since it was commissioned, paid for, and 'eaten.'"

Emma had been right. Mrs. Hall made her appearance in May. Claude proudly exhibited his sketch in pencil and once more assured her that the final composition would not take long. His resolution weakened, however, when he attended a concert at which she played Vincent d'Indy's *Choral Varié*. She was by no means a poor instrumentalist; but the entrance upon the platform of a buxom lady dressed in a light-pink evening gown appealed to the sense of humor of that Parisian audience. When she began inflating her cheeks and blowing conscientiously into the ungraceful saxophone, the merriment of the audience and of the orchestra itself was expressed in a wave of discreet chuckles. Claude came out with an impression of ridicule and the concert acted like a cold shower on his good will.

August found him once more near his old friend, the sea. It was close to Dieppe that he and Emma had located this time, in the little village of Puys, only two or three miles distant. From the high cliff, the view was admirable, and the hotel, the only one there, stood not far from the edge. His delight was as great as ever when he contemplated the sea from some lonely spot. But when they went to Dieppe and happened to stroll along the beach at the bathing hour, he felt indignant.

"It's a desecration, really! A law should be passed to prohibit the exposing of such ugly, shapeless, distorted bodies. Look at those arms, those legs gamboling around crazily! And those fat women with their tight-fitting bathing suits. Isn't that enough to make the fish weep? In the sea there should be nothing but sirens!"

As for the hotel, it was very primitive. The table at his disposal was about thirty inches wide. On that miserable piece of furniture Claude was expected to write something that would revolutionize the world. Then the cooking! Having no competition to fear, the proprietor felt absolutely no pride in his cuisine. Claude expressed genuine indignation:

"That man is dangerous, Emma. He does his marketing himself and brings back the most atrocious groceries. Protesting does no good; he just smiles and continues his sinister business. I believe he brings bad luck to the meat and to the fish. A licensed murderer, that's what he is! When I think that Carlyle contended that an artist must be better fed than any other human being . . . Heavens! What can be done? What can we do?"

What they did was very simple: they shortened their stay and suddenly decided to go back to Paris.

Everything in the mansion was still packed or covered with slip covers and newspapers when they arrived, owing to lack of notice on their part. But never mind the pungent odor of moth balls. It was home, the finest place in the world where everything is familiar, where the body fits in every seat, where the hand knows the particular feel of each doorknob!

Continuing its conquest of European opera houses, *Pelléas* invaded Germany during the following winter. A series of performances was given in Frankfort, Munich and Berlin, but Claude attended none of them. Translating Maeterlinck's text into German had been difficult despite the ability of Dr. Otto Neitzel of Cologne, who spoke French fluently and was a true francophile. The reception was rather favorable with the exception of Berlin, where the "reactionaries" manifested irritation. Nevertheless, a courageous commentator wasted no time in paraphrasing the famous comment of Schumann on Chopin:

"Hats off, gentlemen . . . Debussy is a genius!"

Italy followed with a dramatic presentation at the Scala of Milan. The uproar was such that at times neither the singers nor the orchestra could be heard. The presence of many conservatory students caused the artistic battle to degenerate into a fist fight. To understand such scenes it is necessary to know that in Italy all matters connected with opera take on phenomenal importance. The result was unexpected, however: the public flocked to the remaining performances out of curiosity, and in the end it was an authentic box-office success! Here also Claude was not present. But he went to London, where he had no contrary manifestations to fear. A few months earlier he had been guest conductor at the Queen's Hall and his personal success had been enormous in spite of his poor conducting. The "unknown" musician whose works were not acceptable fifteen years before had suddenly become a "lion." He was treated as such and invited to direct performances of his works with a number of orchestras in the provinces.

There was something in the atmosphere of London which appealed to Claude, despite a persistent lack of comfort even at the Hotel Cecil where he found the beds "very stern." He loved to stroll along Regent Street and Piccadilly, and enjoyed more than ever the shows at the Empire, the Coliseum, and the Alhambra. Claude found the "music hall" formula more entertaining than that of the Parisian "café concert" and also less vulgar. Whenever he attended the latter he was shocked by the low standards and the plebeian atmosphere; in the English music hall, on the contrary, everything was on a higher level. Besides, there were those inimitable comedians and clowns. He never tired of watching them and found more finesse, more histrionic ability in their performance than in the heavy acting of stage or opera stars who took themselves too seriously.

Theatrical atmosphere disgusted Claude thoroughly, and Covent Garden was no exception. He never could feel at ease among those people, so pompous, so unnatural, so flippant, so rude. He simply hated it, and his hatred grew with each rehearsal.

"Detestable!" he stated in answer to Emma's question regarding the last rehearsal. "Detestable, and I can do nothing with them, with the best will in the world. Something always happens that is mediocre, irritating. I will not go to the première."

He stayed at home quietly, but the news arrived in the form of Maestro Campanini who knocked excitedly at the door, bounced in and started running around the room, throwing up his arms:

"The opera is a success! . . . The opera is a triumph!"

Then he embraced Claude, kissed Emma's hand and, recovering his composure, gave the details of a perform-ance which, according to him, had been most satisfactory. It must have been true since the newspapers published en-thusiastic reviews and *Pelléas* was granted the high honor of being analyzed and commented upon at a session of the Royal Academy of Music. Claude had captured the Brit-ish metropolis.

As to New York, Hammerstein presented *Pelléas* at his new Manhattan Opera House and the reception was quite sympathetic. Two visitors called on Claude as a result of this American presentation.

The first one was Giulio Gatti-Casazza, director of the Scala of Milan, who had just been appointed manager of the Metropolitan Opera Company. Having mounted *Pelléas* at the Scala, he was much interested in securing Claude's next lyric work for the famous New York institu-tion. In answer to his inquiries, Claude spoke to him about *The House of Usher* and also mentioned *The Devil in the Belfry*.

"But," he added, "no music is written as yet. The li-bretto of the *House of Usher* isn't even completed."

"Never mind that. Why not sign an option? I will ad-vance you a certain amount."

That was music to Claude's ears. The contract was concluded.

The second visitor was a publicity agent from New York, a typical salesman, loud, high-pressure, "shooting at the bull's-eye like a bullet out of a rifle." Evidently, he had been tipped off about Gatti's plans and took it for granted that Claude would come to America the next season.

"Hello, Mr. Debussy," he began in the usual offhand manner and in broken French. "I come to see you about some publicity. You know . . . it's about that new opera of yours that's going to be put on at the Met."

"But there is no opera of mine."

"D'you mean to say that you don't know? You can't put that over on me. . . . You've got to have some advance publicity on that. I can take care of it for you, and since you pay in francs, I'll give you a special rate."

"I really do not see—"

"Besides, a man like you will surely have something of a tour, if only for the sake of boosting your music. But you've got to put yourself on the map first; otherwise no manager would be able to sell you!"

In his wildest dreams Claude could not begin to understand what kind of connection there could be between himself and a sale; and he was alarmed by the growing ashes of the enormous cigar which stuck in a corner of his visitor's mouth. Sure enough, before he could reach for an ash tray they dropped on the rug; on the rug so carefully kept free from even the tiniest bit of lint.

Luckily Emma came in, having sensed that her intervention was needed. She told Claude that he was wanted in the drawing room; then with gracious diplomacy she brought the interview to a close.

Later in the season the saxophone lady came once more. Her tenacity was really admirable, Claude thought. He made an effort, and in a few days the orchestration of her "rapsodie" was sketched; he handed her this manuscript "as is," and she was quite agreeable to having it developed by a professional arranger.

While Claude's music continued its conquest of Europe and the New World, the situation in Paris remained one of heated polemics. The atmosphere of mystery which surrounded him was an incentive to all sorts of fantastic stories. When Ravel produced his *Rapsodie espagnole* for orchestra, there was a renewal of the former accusations of plagiarism against Claude. Ravel had used for the second part the "Habanera" from *Les Sites auriculaires*, and the date of its composition, 1895, was given special prominence on the program. So once more there was a storm on the little pond. It was aggravated by the presence of another element, so low that its name can only be whispered. Envy! They were not few, those who were jealous of Claude's ever-growing success and perhaps still more of his new social prominence and wealth. In their desire to hurt him they resorted to the most abominable calumnies:

"Do you know what happened after his first wife's attempted suicide?" said one of them. "Well, Dr. Desjardins saved her life, as everyone knows. Debussy met him one day and told him it was a very poor favor, since now she would get after him and he would never see the end of his troubles."

While such rumors were circulating, Claude pursued his life of devotion to his wife and his child, surrounded by the tender understanding so long craved in vain. While he was accused of being a monstrous egoist, he found a naïve joy in watching little Chouchou grow. He played with her, took her on his lap, his face glowing with pride. For her forthcoming third birthday he wrote a little cantata consisting of two pages of music, with Emma, Chouchou, and himself as characters. Then he rolled it in a piece of carefully chosen colored paper tied with silk ribbons, and presented it on the morning of the anniversary.

The life of the family would have been quite happy if Emma and Claude had been endowed with a little more practical sense. But both were unable to establish a relation between the cost of their desires and their financial resources. What did it matter to have a considerable income, if the expenses were still greater! Consequently, they were hard pressed for money, bills accumulated, and it was not rare to hear, at the service door, the loud voice of a collector anxious to obtain immediate cash. Also the general was still active, hoping against hope that he would succeed in recovering something.

In order to augment their income Claude decided to accept several offers for personal appearances. The mystery in which he lived made his actual presence a great drawing card. Edouard Colonne, great conductor and astute businessman, took advantage of this new disposition. It proved to be an extraordinary Sunday afternoon.

Since early morning the Châtelet theater had been surrounded by a long queue. The vast auditorium was jammed and despite Colonne's prestige, there was but little attention until Claude walked on to direct *La Mer*. The manifestation which followed may never be repeated in concert history, and to any listeners of Anglo-Saxon birth who might have been in the audience such an uproar

probably came as a shock and a surprise; surprise that music, which supposedly exalts life and brings sweeter understanding, could be the cause of such a near riot, and that
the public could let artistic passions dominate so completely the requirements of good manners. Anyhow, the
pandemonium lasted for ten full minutes. When a relative armistice came, Colonne brought on the next number; but hardly had he begun when, like a boiling pot over
a strong fire, the tumult flared up all over again. It was an
unforgettable scene and will remain in the memory of all
those present.

In Vienna, on the other hand, success was unanimous.
Claude greatly enjoyed this, not having in the least expected it. But he was annoyed at the rehearsal because of
the necessity to have his instructions translated. Could he
be sure that the interpreter did it accurately?

"My nerves were in sixteenth notes," he said afterward
to Emma. "I wish you had been there and could tell me
what I looked like during that rehearsal. I can't remember
the technique I used, or rather, which one I *did not* use: I
sang, yelled, and gesticulated like an Italian marionette.
Enough, honestly, to soften the heart of a buffalo! Finally
I had the last word."

From the concert itself Claude came back excited and
satisfied.

"A fine success, really! They recalled me like a star
ballet dancer, and when I came out there was a crowd
waiting to see me. If they didn't unharness the horses
from my carriage, it's only because I rode prosaically in a
plain auto-taxi!"

The next day a banquet took place at which many
high officials were present. At the hour of champagne sev-

eral of these gentlemen made speeches. One of them, speaking in German, made a remark which must have been striking since everyone looked at Claude; many applauded, while others looked rather disapproving.

"What was that? What did he say?" Claude asked.

"He lifted his glass 'to the glory of the master who has removed melody from music.' "

"But that's impossible! I must correct that right away." Claude rose and there was a great silence.

"This is a serious misunderstanding, gentlemen. All my music, on the contrary, strives to be nothing but melody!"

From Vienna Emma and Claude went on to Budapest, where the program was composed of smaller selections. It included *Children's Corner*, performed by the composer, and over two thousand people listened to these miniatures, a fact which he found astounding. They thought the Hungarians very charming, with a "French touch" in their hospitality that made one feel at home. They rode along the Danube, but did not find it the least "blue."

However, it was during their last night that they gained the deepest impression. While taking a walk, looking for some genuine Magyar atmosphere, they entered a café decorated in rustic style, where pipe smokers sat around their mugs of beer, listening to an orchestra composed of a dulcimer and a violin. But such a violin! Claude had never heard anything comparable.

"This Radicz is a truly great artist," he repeated over and over. "He loves music more sincerely than many famous musicians. Listen to his expression, his phrasing! Doesn't he play as if he were in the shadow of a forest, trying to awaken in the soul a rare and precious melancholy? And that tone, so rich, so intense! Why, this Radicz is a *violin* himself!"

The chestnut trees along the Avenue du Bois were white with blossoms as Emma and Claude drove back from the Gare de l'Est to their home. He basked in his success, but was glad to be in Paris again. Little Chouchou was in good health and was overjoyed at the return of her father and playmate. She was growing fast, and as he looked at her he was astonished to see how definitely her features began to resemble his own. Strikingly similar were the dark hair, the large forehead, the mysterious eyes of velvet and onyx. Her intelligence was well above her age, so Emma and Claude decided that the time had come to think of her education. During their vacation at Pourville, near Dieppe, they corresponded with an English governess who had been recommended to them, with the object of securing her services permanently.

In the autumn Miss Gibbs arrived. She was a frail little lady, looking around thirty, though it would have been difficult to make a precise guess as to her age; incredibly slender, she wore impersonal clothes, impersonal hats, and everything about her was subdued and unobtrusive. She glided over the floor like a sylph, made no noise, and her presence was hardly noticeable. Besides these qualities, Miss Gibbs was intelligent, trained to housekeeping, and a college graduate. Claude and Emma felt they had discovered just the right person and that little Chouchou would be in good hands.

Musically, a big project was in the making. Ida Rubinstein, the Russian dancer, had requested Claude to accept a commission to write incidental music for *Le Martyre de Saint Sébastien* by Gabriele d'Annunzio. This project aroused his immediate interest, but could he be ready in time? The date had already been set for the following Grande Saison and he had only six months to complete this important score.

Claude had an idea. Recently he had become acquainted with a young Prix de Rome, André Caplet. He could probably be engaged as assistant, as an instrumentation expert such as Wagner himself had used for the elaboration of his gigantic scores. With this in mind he signed the contract with Ida Rubinstein.

With real fervor he set to work. Soon, however, despite his enthusiasm, he began to feel the yoke of that precise date. It weighed terribly upon him, and the days seemed to slip by with redoubled haste. He was caught in the machinery of Time, and there was no way out but hard work, work by day and by night.

Emma, too, was the prey of great concern. For a few months she had worried about Claude's health. During their stay at Pourville he had complained of painful intestinal trouble, but after a few days of careful diet it had disappeared.

Now he was suffering again, and at times he had to stop writing and lie down on the sofa. He did not like to complain, but it was easy to detect from the expression on his face how severe the pain was.

Dr. Desjardins prescribed a stricter diet, and above all, plenty of exercise. Claude ought to go out more, walk in the Bois for an hour or two every day. There could be no better remedy, and Emma tried her best to convince him that it was absolutely necessary. But it was of no avail. *Saint Sébastien* held him in its grip, and with time press-

ing more and more, how could he conform to medical
orders?

From time to time, Manuel and Victorine came for a
visit. They never stayed long, for they hardly knew how
to behave in such luxurious surroundings and were frightfully intimidated by Emma's patrician manners. Manuel
was getting along in years and now he was enjoying his
"retreat" pension; his hair had turned white and he had
grown quite stout, but he still retained his boyish good
humor of the past. During these last years of his life it was
a crowning achievement to watch the fulfillment of the
dreams he had formulated for his son.

Following the course of their own lives, the other children were scattered elsewhere, leaving their parents alone
in the now quiet and restful apartment.

As a short diversion during his hard work on *Saint
Sébastien*, Claude sometimes accompanied Emma to the
bar of the new Carlton Hotel, where a quintet of musicians played. He loved to listen to them. The leader was
called Léoni and reminded him of Radicz.

Those whose memory goes back to 1910 certainly remember the enormous popularity of the "valse lente," the
slow waltz. *Amoureuse, Sourire d'Avril* and the *Valse
bleue* were on all the pianos, and Rodolphe Berger, Maurice Dépret, and Alfred Margis were the kings of the hour.
Claude felt intensely the appeal of those melodies lulled
by the languorous rhythm of the accompaniment. Once,
as they came out, he said to Emma:

"Léoni is another great artist. I think I shall write something for him. It won't take me long, for I am full of my
subject."

So he did. Instead of complying with the doctor's orders, he created for himself more hours of work. And soon an exquisite pastiche of the valse lente was completed, to which he gave the appropriate title, *La plus que lente* (more than slow).

Claude presented his manuscript to Léoni. On the front page was his autograph. Did the violinist know the celebrated name? Perhaps not, since he looked at it casually, said "thanks," and tossed the manscript on top of a pile of music that lay behind the grand piano. Of course, he never played it. Once more pearls had been cast before swine.

Among the playwrights whose new productions were eagerly awaited each season by the Parisian public two names were of particular importance: Henri Bernstein and Henri Bataille. For their subjects they drew mostly upon the tragedies of everyday life. Their sense of drama, the intensity of their dialogue, their ability to build a thrilling climax lent to anything they wrote a profound human appeal. When Bataille announced *La Femme nue* (A Woman in the Nude) there was much curiosity. The title was a puzzle in itself, and as usual all kinds of comments were going about.

The play, beautifully acted by Berthe Bady in the role of the heroine, depicted the pathetic story of a woman abandoned by her husband. She was a good woman, intelligent and kind, and she loved him devotedly; but he belonged to that class of climbers who wouldn't hesitate to trample on their father's body in order to "arrive." So he deserted his wife who was poor, who was "in the nude," and married a wealthy woman who could be a stepping stone toward the realization of his ambitions.

Bataille's play was a masterpiece and on several occasions the audience, gripped by scenes of intense emotion, almost rose from their seats. But during the intermission a rumor spread among that audience. The first act sounded strangely like a story they all knew.

The last two acts dispelled all doubts. Names were being assigned to each character. From all over the theater came an explosion of indignation:

"Debussy. . . . Debussy . . . It's the story of Debussy!"

So Claude's name was again flung around, plunged in the mire under the merciless censure of many who would have done better to examine their own conscience and judge if they were qualified to throw the first stone!

Despite his absorbing occupations, Claude found time to keep himself informed on up-to-date musical trends. From the publishing houses he received packages containing the latest novelties. Some of them were read while he lingered at the table over his coffee, or in bed at night before going to sleep.

Once after lunch he examined the score of a new lyric comedy which had just been presented with success at the Monnaie in Brussels: *La Farce du Cuvier* by Gabriel Dupont. The libretto was based on a medieval story and written by Maurice Léna, author of the words in Massenet's *Juggler of Notre-Dame*. Claude liked the work because of its life, grace, and humor; and it was so strikingly French, in the best sense of the word. He took his hat and cane, slipped the score into his brief case and went straight to the Opéra-Comique. Introduced at once into the directorial office, he laid the score on the table:

"Here is an *admirable* work. You ought to play it!"

Thus Claude could sacrifice some of his precious time, even in those rush hours, if it was a matter of artistic value; hard pressed and with each minute counting, he would not have felt right unless he had paid his tribute to the genius of a younger composer with whom he was not even personally acquainted.

The month of March was well advanced and it was with terror that Claude now looked at the calendar. He had to send in his score of *Saint Sébastien* by the end of April. He felt nervous about this new contact with the critics. What new experience was in store for him? Would he again have to stand the torture of incomprehension and sarcasm?

The publicity was already in full swing, cleverly built up by the promoter, Gabriel Astruc. Claude was working like a Trojan. Rehearsals were in progress. Scene by scene, the music was sent to the theater while Claude, shut up in his studio with André Caplet, hardly knew any rest and worked fourteen or fifteen hours every day. To gain time, he noted his instrumentation on three staves, then passed the sheet to Caplet who developed it into a full score. No one could see him now and the door was closed to all except his collaborator.

Lucky it was that during this period of strain Claude's health remained fairly satisfactory. He suffered slightly at times, but not enough to interrupt the flow of his activity.

Finally *Saint Sébastien* was completed, but the composer was exhausted in mind and body.

Good luck did not continue. Like a thunderbolt, a condemnation by the archbishop of Paris was published in the newspapers. *Saint Sébastien* was declared "offensive to Christian conscience" and Catholics were ordered to stay away.

This ostracism hurt Claude's deepest feelings; he had conceived his music in all sincerity. He, who never went to church, had raised himself to the greatest heights of mysticism. Inspired by the text of the poet, he had adorned it with a touching, if grandiose musical setting. He was convinced that his music expressed deep faith. Was it orthodox, or unorthodox? He did not know and he did not care. All he knew was that it was his own, and that was enough for his peace of mind.

Another dramatic incident disturbed the dress rehearsal, to which the élite had been invited as usual. At an airplane race the War Minister, Maurice Berteaux, had been hit by a propeller and killed instantly. The government declared official mourning and the rehearsal, which was featured as a gala, had to be given "with closed doors." Most of the audience, however, were unaware of this change, so they came, protested loudly, and ultimately forced the doors. The police ejected them, but this was not done without a fracas, and the rehearsal suffered accordingly.

Meanwhile, Claude and Gabriele d'Annunzio had resolved to challenge the archbishop's anathema. They voiced their protest in a note sent to all newspapers. Its conclusion was particularly emphatic:

"We affirm in all conscience and honor that our work is profoundly religious and is the glorification not only of the admirable Christ-athlete, but of all Christian heroism as well."

In spite of this the condemnation remained and *Saint*

Sébastien proved a financial failure, since it was boycotted by the higher circles of society.

The closing left Claude absolutely worn out; his fatigue was so great that at times he sank into a big chair, let his head drop on his arms, and whispered: "Je n'en puis plus" (I can do no more).

Still, he had signed a contract to go to Turin and direct a concert. The summer vacation was in sight, with all its expenses, so he decided to make one more effort and left for Italy. It so happened that prolonged heat was turning Europe into a furnace. For nearly a month the temperature hovered between eighty and a hundred. On the trains it was so hot that passengers removed their ties and collars; at each stop they rushed to a fountain, dipped their handkerchiefs in the cool water and tied them around their foreheads. Southern France and Italy were still worse, and for Claude the two rehearsals and the concert were a real crucifixion. The return trip was equally bad. Everyone looked at the sky, hoping to discover some little speck of cloud, the vanguard of rain and relief perhaps. But nothing was in sight except burning, implacable sunshine. When he arrived, the combined effect of heat, overwork, and nervousness sent Claude to his bed for several days, and the doctor ordered absolute rest for one month, if possible out of Paris.

This time Claude and Emma selected lower Normandy. The hotels at Puys and Pourville were decidedly too primitive; so they engaged an apartment at the Grand Hotel in Houlgate, a resort located between Deauville and Cabourg and famed for its distinction and tranquillity. Claude liked it immensely; he found the air light and invigorating, the sea soothing, the people quite acceptable.

The only blots were a little orchestra which played miserably, and a lady who had a piano in her room and rehearsed one whole Massenet opera every day. But these were small annoyances compared with the pleasure he derived from the wonderful situation of Houlgate. He often sat on the beautiful beach of golden sand, watching the games of little Chouchou and the other children. Sometimes he took a shovel and helped her build a fort surrounded by a moat, which she defended against the invasion of the incoming tide. When the wavelets closed in, filled the moat and began battering the embankment, "Miss" (as Miss Gibbs was always referred to) became nervous; wringing her hands, she begged Chouchou to come back at once. Chouchou laughed, shrieked joyously, and only gave up the fort when the water broke inside.

"You're a naughty little girl! Don't you know it was dangerous to stay so long?" Miss said as she shook her finger at Chouchou. The latter grasped her father's hand and felt proud of her fight against the elements.

Claude and Emma also took a number of excursions. They went to Trouville-Deauville; they visited the little city of Honfleur, asleep along its old docks. On the other side of Houlgate, and almost adjoining, was Dives-sur-Mer, where William the Conqueror assembled his fleet for his conquest of England. Claude took great interest in these landmarks: the old church where the names of Duke William's four hundred knights are engraved in the stone; the hostelry named for him, with its bowers nestling among roses and geraniums. They ate lobster mayonnaise, an incomparable juicy steak, haricots verts fresh from the garden, cream just out of the dairy. Claude also enjoyed the sparkling cider of Normandy, so cool and appetizing.

The days passed quietly and they had little contact with the outside world. On the beach Claude snapped many pictures of Chouchou at play, at rest, or in the water; then he took the film to be developed and if the result was good his joy was naïve and touching. Such simple pleasures helped him stand more easily certain social obligations to which he had to submit, for instance, the necessity of dressing for dinner. Emma never liked to eat in their apartment, so Claude had to wear his dinner coat when they went to the main dining room. They spoke to no one, but the people were quiet and distinguished.

Very little mail came, apart from a few business letters from Jacques Durand and a picture postcard from d'Annunzio, who was at Arcachon. It expressed gratification over Claude's improvement.

"I am so happy over the good news, dear brother. I send you all this beautiful golden light which is the breath of the oceanic spring!"

They remained at Houlgate until the first week of September. Both enjoyed those last days intensely. Leaving the beaten track they took rides into the real Norman countryside which extends some twenty miles between the sea and Lisieux.

"We saw some really beautiful spots," Claude reported later; "rolling hills, cottages with thatched roofs, gardens resplendent with flowers sloping toward the sea. And nobody around; no Casino on the horizon! Isn't it strange that so many people who own an estate in such a paradise think of nothing but leaving it for the cosmopolitan tumult of Trouville-Deauville. Heavens, heavens!"

October came and the doctor permitted Claude to work again, though with discretion. He made a thorough checkup and the result gave him some concern. Claude was apparently better after his prolonged rest and the intestinal crisis had not returned; but at times he felt within him a dull pain, at other times a kind of quick stabbing, both accompanied by a sensation of growing weakness. The doctor put him under observation but for the present refrained from using any medicines.

More offers, however, continued to pour in for Claude to participate in various concerts in France and abroad. Rome, Brussels, The Hague, Amsterdam, London, and even Russia clamored for his services. His reaction was alternately favorable and negative. He knew his limitations in the art of conducting; as a pianist, on the other hand, he was supreme. But he always felt so tired, and so weary. At the approach of his fiftieth birthday it seemed to him that soon maturity would be over and old age would take its place. Instead of looking toward the coming years as a period of riper fulfillment, he allowed the first symptoms of fear to creep upon him. Sometimes in his conversations with Emma he was very melancholy. The balance of his life appeared so short in comparison with all his unaccomplished projects! He had not yet been able to put the final dot to his libretto for *The House of Usher*. And there were so many others: *The Devil in the Belfry, As You Like It,* a ballet called *The Palace of Silence*, plus a lyric work on a Hindu legend in collaboration with d'Annunzio. Where would he ever find time to do justice to these? Sometimes he thought of Massenet, who retired at eight o'clock, rose at four and considered his work done by the time Claude awakened; Massenet, who wrote at least one opera every year, and sometimes more. Of course, one felt in them the haste, the facility of improvisation; but what a tremendous figure he had been, anyway, that man who in the last year of his life and desperately ill found the energy to write one last opera, lying on the floor with cushions under his chest, manuscript paper in front of him and pencil in hand. Claude compared himself, his hesitations, his waverings. He remembered a piano piece which for six weeks he had refused to release to the publisher because he could not find four closing measures that sounded exactly right. Did he not also vacillate between two possible chords for days at times, not knowing which one to choose and wondering if he would not have to throw up a coin and let heads or tails decide? Instead of considering such artistic scruples as a virtue, he gradually turned to pessimism and it seemed to him that his brain became encircled by shadows of sterile impotence. To Gatti-Casazza, who called on him on his way from Italy to New York, he said:

"I haven't done a thing since last year. Please remember that I was very frank with you when you asked me to sign that contract. Perhaps you will never get anything."

Through that period of uncertainty Emma watched over him with tender devotion. The doctor had recommended more regularity in the hours of his meals. When she realized that the clock had already struck three and Claude was still in his studio, Emma quietly turned the knob and pushed the door ajar. The fumes from the kitchen stove would then make their way through the opening and insinuate themselves into Claude's nostrils. It seldom failed to make him realize that he was long overdue and perhaps the simmering dishes would be ruined.

Emma and Miss also kept close watch on the front

door and on the ever-growing number of hero-worshipers, autograph hunters and upstarts of all descriptions who tried to gain entrance to the "sacred abode." Admission was limited to a few select friends. The faithful André Caplet was one of them and also Arthur Hartmann, the violinist, who was engaged in the work of transcribing for violin a number of Claude's piano compositions. When Hartmann came with his instrument and played his arrangements, it was an hour of relaxation for Claude. The new aspect given his music refreshed him. He played the accompaniment, offering an additional suggestion here and there. He had taken a personal liking to the violinist and said to Emma:

"I admire Hartmann greatly. He is a rare character, a real man who is not afraid to speak his mind. He may harm his career by doing so, but it is good to see an artist who is unafraid in this musical world of ours, so full of politics and corruption."

Once a newspaperwoman presented herself with a letter of introduction. Her name was Miss E. F. Bauer and she wanted to interview Claude about some problems of musical education in the United States.

"Of course, M. Debussy, you know that the world is moving westward and future discoveries in music are bound to come from America. We are a young nation; for this reason we must break with tradition and find new ways of our own."

"I see."

"Our young people are dynamic, red-blooded, full of life. They want to lose no time. They want to do away with the prejudices of an old, tired world."

"I see."

"We want to decide on the future of our young musicians between the ages of eight and ten. They are full of talent and they want to get there quickly. What do you think would be the best short cut?"

"The best short cut, mademoiselle, is a machine which the genius of your wonderful engineers will certainly devise one of these days. Students will enter at one end, and five minutes later they will emerge at the other end transformed into full-fledged musicians!"

During those unforgettable pre-World War years the main feature of the Grande Saison probably was the performances of the Ballets Russes under the direction of Serge de Diaghilev. Nijinsky and Karsavina were the stars of the company and whenever *The Specter of the Rose*, with Weber's music, was on the program it was impossible to secure a seat. Rimsky's *Scheherazade*, Borodin's *Prince Igor*, Stravinsky's *Fire Bird*, and other Russian works constituted the standard repertoire. But Diaghilev was a dilettante whose eclectic taste looked for opportunistic variety. Claude's name being much in the limelight, he was asked to write a special ballet. In the meantime Diaghilev would stage an adaptation of the *Afternoon of a Faun* with Nijinsky in the title part.

Claude accepted this commission. Once again it would help balance a budget which was always in the red despite the good care Miss took of the household.

For the *Afternoon of a Faun* Nijinsky prepared an impossible choreography. His misconception was aggravated by certain postures which shocked the public and caused a violent reaction. The music, of course, had become so well known that it could not be harmed by this experience.

For the following year Claude composed a ballet, *Jeux* (Games), illustrating a queer scenario invented by Nijinsky himself. The story revolved around a tennis match between a young man and two young ladies, followed by other games somewhat less innocent; at one point a tennis ball fell, thrown by an unknown hand, and the participants ran into the sheltering darkness of the woods. At the rehearsal Claude lost his temper as never before in his life. Rising from his seat he stopped the orchestra and the dancers:

"This is impossible! I want the choregraphy changed at once."

"It cannot be done. It will go on as it is," declared Nijinsky.

"Then I withdraw my music and I want my score!"

When he started to walk down the center aisle, Diaghilev grew nervous. There was a nasty look on Claude and Nijinsky's faces. Fearing that the stage might turn into a boxing ring, Diaghilev beckoned to the stagehand: down came the fire curtain, and the opponents were separated by actual steel. But Claude had only his score in mind. He grabbed it from the conductor's stand and started toward the exit. Whereupon Diaghilev ran after him, put his arms about him, besought him and finally succeeded in recovering the score. But Claude was peeved at Nijinsky and did not attend the performance.

Also, because of material considerations, he finally accepted the offers from abroad. His tour would begin in November, and in Russia. This meant another postponement of his projects, including *The House of Usher*. In the meantime he played some of his new *Préludes* at a concert organized by the Maison Durand. It caused another outbreak of unfair vituperations and these were mailed to him by the same untiring hand. One was short and to the point:

"M. Debussy in person played three of his new *Préludes*. The first one contained little. The second one contained less. The third one contained nothing at all."

And this from another critic:

"Can M. Debussy honestly believe that his little ditties deserve the same kind of ovations that greet the master works of Mozart and Beethoven?"

"Will they ever leave me in peace?" Claude murmured, as he reached for Théophile Gautier's pamphlet, the best antidote to the venom.

Another diversion soon came, and it was a lovely one. André Hellé, the painter who specialized in illustrating children's stories, approached him regarding a ballet, *La Boîte à joujoux* (The Toy-Box).

Nothing could suit Claude better than this delightful short story, which appealed to his sense of humor and philosophy as much as to his paternal instincts. He would write it for his beloved little Chouchou whom he adored more and more.

In November he left for St. Petersburg, where he found Koussevitzky's orchestra "purely admirable" and spent several enjoyable days in the great city known for its friendliness to art. The concert was repeated in Moscow, and before he left he was presented with a testimonial signed by some twenty-five of the leading Russian musicians. The text was written in French:

"Illustrious Master,

"For a long time we awaited impatiently the moment when you would come and direct your works for us; for a long time we looked forward to the joy which would be ours when, in your company, we could penetrate the captivating charm of your music; and our dream has finally come true. The days spent with you will never be erased from our memory and they will dwell within us as the kindling of a light which will shine everlastingly upon our musical careers."

Claude had hardly returned from Russia when he left for Rome. Thirty years had passed since the night when, at the same Gare de Lyon, he boarded a stuffy train en route to the Villa Medici. Now he came back in triumph, eagerly awaited by musicians and the public.

On the platform at Rome a little man walked up and down briskly. The face that emerged from a woolen scarf was intelligent, winsome, with at times a shade of frolicsome spirit in the sparkling blue eyes. It was Bernardino Molinari, regular conductor of the Augusteo orchestra. He had never met Claude and knew him only through his photographs. Perhaps it would not be easy to detect him among a crowd where Florentine types were by no means a rarity. But Molinari's instinct spotted his man. He walked up to him, stretched out his hand:

"Debussy?"

"Molinari?"

A cordial handshake sealed the friendship at once established between these two brothers in Latin art. The concert was more than a victory: it was a compensation for the scandalous reception of *Pelléas* four years before. After the *Afternoon of a Faun* the Augusteo almost collapsed under the thunder of applause and at the end the public became well-nigh frantic.

Claude took time to drive up to the Villa Medici. It looked just the same; he did not go inside, however, and spent only a few moments in contemplation of the city below.

He also wandered through the old streets; the store where he had bought the statuettes was still there but it had changed hands. Gone was the Punch and Judy show; a new building stood in its place and most likely the funny old contrabassist had departed from this world.

His next appearances were to be in the Netherlands, but on his way Claude stopped over in Paris and took part in a concert given by Hartmann for the presentation of his transcriptions. He also played with Hartmann one of the Grieg sonatas, for the purpose of asserting his admiration for the Norwegian composer who was then the object of attacks by the Schola Cantorum clan.

The concerts at The Hague and Amsterdam gave Claude an opportunity to hear his orchestration of the *Marche écossaise*, former march of the ancient Earls of Ross. As he conducted it he recalled vividly the silent interview, the whisky-sodas, the fifty pounds sterling. The march gave him a pleasant surprise. "But . . . it is quite lovely!" he muttered to himself after the performance of this new version.

For a few days he was undecided about making a trip to London. He was going there simply to accompany his songs and play a few pieces at a musicale given by Lady Speyer, wife of the well-known financier and multimillionaire. He was not pleased because his fee had been disputed and somewhat reduced.

"I should not have accepted," he told Emma. "Caruso would demand more for his accompanist than I am to receive!"

But, as he put it, it would be "a drop of water in the desert of those unpleasant summer months." So he finally went.

When he came back Paris was enveloped in an atmosphere of anxiety and unrest. The agitation caused by the Sarajevo assassination had not subsided; it changed, on the contrary, to a slowly mounting anger which threatened to spread war all over Europe. The situation in France was one of political uncertainty. One after another ministries were overthrown, and this created rage among the people. War talk was going on everywhere. Mobilization was already under way and men were being called to the colors discreetly, by individual orders.

It was on one of those troubled days that Charles-Marie Widor, newly elected "perpetual secretary" of the Academy of Fine Arts, came to see Claude.

"I am glad to find you at home, Debussy," he said. "I wanted to see you urgently. My election as secretary makes my seat vacant for a new member of the Institut. I have come to offer you my place. No one could be worthier. You are now honored by the whole world."

"I . . . a member of the Institut. *I!*"

"Certainly. I have consulted the majority of our members. Your election is assured."

"But . . . my break with the Villa Medici . . . my resignation . . . my harsh words later on?"

"All forgotten. Let's shake hands, my future colleague!"

The political outlook, however, grew more ominous every minute. Events of international significance succeeded one another at whirlwind speed. Crowds stood before the offices of the newspapers, looking anxiously at the bulletin boards. Parades marched along the boulevards. President Poincaré, back from his official visit to Russia, was greeted at the Gare du Nord by a cheering multitude. Then the tragic night, the murder of Jaurès, artillery convoys rolling through Paris streets, general mobilization, war.

In the great confusion that ensued the session of the Institut was forgotten and his election was postponed.

6

The Last Years

CLAUDE'S sensitiveness was tremendously affected by the gigantic drama in which the independence and very life of his beloved country was at stake. He wanted to do something, to take some active part, to aid in some manner. But at his age, with his poor health, he realized how helpless he was.

Paul Dukas called hurriedly, declaring his readiness to sacrifice his life if this could hasten victory. From him he heard that Ravel was in the automobile service and quartered at the fire station in the Avenue La Motte-Picquet. André Caplet was at his native Le Havre, and Jacques Durand at Fontainebleau. Emma's thoughts, despite her new situation, turned to her grown-up son and she wondered where he was, what regiment he had joined. Little Chouchou, though only nine years old, discerned the gravity of it all, and her dolls were relegated to a chest. Even the birds were sad; they sang no longer, and the two dogs, the fox terrier and the collie, rubbed themselves against their master as if looking for protection.

When hostilities broke out Claude gave up all musical activities. The piano lid remained closed and the manuscript paper unused. How could his mind concentrate on anything when France's finest sons were falling every minute, when the whole country was passing through such terrible hours of anguish?

The scant news that filtered through the censorship was alarming. The fighting was taking place in Belgium, already invaded by the German army.

Then one Sunday Claude bought a newspaper and read the terrible words:

"Our front, from the Somme to the Vosges . . ."

He rushed back home.

"Emma! Emma! What does this mean? Last week our army was at Charleroi. Now look at this. France is invaded!" And he gave way to utter despair.

When the German army continued its advance and Paris was threatened, the government fled to Bordeaux. It was the signal for an exodus en masse. The railroad stations were taken by storm, the streets were filled with taxicabs, delivery wagons, pushcarts loaded with all kinds of household belongings. While confusion increased, optimistic rumors were circulated in an attempt to restore confidence: the Russian steamroller had started; a hundred thousand Cossacks were within two days' ride of Berlin.

Claude refused to yield to the near-panic. Like Myron C. Herrick, the American ambassador who endeared himself to the hearts of the French people through his courage, he declared that he would stay in Paris happen what may.

A few days later, however, when the danger increased, Claude was invited, almost ordered, to leave. The presence of women and children was no longer desirable. A family passport once secured, he, Emma, Chouchou, and Miss left for Angers, the conservative city on the Loire. The train was overcrowded and the trip lasted the whole day instead of the usual seven hours.

They rented a furnished apartment, comfortable only to a degree, and began living long, dreary days brightened only by the arrival of news. Claude sank deeper and deeper into despondency.

"I am heartbroken, Emma. For two months I haven't touched a piano nor written one note. It has no importance, I know, in the face of events that are going on. But just the same, I can't help thinking of it and it makes me feel sad. At my age, any time lost is lost forever."

A letter came from Jacques Durand, who had left Fontainebleau for the island of Noirmoutiers. Now he announced his impending return to Paris: the Marne victory had removed the menace; conditions tended to become stabilized and, in many ways, normalized. Durand's decision was wise, Claude thought, and after consulting with Emma they decided to do the same.

They reached Paris at the end of October and found the capital quite changed. Everything was serious, grave, and war was being brought down to a matter of administration and routine. Schools and colleges had reopened and the theaters were in the process of doing so. Uniforms were noticeable everywhere.

Claude decided that, after all, the best way to serve his country was to resume his work and try to enrich its musical treasure. Vaguely, he thought of composing a *Marche Héroïque;* but he abandoned the idea, not being fitted for that kind of music which is necessarily bombastic and trite. In his mind several projects began to take shape: a suite for two pianos, introducing the Luther choral and the *Marseillaise*; a series of short sonatas and concertos renewing the tradition of the eighteenth century. Once again his brain seemed to become productive.

He was at his desk one day, struggling against the disturbance of a military school for drums and bugles recently created in the moat of the fortifications directly across the railroad tracks, when the bell rang and a messenger brought the news that his mother was very ill. For some time she had been suffering from an incurable disease and Claude knew well there was no hope of her recovery.

When he arrived at the little apartment she was almost unconscious, and a few hours later she passed away. It was a hard blow, for to any sensitive man, even when age grows upon him, is not a mother always the greatest being on earth, before whom he remains the little boy and bows with reverence and respect?

In spite of the war, the house of Durand continued to pay Claude his monthly allowance. This began to worry him: it had been a long time since he had turned in a manuscript and he felt embarrassed at taking the money and giving nothing in exchange. So it was with pleasure that he acceded to Jacques Durand's request that he make a revision of the entire works of Chopin. They were preparing a "National Edition" destined to take the place of German editions banished from Allied markets, and here Claude thought that in accepting he would be contributing to his patriotic duty.

During that first winter of the World War, the disbanded orchestras tried to reassemble in one unit, using

musicians not called for military service. They announced
a series of concerts at the Théâtre Sarah-Bernhardt, with
the assistance of guest conductors who generally gave their
services for the good of the cause.

Claude was invited to attend the final rehearsal when
his *Nocturnes* were featured under the direction of Al-
fredo Casella, the Italian pianist and modernist composer. These Saturday morning rehearsals as usual were
attended by a number of critics and musicians. About a
hundred of them were scattered about when Claude and
Emma entered the theater and took their seats in one of
the front rows. The first two nocturnes, *Clouds* and *Festivals*, are most often played, and they fared pretty well.
But from the beginning of the third one, *Sirens*, Claude
began to show signs of nervousness. Casella stopped repeatedly, tried once more, stopped again. Claude's voice
rang out:

"I have not heard the third horn."

Whereupon the "third horn," hurt in his artistic pride
and forgetting discipline, replied directly:

"What's that? In the first place, I'd like to know if we
are supposed to use mutes in this thing."

Claude already was standing up:

"Never mind the mutes. I did *not* hear you. And I do
not write 'things'!"

Then he turned to Emma:

"Let us go."

But she took his arm and made him sit down again.

"Claude, listen to me! You cannot do that to Casella,
with all those people watching you. It would be a serious
offense."

A few moments passed, during which Claude remained

quiet. But he was boiling inside and soon his patience broke before so much ill-will on the part of the horn section. Suddenly, and almost aloud, he broke into profanity:

"Come on! Let's get out, in the name of God!"

There was nothing for Emma to do but follow him as he walked out. His feelings must have been terribly hurt when he used language so little in keeping with his dignity and reserve.

The practicing of the drums and bugles in the fortifications soon became most annoying. Soldiers rise early, and with the days growing longer, they began their exercises at six o'clock in the morning. Nothing could be done about it and any complaint would have been received with the fatalistic "C'est la guerre!" So the shutters, the windows, and the curtains were kept tightly closed. Meanwhile, Claude progressed with his revision of Chopin's works. At the same time he started a series of *Études* of his own.

War conditions caused many charitable organizations to seek new ways of raising money. One day a committee called on Claude and asked him for a manuscript, one that could be sold at a forthcoming benefit auction. He responded at once, but instead of handing his visitors an unimportant fragment from his files, he had a delicate and unique idea. Asking them to kindly wait, he went to his studio and improvised an exquisite little waltz. Then he made a beautiful copy of it and presented it to the delighted ladies. This *Album Leaf*, in its conciseness, is a rare gem of daintiness, spontaneity, and charm.

The first winter of the war was marked by an epidemic of grippe. For two weeks Claude was laid up and completely incapacitated for any work. But Emma's company alleviated many long hours. Between his periods of rest she sat by his bedside and they quietly conversed of things musical. For him it was a rare pleasure to exchange ideas with one who understood him so well, one in whom he could confide without fear, one who would never misinterpret his words. He was still affected, and profoundly so, by the part his very admirers made him play.

"If they only knew how they hurt me by idolizing me as they do. These polemics, these controversies, these futile little arguments are so ridiculous! I have often said so and I will repeat it until the end of my days: I am not the chief of any school. I just write because I believe that what I have to say is worth saying. But I am myself, just myself! Honestly, the 'Debussyists' are killing me."

Claude also knew how his enemies took advantage of his supposed disdain for Bach and Beethoven to represent him as a revolutionist and an iconoclast.

"It's all so unjust. No one loves Bach more than I do. But does this mean that I must admire everything in Bach because of his name? I don't think so. When I hear the andante from the E major violin concerto, for instance, I find its beauty so entrancing that I don't know how to sit in order to be worthy of listening. But in some other cases, and since Bach made composing a daily duty, he started on anything when he had no ideas, and not being admirable, he became unbearable. Oh, those pages without joy, those measures that pass by unmercifully, with always the same little rascal of a 'subject' followed by its countersubject!

"They also say that I despise Beethoven, that I insulted him, called him 'the deaf old man.' Here, again, I believe Beethoven was too prolific and some of his sonatas or variations are also without joy. But let's take the Ninth

Symphony: the idea has prodigious beauty, the development is magnificent, each progression is a new joy. In
this work of enormous proportions, not one bar is super-
fluous."

Once he said, speaking of Wagner:

"Had he been a little more human in his splendor, he
would have been great for all time."

Claude recovered slowly and incompletely from his illness. His intestinal trouble had come back, and worse than
before. The least effort tired him. Although he said little
about it, the war and his prolonged inactivity continued
to depress him. Even his home began to weigh heavily
upon his shoulders, and he longed for open spaces, wide
horizons, and his old friend, the sea. There, at least, he
would not be obsessed by the melancholy of the Paris
streets; by the idle talk of the bourgeois wanting the capture of a German trench at each breakfast; by the stupidity of the amateur strategists who fought the war vigor-
ously on café tables by means of matchsticks representing
brigades and divisions, and blamed the high command
for not moving an army corps as easily as they moved the
chairs they sat on.

"I would like to go to Pourville again," he said; "my
brain will dry up if I stay here much longer. For two or
three days it appeared as if a few ideas were coming back
to me. I feel I'll be able to work there. Would you mind
leaving at once, Emma?"

They left on a rainy morning in July, taking more baggage than usual because of their wish to settle in a house,
instead of patronizing the dismal local hotel. Claude was
anxious to reconstitute a little of his familiar surround-

ings. A special trunk contained his favorite prints, small boxes filled with pencils, pens and erasers, an ample supply of "quarto papale" manuscript paper, and, of course, Arkel-the-toad, all wrapped up in cotton so that his precious limbs wouldn't get fractured.

It still rained when they arrived. A real estate clerk took them on a round of the vacant houses. One of them, called Mon Coin (My Corner), appeared suitable; it was a Norman cottage with brown rafters and a tile roof. There was a garden in front, not too neatly kept but full of flowers, and best of all, a terrace upstairs from which one enjoyed a splendid view over the sea. This caught Claude's fancy and at once they signed the lease.

Claude began the installation of his worktable, which was of decent size. In the church tower of the village the Angelus rang timidly, as if conscious that it could bring no peace into the hearts of men. The sky hung low and the sea was gray. But Claude felt relieved. At last he was away from Paris! The coal stove purred gaily in the kitchen and Miss was setting the dining-room table when twilight crept in and he went down to light the lamps.

In normal times, Dieppe would have been buzzing with vacationists, its musical season, and the crowds coming over from England for the week ends. But war had changed all that, and a hospital was installed in the Casino. On the sea front wounded soldiers took their walks, some in bandages and others aided by canes. A few were being wheeled in Bath chairs. All wore old uniforms with red trousers and képis, the new stock of "horizon blue" being reserved for the fighting units. The harbor was at a standstill: the fishermen were in the navy; their boats were disarmed and lay at anchor; even the traffic with England had been considerably curtailed.

After their visit to the piano house where they rented a piano, Claude and Emma roamed along the streets that once had known so gay a life. From now on they would remain at Pourville, and try to forget.

"Here's some good news, Emma. I have just finished my revision of Chopin's works! And I'm sure it can stand the examination of the 'Doktors,' even if they put on their unfriendly supergoggles."

Claude was also at work on his own *Études*, and as Emma watched their progress a hope grew in her that perhaps her beloved patient would conquer his sadness, that his creative days would return again. If only the war could come to an end! She knew that Claude worried over the thought how long, how cruel, how unmerciful this war threatened to be. Still, he was doing his utmost to check his anguish, to use all his remaining strength for the beauty toward which all peoples on earth instinctively aspire.

Sometimes he was afraid to open the newspapers for fear of the news they might contain, inaccurate, sensational. Once he confided to Emma:

"I think I won't read anything any more; otherwise I would relapse into the condition I was in before leaving Paris. This mustn't be; I want to prove that even a hundred million enemies can never destroy the culture of our France. My thoughts go out to our heroic youth, mowed down day after day on the battlefields. Every note I write is offered to them in fervent homage."

This stimulant restored his powers to an unexpected

degree of efficiency and it was with juvenile buoyancy that he expressed his joy:

"How wonderful, to feel myself free from that horrible shroud of impotence! I'm active again, like an ambitious college boy!"

He was at his table day and night, just as in the good old days. No leisure hours, even for the little gardening advised by the doctor. Anxious not to interfere, Emma spent much time on the beach with Chouchou. Claude rested only when it was forced upon him: a wasp stung his right hand and it became so swollen that he could neither play nor hold his pencil. Nevertheless, it was a matter of only two days before the "good spell" was resumed, never slowing down until the end of the season.

Early October brought its rainy days, its short twilights; nights became chilly and Mon Coin, without a heating system, appeared less hospitable. It was time to return to Paris. Good-bye, sea. Good-bye, tranquillity. Again the trunks were brought out, the windows shorn of their curtains, amid the haste and melancholy suggestive of impending departure.

In Paris Claude kept up a high pace, and in agreement with Jacques Durand he selected a new type of presentation for his works. The cover of the *Sonatas* would emphasize his nationalism, with its lettering somewhat altered but in authentic eighteenth century style. There was a florid vignette in the corner, and the music was "composed by Claude Debussy, musician of France," "for sale at the house of Durand and son, located at No. 4, Place de la Madeleine, near the Grands Boulevards," and "dedicated to Emma Claude Debussy (p.M.) by her husband, C.D."

This created another flurry of bewilderment. Here was that puzzle again—"p.M." What on earth did he mean by that?

Claude's spirits constantly rose higher. The unfinished libretto of *The House of Usher* was taken out of the files and placed prominently on the desk. Musical ideas were already incubating: for the accompaniment of Roderick's monologue he would use a queer formula, a mixture of lower oboe tones and high harmonics of the violins. His head buzzed with new schemes, new dreams.

But it was all in vain. What can be done against impossible odds? The disease, rampant for eight years, had continued to corrupt his body. It broke out with unrestrained violence. One afternoon, early in December, Miss ran upstairs:

"Madame . . . madame . . . come down at once. Monsieur is very ill!"

Claude was in his studio, lying on the sofa. Never before had his loss of weight been so noticeable. His eyes were glassy, his arms extended beside him, one hand dangling from the wrist and swinging as if to chase away pain too fierce to endure.

Emma rushed to the telephone and begged Dr. Desjardins to hurry over.

In France it is not customary for doctors to inform a patient accurately about his condition when the trouble is serious; even to close relatives much euphemism is used. After the consultation Emma and Dr. Desjardins retired to the drawing room.

"Tell me the truth, doctor. I want to know."

"I can't tell just yet. His strong constitution will help. But an operation must be performed at once."

Claude was told not to worry: as soon as the neglected fistula could be removed he would feel all right again.

The same day he left for the clinic. His good spirits had not left him and he had implicit faith in the great skill of his surgeon. Even on his sickbed he wrote a few letters:

"It is decided that tomorrow I will be operated on," he said in one of them. "I haven't been able to send out invitations, owing to short notice. The next time I'll try not to forget."

Claude remained one whole hour in the operating room. Apart from the removal of the tumor itself they had to insert a silver tube, necessary for the draining process.

As those who have been under ether will understand, it was not the operation itself that was painful, but the dressings that followed, for which no anesthetic could be administered. He stood it all bravely, finding new courage in the short visits of Emma and Chouchou. Once they brought him the first copy of his new song, *The Christmas of the Homeless Children* and his joy was touching. The words were his own, inspired by his immense, simple, and naïve patriotism:

"Our home is no more, the enemy has taken all, all . . .
Even our little beds.
They burned the church and Mister Jesus Christ,
And the old beggar man who hadn't time to get away."

Claude remained at the clinic for a few weeks; then he was allowed to return to his home where special treatments would soon begin. It was, they told him, a new element of extraordinary and even mysterious healing power. One of its disadvantages was its high cost.

Emma sold some of her securities. Since the declaration of war she had received hard financial blows and part of her fortune invested in foreign bonds had been wiped out. But Claude's health being at stake, she was ready for any sacrifice. The treatment would be a long one because of his weakness and the necessity to use small doses.

It was a shock to Emma when she learned the name of that mysterious substance. Though the use of radium was a rather recent innovation, she knew that it was associated with that greatest plague of humanity—cancer.

Anxiously she questioned Dr. Desjardins. She hardly dared to pronounce the dreaded name, but the doctor held her hand in silence. She had guessed right and now tears streamed down her pale cheeks.

Three physicians were taking care of the patient, supervising the treatments and meeting in conference from time to time. Claude was suffering and it became necessary to give him morphine, as sparingly as possible, of course. How he hated that drug which "transforms a man into a walking corpse, makes him go left when he wants to go right, and annihilates his will power!"

Emma had kept her financial worries to herself, but Claude had overheard a few words spoken downstairs; it made him wonder and worry, increasing the heavy burden of fretting which already harassed him.

Has Claude Debussy any reason to exist if he no longer can compose? he sometimes thought. He could do nothing else, had no hobbies, and had been taught nothing but music. To be tolerable, life had to be filled with activity and he had to write, write all the time. But how could this be done when his brain became a void, like a cracked drum?

Often he smiled at the irony of fate. They were many, those who envied his genius, his fame, and who looked upon him as one of the fortunate few. What was he, in reality? A sick, aging man, a subject of experiment for surgeons, a hopeless invalid with a foot already in the grave.

In May a slight improvement took place and it came just in time to prevent his sinking into further melancholia. But it was short-lived and one day he called Emma.

"Is there really any hope that I will get well? It has occurred to me that perhaps there is no cure for my illness . . . If so, I would rather know it at once. Then, as Golaud said, oh, then!"

When the second anniversary of the war arrived, they were still in Paris and the treatments were still going on. Whether they were effective or not he could hardly tell. But suddenly he made up his mind to stage a fight, to resume his work happen what may. Why should he be a slave to this disease? Why not disregard it, shake it off? At least he could try, and if his doom was sealed he would depart with the satisfaction of having attempted to do his duty.

In October the doctors advised a change. The autumn was a rainy one and a few weeks in a more invigorating climate would help him. The treatments were completed for the time being, though another series would be administered later on. They recommended Arcachon, and this choice was quite agreeable to Claude who had not forgotten the peaceful atmosphere of the southern resort.

To avoid crowds they traveled by night despite the discomfort. It was wartime and no sleeping cars were in service; but on the French trains one can always rent pillows and blankets. They made the best of it and if they did not sleep much, at least they were not disturbed, since they were alone in their compartment. Upon their arrival they drove to Le Moulleau, where a new hotel had been built in the heart of the pine forest.

Once more Claude had to live in a "numbered box," as he pleasantly put it. The figure was an accurate description of the Hotel du Moulleau. On both sides of a long corridor rooms opened, with a number painted on each door. Everything was plain, uniform, without any trace of originality. The sound of several pianos was audible. Was this a hotel or a conservatory? Claude thought, annoyed by the din in which he recognized the presence of his "Delphic dancers."

In the afternoon, as he sat downstairs in the lobby, a gentleman walked up and introduced himself. He was a composer, a former student of the Schola Cantorum, above all, the scion of a wealthy southern family, a circumstance which enabled him to act and speak with arrogance. He expressed much interest in Claude's projects and questioned him about his immediate activities.

"Right now I am busy with a sonata for violin and piano," was the answer; an answer which must have surprised the visitor since a hint of a sneer was noticeable in his smile.

"A sonata! Oh, indeed? A sonata."

He shook his head several times and continued:

"A sonata is so difficult to write. The most difficult thing in the world. It takes such experience, such technique, such craftsmanship. Such preparation, too! At the Schola it's a rule that you must write many sonatas before one of them is considered worthy of performance."

When he left, Claude was completely cast down. He well knew that his visitor was nothing but a would-be composer, a conceited upstart, an amateur filled with over-bearing ego whose opinion was of no consequence.

Still, there were those remarks he had just made. Was Claude so sure that they were entirely unjustified? Then he stopped and pondered: Yes, he knew he had written *Pelléas*, songs, piano pieces . . . but what had he com-posed in the realm of chamber music? His string quartet? Chausson had not liked it, and Claude realized that now he was not far from agreeing with him. To his dismay, it occurred to him that perhaps there was some truth in those remarks; perhaps he was unfit to write a sonata; perhaps it would be a failure even before it was com-pleted.

This state of mind caused him to long for his home and wish that at once, by some miracle, he could be trans-ported to his studio where at least he was protected from such intruders. Even the noisy trains, the drums, the bu-gles were heavenly, compared with such poisonous words which seeped through his brain like slow venom, under-mining his confidence, destroying his faith, and making him doubt himself.

Under such conditions it would have been useless to try and do any work on the sonata: better to go out and seek relief in the solitude of nature.

For some time Claude roamed woefully through the avenues. He stopped in front of an entrance gate leading to the villa where Gabriele d'Annunzio had lived for several years; everyone in Arcachon still spoke of his ex-traordinary wardrobe, his panama hats with wide brims. On Sunday afternoons, when out for a promenade, the natives often went to see this villa, so quaint with its triple enclosure protecting the poet against undesirable callers.

The little stone rabbits were still sitting at each side of the gate, but the owner had gone back to his sunny Italy, taking his two Russian hounds with him. The shutters were closed and weeds grew high in the garden. There d'Annunzio had written his last novel, *Leda Without Her Swan.* The townsfolk identified Leda as the poet's last "flame," a young and pretty divorced countess.

It was on the beach near by that d'Annunzio had suffered a bad affront, one Sunday, as he met a crowd of young excursionists from Bordeaux, mostly shopgirls and clerks in gay and noisy spirits. As the great man passed by, one of the young women, unaware of his identity, turned to her companions with: "Heavens! Look! What a homely man!"

It was a hard blow to the pride of the famous lady-killer. What is glory?

Near the seashore Claude passed the Villa Florida where Gabriel Dupont, the young genius prematurely carried away by consumption at the age of thirty-six, had composed *La Farce du Cuvier* so much admired by him.

Twilight had set in when he reached the sand dunes, and the wind began to blow, presaging a stormy night. The sky was overcast with dark clouds; no sunset was visible and the sea was leaden. A queer feeling pervaded Claude; this landscape was not strange to him. Somehow he was familiar with that outline, the "grande dune" there, the Cap Ferret across the lagoon, the lighthouse already twinkling on the horizon. He was startled as he turned to the right, then to the left. The pines . . . the two pine trees!

Now he remembered. He had stood on this very spot almost forty years before. He was young then, rich in all his hopes, and the sun shone gloriously. Now everything was in the past and he looked back on his life, a life which he felt had been wasted, during which but a small fraction of his aspirations had been achieved.

Overpowered by the immensity of his present helplessness, by the ominous silhouette of those two tall pines formerly so cheerful and now looking like gibbets, the man in black turned away, pulled up the collar of his coat and disappeared into the forest, while through the chilly air echoed the shrill call of buzzards hunting for some carcass along the deserted beach.

Back in Paris, Claude and Emma were confronted with their first real difficulties caused by the war. It was a cold winter and fuel was getting scarce. Like foodstuffs, it was rationed and could be obtained only on presentation of individual cards. Being the head of the family Claude had to go in person to the City Hall where a long line waited on the sidewalk. He caught cold and had to go to bed when he came home. For many days he was laid up with severe pain in the kidneys and again the completion of the sonata was postponed. With all this trouble and his morale lower than ever, he was asked to organize a charity concert. This took much of his time and strength, and left his nerves in pitiful condition.

The shortage of coal was relieved when spring set in. With the rising temperature came a series of inter-Allied propaganda concerts. Bernardino Molinari, Claude's former host in Rome, conducted one of them which featured *La Mer*. The author was carried away by his dynamic leadership and voiced his enthusiasm in rapturous terms:

"I don't think the Parisian public has ever heard a performance that can compare with this one. Molinari is a sort of wizard. He succeeded in shaking the apathy of this orchestra, which in itself is a feat. Of course, our musicians are fine, if they only want to play. Well, today really they played like angels!"

Before leaving for the summer vacation, a request came to Claude from the Nationale: Would he agree to play his violin-and-piano sonata at the first performance in November?

Once more the family took the train at the Quai d'Orsay and descended in the picturesque little city of Saint-Jean-de-Luz, on the Bay of Biscay and only a few miles from the Spanish border. They had leased a house through a mutual friend of the owner, General Nicoll of the British War Office. It was a great surprise, and Claude found the "Chalet Habas" very pleasant as they inspected the various rooms.

"Look at those spears from Zululand. Those awe-inspiring rifles which never shoot. Those pictures of Christiania. And those ancestors' portraits—that one over there especially. The old gentleman looks handsome, but oh, so stern! Nevertheless, I feel I could have got along quite well with him. I could almost believe that S. Pickwick, Esq., is going to come down these stairs. The garden is restful and easy to get acquainted with. Then, look at those little mountains over there, so discreet. They have no desire to attain the fame of Everest or Mont Blanc! I like it here. I think I will enjoy this Biblical calm, this 'extraordinary silence,' as Maeterlinck would say."

But still Claude could not work. Always with him was a terrible fatigue and that same old impotence. There were mornings when his weakness was such that the simple act of dressing seemed to him a Herculean labor; and he waited, waited, expecting he knew not what, a revolution, or an earthquake that would save him the trouble of going through with it. Without undue pessimism, this continual struggle against illness and against himself was hard to bear and he feared becoming a burden to everyone. Little by little he was taking note of his real condition:

"If anyone is needed to direct the music of the spheres, I think I am quite fitted for this 'lofty' job," he said to a friend.

It was another rainy season. Something had gone wrong with nature's machinery; every day at the approach of the incoming tide heavy clouds came from the west and soon the rain began to patter on the roof, preventing Claude from taking his siesta in the garden. Life was not a bit worse in Paris, he thought, so why was it that so many people, including himself and his family, found it imperative to leave the capital?

In September Claude presented his *Sonata* at a charity concert given by Gaston Poulet, the violinist. This was a good opportunity to test it in public prior to its performance at the Nationale in the fall. When he appeared on the platform he was greeted by salvos of applause, but the shock caused by his physical appearance was noticeable. His skin had turned ashen, with waxy reflections here and there; a faint smile of acknowledgment was forced to his lips, but behind it lingered great resignation and weariness. He sat down, turned his head slowly, and as he looked at the audience one could sense some apology for his pitiful condition.

A few days later he dragged himself to the recital of

Francis Planté, dean of French pianists, contemporary and rival of Liszt and Rubinstein, and landowner in the surrounding Basque country. Those were hours of pure delight for Claude, and he greatly enjoyed Planté's rendering of his *Toccata*. This concert took place at the end of September. Soon it would be time to leave. Three months of complete inactivity was all that Claude could inscribe on his musical balance sheet. The pile of manuscript paper was intact; his pen had never been dipped in ink, and even Arkel-the-toad seemed to look at him with reproach.

Paris was preparing for another winter of war. After the tremendous offensive against Verdun, the fight had settled down once more to a matter of long patience. In view of the economic situation, all restrictions were tightened and it became increasingly difficult to secure gasoline and coal.

Despite their splendid stamina, the French people showed some evidence of weariness; this conflict was so interminable, and even the stanchest optimists could detect no signs that peace was in sight.

One of the Paris managers sent Claude a proposition for an extensive tour of the British Isles. But this could not be considered, since now he was hardly able to walk. Caplet, Dukas, Satie, and the few other faithful friends, who were admitted, were profoundly distressed at the sight of his misery. Emma, who still hoped against hope, had succeeded in making him take a few hours of rest every afternoon, but recently his nervous system had become supersensitive to the slightest noise. Each passing train sounded to him like gigantic roaring thunder. And those bugles!

Their high notes were so many sharp knives cutting through his ears into his brain.

All was exasperating, nerve-racking, as cruel as slow torture invented by the refined barbarism of Oriental tormentors. The inoculations of morphine had been resumed, to keep the physical pain under control. Of course, the concert at the Nationale was canceled.

Claude knew the gravity of his condition. To friends who tried to comfort him, he replied with a cryptic smile:

"No . . . no . . . I am through. It's no use. Never before have I felt so fatigued by this pursuit of the inaccessible. I am like a weary traveler waiting for a train that will pass no more."

With the New Year the German aviation increased its activity, as a prelude perhaps to the forthcoming offensive. One night the sinister blowing of the sirens sounded all over Paris, followed by the droning of the Gothas and the crashing noise of the explosions.

Emma rushed to Claude's room, while Miss awakened Chouchou, whose youthful sleep had remained undisturbed and hurried her to the cellar, equipped as a shelter in conformity with government orders. Emma wanted to call for help, fearing that Claude was too weak to walk and would have to be carried below. But he refused to leave his bed. His strength seemed suddenly galvanized. Like Cyrano de Bergerac putting his back to the tree and drawing his sword, he would fight to the last against the Philistines, the demagogues, incomprehension, prejudice, abuse, death itself! Now was the time to do it, to try to shake off that soot which clogged his brain. Why, after all, should he yield to this tyrannical disease and let it force its will upon him?

"Bring a pencil and my manuscript of *Usher*," he said.

Emma, realizing how stirred he was, brought the libretto, then left the room; but she waited outside, ready for any emergency.

Claude grasped his pencil, pondered for a little while, and started scribbling feverishly:

"Do you not hear? Yes, I hear! Oh, have mercy on the miserable unfortunate that I am! He has locked her alive in the vault. I know it, I tell you that I know it, I tell you that I am sure of it! Don't you see her, in the vestibule of copper? Don't you see her poor little hands bleeding? Her dress is bespattered with blood! She cannot walk any more! Ah, ah! Roderick, will not your beloved be here soon? She is climbing the stairs. I hear her steps, I hear the horrible beating of her heart. You are mad, insane! I tell you that she is now behind the door!"

Frenzied, nearly delirious, Claude had spoken aloud the last words. The door opened and Emma rushed in.

Then he dropped his pencil and fell back on the pillows, haggard, panting for breath, only half conscious.

One after another the weeks passed. Claude now remained in bed and grew weaker daily. His pain was becoming unbearable; it was like a wild beast within him, gnawing at his flesh. Mercifully, the doctors increased the dose of morphine.

The air raids occurred more and more frequently, but he still refused to be carried downstairs. One day around noon he was dozing when a low, heavy, rumbling sound was heard. Emma was seated near the bed, watching over his rest. Miss came in quite alarmed. What was that new

noise . . . an explosion? All was quiet again, and no droning was audible from above.

Some minutes passed, then again came that sound. Still
there was no air raid alarm, no siren blowing.

The noise occurred six times in two hours and was
hardly ended when a great rumor spread throughout Paris.

"We are being bombarded by guns, not by airplanes!"

The populace already filled the streets. Surely the government had lied and the enemy must have advanced to
close positions. There was no panic, however, among those
Parisians hardened by nearly four years of war.

It was the first appearance on the scene of "Big Bertha,"
that monstrous cannon capable of shooting almost a hundred miles, and the round marked the "H hour" of a great
new German drive. Each day, but at different hours, another volley began, and one shot was fired every twenty
minutes. This was hard on nerves. No one could tell where
the shells would fall, as the aim constantly changed. On
these occasions Emma sat by Claude and held his hand.
Having made a sacrifice of their lives, they were neither
nervous nor afraid. If they died, it would be together.

In a moment when Claude's mind was still lucid, when
the morphine had not spread too thick a veil around his
brain, he spoke to her softly, with a voice that seemed to
come from beyond:

"Soon I will lay myself to rest, Emma. I have one wish
. . . I want my resting place to be at Passy."

He liked the atmosphere of that old, unused cemetery;
its venerable trees, its location close to the Trocadéro, its
aristocratic atmosphere, all had combined to catch his
fancy.

Alarming news reached Paris. The first push of the German offensive apparently had succeeded. The Allied line was broken on the Somme; Amiens was threatened; the front was heavily pounded in other sectors. But the American troops were pouring in, bringing a new element of freshness, and already they were fighting gallantly near Château-Thierry and Saint-Mihiel. This thought, the hope and even the certitude that it aroused, was one of Claude's last perceptions among the shadows that more and more enveloped his mind.

One afternoon toward the end of March, as a cold raw wind blew outside, Emma entered his room. Claude was resting. Already he seemed to have lost contact with this world. His face was frightfully emaciated, his hair had rapidly thinned out, his hands had taken on the shade of old ivory.

Dr. Valléry-Radot, one of his devoted friends and physicians, came to visit him at four o'clock. As he stood by the bedside Claude awakened, smiled at him, uttered a few words of affectionate greeting. When he left, Emma rose in order to accompany him downstairs. But Claude feebly articulated a few more words:

"Please stay near me . . . do not leave me, petite Mienne."

These were the last words he spoke on earth, his last token of devotion to the adored and faithful companion of his joys and sorrows. "Petite Mienne" (My own Little One), as he had tenderly called Emma since the early days of their great love, since that mysterious dedication had appeared for the first time and puzzled the musical world: "A. l. p. M.," . . . "A la petite Mienne" (to my little One). . . .

So true it is that sometimes a few naïve words can contain more fervor than a long poem, and deepest feelings can be expressed in simplest fashion.

As the hours passed Emma still held Claude's hand. From time to time he lifted his eyelids, gazed vaguely in front of him, as if coming out of a dream. Probably a haze already dimmed his thoughts. His hand trembled slightly. Apparently he suffered no longer.

With the striking of ten o'clock he opened his eyes once more; they seemed lifeless, as if reflecting the bluish-given shadows of stagnant waters. Emma noticed that his hand grew cold, ceased to tremble.

Claude Debussy had entered eternity. Now he would be "Claude de France."

Epilogue

Only fourteen persons walked behind the hearse from the Square du Bois de Boulogne to the Père-Lachaise cemetery, where Claude's remains would be placed in a temporary vault pending negotiations for final burial at Passy. The distance is almost four miles. Emma and Miss, unable to stand such exertion, followed in a funeral coach.

The day was cold and at times a drizzle fell. Life in the streets was subdued, grayish, muffled.

Suddenly, as the procession circled around the Arc de Triomphe, the growling roar of Big Bertha was heard. Passers-by hurried to shelters. Every twenty minutes another shell fell and by the violence of the crash one could judge how near it had hit the mark. The slow march to the resting place lasted nearly three hours through a Paris almost deserted and a silence broken only by the rumbling of the bombardment.

At Père-Lachaise there were no speeches, no oratory of any kind. Four men in black awaited the convoy. As the casket was lowered into the vault one of them said: "It seems that he was a musician."

For Emma a new life began, made up of cherished memories and tender care for Chouchou who was now thirteen and more and more a striking likeness of her father.

318

The difficult matter of obtaining a plot at the cemetery of Passy had to be arranged. Emma, fortunately, could rely on her devoted friend, Magdeleine Greslé, who had volunteered to attend to everything in order to spare her the agony of that ordeal. She went to the City Hall and was directed to the office of an official to whom she explained the case.

"Sorry," he answered, "but it is impossible. The cemetery is unused and no more lots can be sold."

"But, monsieur, could not an exception be made, when it is for Claude Debussy?"

"Claude Debussy. Who's he?"

It wasn't until close to the first anniversary of his death that permission was granted, and it took all the perseverance of which Magdeleine Greslé was capable. Accompanied by a friend, she practically forced her way into the office of the prefect himself. Information was gathered, and the burial was allowed.

Then Emma moved to an apartment on the Rue Vineuse. Their mansion held too many sad memories and it was too large and too far from the cemetery.

Every day, summer or winter, in fair weather or foul, Emma visited the grave and spent moments of meditation before the simple slab.

But she knew only part of her misfortune and soon fate was to strike her another terrible blow.

Like a flower fading away, Chouchou became ill and, despite all that human science could do, she followed her father into the great beyond at the age of sixteen.

Emma remained stoical under this new disaster which tore at her heart. Mustering up her courage, she devoted her life to the collection of souvenirs. Claude's grand piano, the prints and pictures he liked best, his favorite books imparted to her surroundings a sense of his actual presence.

Meanwhile, Claude's world-wide fame continued to grow. In 1926 the directors of the Opéra-Comique had a touching idea: twenty-four years after the première, they arranged three performances of *Pelléas* with the original cast headed by Mary Garden. André Messager, now a grizzled veteran, once again conducted. This sentimental aspect increased the meaning of the performance, and such a reunion, after so many years, added an emotional element in the thunderous applause which greeted the work itself. Emma was moved to tears, as she commented on the glorious event:

"I can hardly express my joy. As Mélisande there's no one in the world who can touch Mary Garden."

Soon afterward the project of erecting a monument to Claude's memory was conceived. But what would it be? From the first the idea of a conventional statute was discarded: something new and fitting should be found for the poet of nature and open spaces. A contest was arranged and the winners were the distinguished architects, Martel Brothers. Originally, their plan was to be carried out in Claude's birthplace. Saint-Germain-en-Laye. But by now the officials at the City Hall had awakened to his glory. They claimed for Paris the honor of paying this permanent tribute, and a tract of land was offered on the former site of fortifications bordering on the Bois de Boulogne and a few steps from the mansion where Claude had lived and died.

The inauguration took place with great pomp in 1932

and much official eloquence was dispensed before the monument:

"A fountain lighted softly by the setting sun . . .
Shining through the leaves, reflected rays are spun,
Perfumes fill the air; see on the water there
A great cathedral's shadow, 'neath which swim goldfish
* fair.*
And through the ling'ring shadows, such sweet nostalgic
* tones,*
Could they arise from Viol or Lute carved there upon the
* stone?*
Through dark'ning forests yonder, shy Fauns pause at
* their play,*
A hunting horn from somewhere far . . . then night en-
* velops day."* *

Emma lived a life of retirement in her apartment. Miss was still with her and continued to manage the house. The royalties from Claude's music increased steadily and in some measure made up for losses caused by the war and its aftermath. At the time of her divorce, Emma had been bitterly criticized by her husband's family who thought it a disgrace to marry a "poor musician." Now things were reversed: ironically enough, the poor musician's spirit came to the rescue, and later it would enrich the very descendants of those whose words had been so sharp.

But it was too late for Emma to reform so far as finances were concerned; besides, conditions had become hectic, prices shot up and down, and the successive devaluations

* Evangeline Lehman, *Bois de Boulogne* songs, by kind permission of G. Schirmer.

played havoc with even the most careful calculations. So her budget continued to remain unbalanced and it was not unusual for the baker or the butcher to come and claim an unpaid bill. This happened regardless of what important royalties she might have collected the week before: in the meantime most of the money had gone for flowers, gifts, discreet help to the unfortunate, lovely attentions to her friends, all that her kind heart considered before anything else.

One day Emma received a letter from Oslo:

"Madame,

"Although you do not know me I take the liberty of writing to you. Many years ago, when I was a little boy, your husband gave me piano lessons. You probably remember that for several seasons he spent the summer with Mme. von Meck and her family. Mme. von Meck was my mother.

"Now, as a consequence of the revolution, I have lost my fortune and am in exile with my wife and four children. The object of this letter, madame, is to beg of you a great favor: among my mother's papers some manuscripts written by your husband were discovered. These songs are now in my hands and I have an offer from a publisher, but we need an authorization which can be granted by you alone. By consenting, you will alleviate the suffering of a family confronted with many hardships. May I hope that in remembrance of my association with your glorious husband you will accede to my request? In advance I thank you with all my heart and remain, your respectful and humble servant,

Von Meck."

Moved by this pathetic appeal, Emma gave her authorization. The songs were published by the house of Eschig in Paris.

Then, like a thunderbolt, an issue of the *Monde Musical* appeared. It contained, side by side, a reproduction of the first page of two songs. Both were the same music and the same words, but the song on the left was signed by Émile Pessard, while the one on the right bore the name of Claude Debussy! The title of each was: *Chanson d'un fou.*

This caused a great scandal and the entire edition had to be withdrawn from circulation. Emma had never seen Claude's manuscripts and she was, of course, completely innocent. Nevertheless she had to take part of the blame. In reality, no one was guilty: the song was one of those copied, just as a prank, by Achille in Conservatoire days and shown to Paul Vidal as his own. He had taken it to Russia and forgotten it there.

Toward the autumn of 1933 Emma's friends began to worry about her health. Repeatedly she suffered liver attacks, though on every occasion she tried to minimize her trouble. Obviously there was more to it than she thought, and toward spring her condition became one of great concern.

At that time the Quatuor Pascal, one of France's best chamber music ensembles, requested her to listen to their performance of Claude's String Quartet. For ten years it had figured prominently in their repertoire and to mark this anniversary they wanted to be granted the honor of playing it for her. Deeply touched by this attention, Emma invited the quartet to an intimate afternoon tea and the audition followed.

Emma lay on her long chair in the softly lighted drawing room; the few others present were Magdeleine Greslé, the faithful friend, Evangeline Lehman, the author-composer whom Emma held in great esteem, and myself. The interpretation of the admirable work by Pascal and his associates was really beyond description and probably will never be duplicated by these artists themselves.

As the extraordinary slow movement was being performed, Emma closed her eyes. Perhaps her thoughts turned back to that evening of long ago, when she met Claude; perhaps she remembered her first words to him:

"At the hour of my death, monsieur, I want to hear the slow movement of your string quartet."

How often had she repeated that statement, even recently to her friends.

As the last measure died away, fluid, evanescent, immaterial, the listeners looked at each other with sorrowful understanding. A common thought had flashed through all minds: Claude's "petite Mienne" had heard the slow movement for the last time.

It came to pass as we had feared. A few days later she was taken to the clinic on the Boulevard Arago. It is a long way from the Rue Vineuse, but during the ride she kept looking out, as if wishing to absorb one last vision of her beloved Paris which her intuition told her she would behold no longer.

The nuns led her to a large room opening on the flower garden. In front of the window a walnut tree spread out its leafy boughs.

"Look . . . how pretty!" one sister said.

"Yes, a pretty walnut tree . . . but not by Schumann," Emma whispered with a faint smile.

She began her fight for life. The head doctor came; then the head surgeon.

"Medicine can do no more," said the doctor.

"Surgery would be fatal," said the surgeon.

Tragic dilemma.

So nothing remained but morphine, to alleviate her last hours.

During all this she remembered her friends. To one of them she scribbled a note in pencil, the last one to come from her hand:

"My blood pressure is low . . . I cannot leave my bed. When, dear friend, shall I see you again?"

We were not to see her any more; the next day she passed away peacefully.

Again it was summer and Paris was deserted. When the hearse left the Rue Vineuse on the day of the funeral, a dozen mourners followed it on its short journey to the cemetery of Passy. It was almost midday and the atmosphere was suffocating. Two rabbis waited in the center aisle, wearing their ceremonial garments. The hearse stopped under the shady trees and they began to chant. The leaves quivered under the torrid heat of the blazing sunshine.

Suddenly the shrill noise of a phonograph broke out. It came from the wide-open windows of an apartment house near by, and invaded the cemetery greatly magnified, like a blast. No attempt could be made to locate the machine, so the ceremony continued and the slow lament of the cantors was mixed with the joyous strains of a French military march.

And why should this not be, after all? Would not Claude himself have wished it so? This mournful dirge, was it not the complaint of his Faun, far away and disconsolate? The martial music, one last echo of his popular night of Festivals?

The coffin was lowered and each mourner passed, dropping a handful of earth according to the rite. Then the slab was sealed, on which already was engraved:

"Claude Debussy, Musician of France, 1862–1918"

Reunited by death, they rested together. And carved in the granite of the Fountain in the Bois, the principles of the Master of Dreams remained as a guiding light for the generations to come:

"Look for discipline within liberty. Listen to the advice of no one, only to the wind that passes and recounts for us the story of the world."